Change Your Mind
A Neurologist's Guide to Happiness

D.V. Pasupuleti, MD, FACP, FAANEM,
DDG, LFIBA, DO, MOIF, AdVMed, IOM, PC

CHANGE YOUR MIND
PUBLISHED BY SYNERGY BOOKS
2100 Kramer Lane, Suite 300
Austin, Texas 78758

For more information about our books, please write to us, call
512.478.2028, or visit our website at www.bookpros.com.

ISBN-10: 1-933538-29-5
ISBN-13: 978-1-933538-29-7

Copyright© 2006 by Devakinanda Vithal Raja Pasupuleti

Publisher's Cataloging-in-Publication
(Provided by Quality Books, Inc.)

    Pasupuleti, D. V. (Devakinanda Vithal Raja)
      Change your mind : a neurologist's guide to happiness
    / D.V. Pasupuleti.
      p. cm.
    Includes bibliographical references.
    LCCN 2005937130
    ISBN 1-933538-29-5

    1. Self-perception. 2. Introspection. 3. Change
(Psychology) 4. Happiness. I. Title.

    BF697.5.S43P37 2006   158.1
                  QBI05-600195

Library of Congress Control Number: 2005937130

Dedication

Dedicated to my loving wife Bhanu, and my dear children Naveen, twins Usha and Nisha, and my baby Sirisha. I am also grateful to my parents, Sree Ramulu and Lakshmi Narasamma, who brought me into this world and molded my qualities.

• *Contents* •

• *About the Author* •

D. V. Pasupuleti, MD, FACP, FAANEM, is a physician who specializes in nervous system diseases (neurologist). He has cared for patients and taught medical students, interns, residents, internists, and family practitioners at university-affiliated hospitals for more than twenty years. Now, his name is attached in the medical literature as "Tetrad of Pasupuleti" to easily identify a rare neurological disorder called Arnold Chiari malformation.

He received the "outstanding teacher award" from the medical students of Michigan State University.

Dr. Pasupuleti has been elected into the International WHO'S WHO, Strathmore's WHO'S WHO, and Sterling's WHO'S WHO.

He is the director of neurology at a teaching hospital as well as past chairman of the neurology department and clinical professor at Michigan State University. He is a member of many professional organizations, a board member of the Genesee County Medical Society, member of many committees, and was an assistant editor for the Genesee County physicians' magazine (*Bulletin*).

Dr. Pasupuleti has written many articles for various medical as well as nonmedical journals. He has appeared frequently on local TV news broadcasts, and has been interviewed by several local newspapers. His extensive teaching includes lectures to the general public, and he is always interested and enthusiastic in learning, teaching, and sharing his understanding of life. He doesn't hesitate to stand alone and address boldly issues like unfairness, hypocrisy, and double standards, as well as moral and ethical issues.

• *About the Book* •

Change Your Mind is a self-help book that deals with self-awareness and self-knowledge. It is *not* about psychology, theology, philosophy, or religion. The author explains a logical approach to experiencing ongoing, everyday happiness. It is presented as nondenominational awareness that can be translated and applied universally.

Secular knowledge of science is like a pair of scissors. It cuts the intellectual knowledge derived by reason into various branches of science. It is a relentless quest for knowledge of the factual state of the natural world. A person requires this knowledge for living in this world.

On the other hand, self-knowledge is like a needle with thread. It joins the branches of science into an indivisible reasonable whole. It is a perpetual search into the primary consciousness or awareness. Self-knowledge nourishes ethical values, which are lacking in our society. A person needs this knowledge to develop the personality with balanced mental disposition by correctly tuning all of his or her faculties that bring fulfillment and meaning to life.

There are about 6.5 billion people on earth and there isn't one person who doesn't want to be happy and live "happily ever after." Every human being wants to be happy without sorrow, misery, pain, suffering, or sadness. Nobody says, "I truly want to be miserable."

But no matter how many material goods we possess, it seems we always desire the things we don't have and look for something more to make us happy.

How can we be happy and content during these times of stress, terrorism, and sorrow from the loss of a loved one, a failed relationship, an unsatisfactory job, or from daily living struggles? How can we achieve a state of contentment? The problem is that people don't know the true meaning of happiness. They do not realize that the solution can be found within—in the awareness of one's self. Everyone is busy with their lives and constantly trying to accomplish something to make them happy, even though that happiness may last only a short while. Few among us stop and think, "Who am I?" or "What am I?" But within the answer to these questions is where true and lasting happiness lies.

The first question people ask me when they learn of this book is, "Did this book come from your own experiences?" The answer is yes! Most of it comes from my lifelong commitment to understanding human life, desires, and struggles to be happy forever; by reading and understanding the nervous system, the human body, and science. I have compared and contrasted various religions going back to prehistoric times and learned their basic teachings. In essence, all the great religions of the world are divine in origin; their basic principles are in complete harmony and differ only in nonessential aspects of their doctrines.

Human beings ever struggle with questions like

1) What is the meaning of life?
2) What happens after one dies?
3) What is our relationship to the material world, the universe, and the Creator?

Human beings want to gain control over the environment, nature, and life. We are born with the urge and desire to search out the "unknown." When we look back into time, even the oldest, most primitive people had the awareness of a "Supreme Being."

Change Your Mind addresses all kinds of questions and the ultimate truth about happiness. This book is about real life, real human beings and teaches how to be happy and content with our lives by understanding one's self. This book is written in a simple language without complex words or themes, so that everyone can understand and easily follow the *Five Golden Rules for Happiness*. Once the reader begins to exercise these Golden Rules on a daily basis, it will become natural and second nature to be happy for the rest of their lives.

A Note on My Writing Style

Throughout this book you will find that some examples or concepts are repeated more than once or restated in a slightly different way. Please bear with me on this and trust me when I say it is meant to help you learn more quickly. Repetition is a technique I have used successfully with my students over the years. As a teacher, I have learned that few things work better than repetition for driving a point home and ingraining it in a person's consciousness. Even then, some students on hearing a concept for a second or third time will protest, "I got it! I got it!" But when I ask them to explain it back to me, they realize they can't. Then they understand my method of repetition. I hope that when you, the reader, come across a duplication of a key idea, you will grant me this liberty of repeating it to help ingrain it deeply within YOU. And I hope that by the end of the book, it will be a part of your knowledge that you definitely will not forget. As such, it will greatly aid you in your pursuit of happiness.

A Note on God and Gender

Some people are more comfortable referring to God as "He." For others, "She" is the preference. And some like "It" because it does away with gender altogether. Initially, I had wanted to use all three, but I soon realized this could cause confusion. For consistency and simplicity, I have arbitrarily chosen to use the masculine pronoun. Whenever you come across "He" or "Himself" in a sentence, please feel free to switch this in your mind to "She" or "It" or *whatever* you are most comfortable with. For myself, I perceive God as an amalgam of all three. But in the English language, there is no such all-encompassing pronoun.

• *Acknowledgements* •

I am in great debt for the understanding of life and the truth about life from the teachings and books of Swami Dayananda, for his gracefulness and unconditional love to human beings, and for the dedication of his life to humanity in seeking spiritual knowledge. His books, *Who Am I, The Teachings of Bhagavad-Gita, Morning Prayers, Values of Values,* and *Dialogues with Swamiji,* have been of immeasurable value to me on my own path to attaining self-knowledge. Also, Ed Viswanathan has been kind enough to let me use some of the sentences from his book *Am I a Hindu?* (Halo Books, 1992).

I would also like to extend my sincere thanks to all of the religious people who patiently discussed and argued with me in their efforts to seek the truth about life from their own perspectives. Also, I am thankful for the basic knowledge I have acquired from great books such as the Bible, interpretations of Koran, books on Buddhism, Judaism, Shinto, Taoism, and Confucianism.

I thank my loving wife, Bhanu, and my loving children, Naveen, Usha, Nisha, and Sirisha who constantly encourage me and lovingly try to make me aware of my deficiencies, my temper, and my occasional "blind spots." They've always been eager to discuss issues without bias and without any reservation, which also helps me to think with broadmindedness in many situations. A special thanks to Bhanu for constantly encouraging my good qualities and capabilities, invoking my inner talents, and reminding me constantly of my strengths, such as straightforwardness and uncompromising moral, ethical behavior.

• *Preface* •

The planet earth is host to approximately 6.5 billion human beings and 50 million species (and the numbers keep growing). There are about 3,000 languages in the world, and we all have different physical qualities, appearances, religions, beliefs, and cultures. As human beings, we all have daily struggles, ups and downs, successes and failures. We struggle every day to achieve security in the form of money, assets, jobs, and relationships. We also seek pleasure in a variety of forms, and the definition of pleasure and happiness is different from one person to another. Many of us are used to depending on somebody else to fix our lives, to give guidance or a pat on the shoulder, or to provide instant solutions to our problems.

Through my life experience, my quest as a brain specialist (neurologist) trying to understand the functions and dysfunctions of the brain, and my constant discussions with colleagues, friends, patients, and acquaintances regarding the true meaning of life and the true nature of one's self, I was encouraged by hundreds of people to write a book in a simple form on "how to achieve true happiness without focusing on material securities and pleasures."

That constant encouragement drove me to write this book. I do realize that I cannot change the whole world, but there is always a purpose in life, and if I share my knowledge with my fellow human beings and make them aware of inner happiness, my purpose is achieved.

It is my goal that through this book you, the reader, will gain knowledge about your inner self and what it is to continually experience true happiness (which is always there within one's self). With a new understanding of the workings of the universe and gaining the insight into our part of this whole creation, the material gains and pleasures we seek will no longer be the primary means of trying to achieve happiness.

May God bless all living beings. I am thankful to each and every person I've had the acquaintance of and who changed my life and thinking process one way or another.

• *Introduction* •

In life, one experiences happiness, sorrows, ups, and downs. And no matter what our race, religion, culture, or socioeconomic status, we are all in constant pursuit of happiness, with a constant desire to live "happily ever after." However, we also realize that it is not possible to be happy at all times. Even if you are a millionaire, or if you have everything you've wanted to have, you will still have moments of unhappiness, sorrow, and frustration. Then what is the secret of happiness? What is the king of all secrets of happiness? It is nothing more than knowing yourself. You must know about your inner self.

This book is for everybody, every human being who has the curiosity to know who he or she is, and to understand where we came from, where we go after we die, what is God, where is heaven, where is hell, how many gods and how many heavens? Every one of us will have these kinds of thoughts, and these questions will pop into our minds at one time or another. You don't have to be a scholar to think this way.

In this book, I have provided a basic means of understanding the secrets of one's self in a simple language, sometimes using my personal, professional, and social experiences as examples, so that the reader can use this as a means of understanding himself or herself. I have tried my best to make this book as simple as possible, in plain language, so everyone can understand. I've tried not to use any sophisticated, complex, psychological or philosophical concepts that might confuse. I use the same technique when teaching my interns and residents about the nervous system (neurology) and neurological diseases as I give a lecture or while making rounds and explaining the patients' problems.

My point is that self-knowledge is not philosophy; it is not psychology, theology, or religious mumbo-jumbo. It is the truth about you as a human being, irrespective of your race, religion, culture, and socioeconomic status. As you learn how to "know yourself," confusion gradually will go away and you will become totally aware of yourself. This is like learning how to talk, walk, swim, or ride a bike. Once you accomplish the skills, you don't have to make an extraordinary effort to do those activities, as they become natural to you. In a similar way, once you learn the secrets of happiness, even in the saddest moments of your life you will be able to overcome those negative feelings and emotions with very little effort.

The ultimate truth and the secret of happiness are in knowing yourself. Knowing that you are limitless, you are awareness, existence, blissfulness, and you are the universe, and you are God because God is inside of everything that exists. This book is aimed at making you "self-aware." Once you understand that you are the source of your own happiness, fullness and contentment, you'll realize that you are free from all the longings and struggles of your life.

I have tried not to overload you with too many religious principles, theologies, philosophies, beliefs, or faiths in this book. However, one thing I constantly remember is from Buddhism (which is nothing but a middle path of Hinduism), which was made available to common man and is based on the realization of the four truths:

1) The truth of pain, which is nothing but birth, old age, sickness, etc. and so on.
2) The truth of the cause of pain, which is nothing but desire and craving.
3) The truth of cessation of pain, which is nothing but eradicating the desire or craving.
4) The truth of the way to this eradication, which is knowing the middle path, for it is here that you can eradicate the pain, of which the root cause is again, desire.

So what is self-knowledge? Knowledge of one's self is based on the following principles:

1) Knowing about the workings of one's inner self.

2) Realizing that "I" is just a physical body with five senses, functioning along with the cooperation and coordination of the brain, and that "I" has limitations.

3) However, the self is not "I," and the self has no limitations. The self is "happiness, limitlessness, awareness, and blissfulness." Self is part of the universe, and the universe is part of the Creator. The Creator is everywhere in living and nonliving existence. So, there is no difference between the self, the universe, and the Creator. You are part of the Creator and the Creator is part of you. You are within the universe and the creation.

4) Learning that self-knowledge is like the light, which lets you see everything as it is by shedding away the darkness. Where there is light there is no darkness, and where there is self-knowledge there is no ignorance because ignorance is the source of all the negatives in life, feelings of pain and unscrupulous desire. Desire is the main root of not only the positive, but also the negative aspects of our life—sorrow, sadness, hatred, frustration, greed, inadequacy, prejudice, and the feeling of being different. All of these sources of pain stem from desire.

5) Exercising self-knowledge on a daily basis will require your voluntary effort for a while, but later on it becomes natural and automatic behavior. Just like the toddler falls several times before learning how to walk properly, or a kid falls from a bike several times before learning to balance, once you learn a skill, it becomes your personal knowledge and it never goes away. It stays with you all the time, whether you use it or not.

6) After awhile, when self-knowledge becomes an automatic behavior, you realize that you are the source of happiness, blissfulness, awareness, and existence.

7) Learning self-knowledge is like learning how to fish, rather than buying a fish for dinner.

8) By using your self-knowledge, your reaction, or behavior toward an action and its result changes dramatically, and you gain the ability to look at things the way they are. You

do not jump up and down wildly for a joyful thing or go into deep slumps for a sorrowful event. Self-knowledge conditions you for a good attitude toward any situation, or action, or result.

Who doesn't smile and forget their problems temporarily when they look at a baby's face, even if it is not their own child? A baby does not even talk; it just looks at you and smiles and you forget everything and smile with him or her, and you enjoy that moment. Why is that? And what power does a baby's smile have that makes one forget everything, feel happy and joyous, and smile along with the baby? The reason is that the baby has innocence and purity and doesn't yet know deep sorrow or sadness. You can smile like an innocent baby when you gain the inner knowledge that you are the source of that happiness.

In this book I explain the positives and negatives of life, in everybody's life, and show you how to look at them in a realistic manner and with clear vision. That way, it is possible to have an uncomplicated, happy mind, even when burdens in our life pull us down. We can overcome the struggles and be happy by mere virtue of changing our attitude toward those problems because we now have a clear understanding of the true nature of life.

I hope that after reading this book, you will better understand your true self and realize that we all have the same qualities, but in different proportions. Yet we can always improve one over the other for the betterment of our life, without seeking material objects as a means to happiness. A swimming pool attendant has to check the pH, the chlorine, and the alkalinity in the water. He or she then adds one or another ingredient to bring one component up or another down to get the water in balance. By acquiring more self-knowledge and understanding of your inner self, you will be able to improve certain qualities and make your life much happier. That is my goal for all human beings on the planet.

God created all of us equal and gave us the willingness to change, or the willingness to choose—in other words, "free will." Even if you are 30 or 60 years old, you still have free will, and you can change your attitude, your thinking process, and your demeanor toward fellow human beings, or toward life itself, and learn how to be happy. It doesn't matter whether you have many material possessions or not, whether you can afford a luxury vacation in Hawaii, or whether you can own a plane or not. With practice of the *Five Golden Rules* in this book, you can achieve ongoing happiness no matter where you are in life.

We all have ups and downs. We all have struggles in life or at our work place. We all have losses—economic, material, personal, or family members. I lost my father to liver cancer when I was nineteen years old, and I was very depressed from that loss. I was scared about my future, how it would be, and I wondered who would support me in finishing medical school, as I was already into my third year. But still, I did not become a burden to my family members, and I did not quit medical school. I went on to graduate and became a physician, after which I came to America and became a brain specialist. Then I lost my mother, nine years ago. The point is, we all gain some things and lose some things throughout our lives. That is the way of "nature's law of balance," and by knowing this, we can maintain a tranquil state of mind.

Human beings forever struggle with questions like, "What is the meaning of life? What happens after one dies? What is our relationship to the material world, the universe, and God?" Even the oldest and most primitive people sought awareness of the "Supreme Being." We are born with the urge to reach out to the unknown and the innate desire to know the unknown. We want to gain control over the environment, nature, and life. This comes with the highest degree of awareness, we, the human beings, are blessed with.

My goal is to make this book available to as many fellow human beings as possible and to have it translated into many languages so that I can share my knowledge and my discoveries with everyone. I wish you all the joy in the universe in your endeavor to understand the truths in your pursuit of happiness. May the Creator bless you at all times!

• Chapter 1 •
The Definition of Happiness

Happiness is a relative term. Depending on your approach to happiness, the definition of it may vary. For example, some people need to analyze it and others need to feel it. If you generally feel great, this may be your definition of happiness. If you have the urge to help your fellow human beings irrespective of race, religion, or culture, this may make you happy because you feel good doing so.

A clean mirror reflects the sun's brightness. But if the mirror is dusty, the sun's reflection is blurred. Similarly, if you have a clear mind, everything it reflects has clarity. And if you have a happy mind, everything looks happy to you. Happiness can stem from the fulfillment of desires, for example, hunger, shelter, protection, or the need to feel safe. On the other hand, there is another type of happiness you can gain with knowing your inner self and realizing that happiness is an integral part of human beings and that it can be cultivated. Even though our circumstances in life may change, we can still be happy. The main goal of this book is to show my fellow human beings how ongoing happiness can be a part of everyone's life.

We continuously look for happiness through actions, desires, and material or monetary possessions. We want these things again and again, whatever form, situation, or experience may bring them to us. By nature we are not sad, sorrowful, or unhappy. That is why whenever you face these negative situations, or whenever your self is experiencing them, you instinctively want to get rid of them. It is inherent in our nature to seek that which brings comfort, tranquility, and happiness. If happiness is not an integral part of your nature, why do you seek happiness all of your life? And why you do not enjoy your sadness or sorrows? Once you fully recognize and understand this, you will not require something outside of yourself to appreciate the moments of fullness within you. When you are incognizant, you attribute moments of happiness to an external object or situation. Even if a new experience gives you momentary happiness, once that moment is gone, you will again find yourself looking for another moment of happiness. On the other hand, if you are realistic and able to acquire the self-knowledge that *happiness is always within you,* then you will not need to struggle to find moments of happiness.

Depending on your belief or religion, the source of happiness comes from a Creator—for example, God. Yet, to fulfill physiological or biological needs, using the human ability to think makes us constantly struggle to try to make ourselves happy. Animals are different because they lack the ability to reason. The animal must follow its natural or survival instincts. For example, suppose you want to entice a cow to come to you. If you wave grass in your hand, it will come to you. However if you wave a stick it will run away, even if the expression on your face indicates no ill intent. This behavior was not taught to the cow. Rather, it is a primitive reaction that makes the animal automatically behave that way. Humans, though, are able to choose and discriminate because of our reasoning faculty. We can make choices based on our analysis of each situation. For example, we can choose between good or bad, pleasure or pain, and hot or cold. Yet, we are seldom content with what we have and will almost always seek to acquire external happiness. But, once we have an understanding of what happiness really is and how we can create our own happiness from within, we may then utilize our ability to think in an ongoing positive way.

Once you gain the knowledge of how you create either happiness or sorrow, good judgment will follow. For the moment, consider what happens when we are incognizant. If you live in a society where cows are valuable, you want to possess more cows. In another society, human power may be a societal goal, so you want to have more power in order to feel important. As you climb the success ladder you constantly seek to acquire more and more power. If you do not obtain power, you will think you are a failure. This self-judgment comes from a lack of self-knowledge. In truth it is not failure, because the varieties of experiences we have teach us how to succeed. Momentarily, we may feel and become sad by a perceived failure, but in reality, we can become wiser from the experience.

Have you ever tried to understand the moment of happiness itself? It is nothing more than something which gives us a "kick" or a "high." During that moment of happiness or the "high" we forget other desires or needs. That particular moment of happiness is actually how you feel. The "kick" or "high" could reflect a gain, or an appreciation of beauty, or even the acquiring of a material item or money. But the state of happiness is in the mind. It occurs for a moment in you "where you are just with yourself." During that moment of happiness, in that quiet clarity of mind your self does not want any change whatsoever. At that moment, you have actually chosen a moment of happiness for yourself. The moment of happiness you choose could be triggered by your favorite food, a baby's smiling face, a kiss or a hug from a loved one, or any such pleasurable experience.

People who throw big parties usually get a certain thrill out of them. Lots of people show up, and the host feels good about himself because he has had an experience of pleasure or happiness. But no matter how many big parties one gives, the happy experiences are short lived and limited until the host becomes bored or unhappy and has to throw another big party to make him feel good about himself once again. On the other hand, if that same person realizes that happiness comes from within, he or she does not have to give a party and spend a lot of money to be recognized. Similarly, people who crave spiritual experiences try to achieve them through meditation, yoga practices, and other transcendental methods. Eventually, they will realize that these are all external events to give a person an "experience," while in fact that experience is already within the person.

The experiences described above are all externally dependent. They depend on money or on people. For example, suppose a person enjoys surfing. She may sit on the beach all day, waiting for the big waves in order to surf. This is an external dependence on the waves. Again, if the surfer could bring herself to realize her true nature, she would not have to depend on an external thing like the waves to be happy.

Instead, she would be just as happy when she is sitting there *waiting* for a big wave, as she is when she's *on* a big wave. It is completely possible for anyone to attain this experience where they are happy just *being* as well as happy when they are *doing* a particular action intended to create happiness.

We all have experienced how negative events can make us unhappy. However, few people are aware that if they can separate the negatives from their self-awareness, they can achieve happiness. This does not mean that they will not have normal reactions like sorrow, grief, and anger. But with self-knowledge when they experience those feelings, they will instinctively know how to resolve them quickly and how to separate them from the self so that the attachment to them will be almost completely diminished.

This book does not attempt to create new knowledge. Rather, it is a logical approach to the knowledge that is already here and can be recognized once you have self-awareness. A crystal assumes color when a colored object is placed in front of it. However, the color within the crystal is not real, but only a reflection. Just like the crystal, your inner soul is clear and filled with happiness because the Creator created you that way. But the external world is filled with sorrow, grief, anger, violence, hatred, and greed. We reflect all these qualities as the crystal reflects color. When you remove the colored object, the color you see in the crystal disappears. In a similar way, you can make all these external sorrows disappear by keeping the inner self clear and transparent. One of the most common problems all human beings have, besides the feelings of inadequacy and insecurity, is a problem in self-judgment: "I am a failure, I am worthless, I am useless, I am ugly, I am poor, I am short, I am stupid," or other types of self-putdowns. We must develop the "attitude" of a crystal and reflect back those external influences and thus keep ourselves clear.

In the annual Miss Universe contest, a panel of judges decides who is "the most beautiful woman in the world." When she is crowned, the whole world accepts her as such. Is she satisfied? Does she recognize the honor and say, "Now I don't have to prove anything to anybody from here on?" Does she dress simply and not wear makeup? No. Instead, she feels more responsibility and thinks that she has to represent beauty, so she spends more and more time dieting and applying cosmetics. She behaves like this because of a self-judgment problem, which many people have.

In my practice, I have observed that when patients use poor self-judgment, they may resort to alcohol or drugs to get rid of the pain or suffering. I try to help them and make them aware or knowledgeable about pain medications and their addictive natures. In fact, I seldom prescribe narcotic pain medications. Rather, I try to make patients aware of pain perception. Often, patients tell me they do not want to be addicted to pain medications, drugs, or alcohol. While they have this insight, when their back hurts or when they have migraine headaches, they say, "Doc! To get rid of this pain I had to drink," or "I had to smoke marijuana." I explain that "escaping" or "slipping into themselves" will not make things fall into place. Retreating within themselves with chemicals is not going to change their situation. Not only will they harm your physical bodies, but the happiness they will feel is temporary. As soon as the drug wears off, reality hits. No matter how many times they escape, at some point they have to face reality.

The purpose of this book is to get you to a place where you need nothing external. Nor do you need to put any substance (legal or illegal) into your body to make you happy. This is because all you need is already inside of you. The happiness you are seeking already exists within. You simply need to use the information and techniques I will show you to discover this.

Once you learn the true meaning of "self," it will help you to face reality without "crutches." To get there, it is necessary to unfold the knowledge of your self until it is clear to you. If doubt, vagueness, or an unclear mind persists, it can be eliminated by a means of self-knowledge that I will impart in this book. Until you see the whole picture and understand the whole meaning of it, the problem will not be solvable.

In self-knowledge, there is no difference between you, the universe, and the Creator. Every thing is seen in totality. Bodily experiences resulting from the 1960s with free love, street drugs like acid, hashish, and marijuana, and body-mind experiences are only temporary escapes from the perception of reality and totality. Acquiring self-knowledge and enjoying oneself are like enjoying nature. Take, for example, the sunrise. You know that the sun does not actually rise in the eastern sky. Still, the beauty of the "rising" sun enchants you. You know the sky is not truly blue; it is an effect caused by the longer wavelengths of light passing through the atmosphere, but you enjoy the "blueness" of the sky. You know a rainbow has no colorful substance, but still you enjoy and welcome the rainbow. This is similar to knowing the truth as a whole that accounts for the world, God, and yourself. And in that accounting, the fact is that you are the whole, the total. Totality is akin to enlightenment. A mere body experience or mind experience does not create a wholeness or totality, but it can be created through self-knowledge.

Nor do cults or similar religious experiences make for totality. You do not require experiencing a cult to feel yourself because your experiences in waking, dreams, and deep sleep are enough to enlighten your existence. The problem with cult or religious experience is that the "I" is not going to figure out that the "I" is timeless. Cult or religious experience is momentary and time-limited elation, which means it is bound to come and go. But self-knowledge is not time limited.

The problem with temporary experiences is that, whenever they are pleasant, one strives for a repeat experience to again engender ongoing happiness. When people do what seems like insane thrill seeking such as bungee jumping, snow boarding, hang gliding, and other extreme sports, they risk their lives for a temporary adrenaline rush or thrill. What is the thrill all about? You can experience the same "thrill" listening to good music, participating in an intelligent conversation, or taking in the beauty of nature.

The situations described in this book are universal. These situations occur in one form or another for all of us. But to acquire the knowledge available, one must go after it. For example, to become a doctor, I had to work hard to obtain the highest grades in school so I could be eligible to go to medical school. Then I had to pass all the exams to become a licensed doctor. In order to become a brain specialist, I had to spend more time learning about the nervous system. While the knowledge existed, it did not come into my head without a lot of work. In fact, one has to develop an appropriate intellectual discipline. Preparing one's mind and practicing again and again will accomplish this. An example is Einstein's discovery of the famous equation $E=MC^2$. Einstein's pursuit of knowledge was not a mystical pursuit. It was based on already existing knowledge.

Learning to be happy is not a mystical pursuit, either. By understanding this, when you face a new problem, you can meet the problem with a new type of analysis and attitude. You will realize that with a change in your attitude and thinking process, your perception toward that problem will be different from the way it was before. This is self-knowledge. It does not come to you from experience per se, but from awareness. To gain self-knowledge means to develop awareness. It is not taught in universities or labs. It cannot be demonstrated visually. You attain self-knowledge by having an open mind, *thinking globally at all times,* and through self-effort.

Being tied to or consumed by what you do not want, such as death or pain, creates bondage. When you work toward happiness, you try to get rid of unhappiness. Happiness becomes freedom from unhappiness. Yet most of us engage in activities to fulfill our desires. Only a few seek happiness by giving up, or dispassion, as monks might. The desire itself is not a problem, rather a "without that I won't be happy" syndrome is the problem. Self-knowledge helps to change one's attitude toward desire. This is key to becoming happy.

You want to get rid of a condition in yourself; you do not want to get rid of yourself. For example, a person who wants to kill himself is in pain, and is feeling so helpless that he does not see another way out. Thus, he thinks that committing suicide will end his pain. But, if he is able to see that he can get rid of his pain in a less catastrophic manner, then he will not want to die anymore. By understanding that your self is nothing but happiness, you can get rid of your pain with self-knowledge.

When you recognize the basic problem, "I am a wanting person," you are already on the way to gaining self-knowledge. Twenty-four years ago, when I came to the United States, I was not the same person I am today. The knowledge I have acquired since then has changed my attitude toward humanity. This is why I am so enthusiastic about sharing this knowledge with you. Self-knowledge is nothing more than recognition, so *it has to take place in your mind.* Incognizance or ignorance is the source of all pain, and it can only be removed by knowledge. When you have self-knowledge, you are the knower. Self- knowledge is not a bodily experience or a kind of near-death or after-death experience. To achieve happiness, understanding is the key. What is happiness? How can I get it? How can I make it last forever? With practice it will become natural, like getting up and walking without thinking and asking your legs to move.

People are many, and their tastes are different. So different people have different paths or pursuits from incognizance toward knowledge. Yet, nothing else resolves incognizance except knowledge. Knowledge is born of a means of knowledge. We all have problems, and all problems are important. Whatever we do in every walk of life is very important. We want to have a stress-free and peaceful life. Salvation here in this world means to achieve peace and harmony in life.

Human pursuit of security, pleasure, duty, and freedom are universal. There are all kinds of security—emotional, economic, or social in the form of cash, liquid assets, stocks, real estate, relationships, home, good name, job title, recognition, influence, or power of any kind.

Pleasure takes many forms. Sensory pleasure can be found in eating ice cream or seafood, experiencing sexual pleasure, or having good restful sleep. The intellectual pleasures include watching a good movie; experiencing nature, sunrise, or sunset; reading a good book; playing games or playing with a child; seeing stars in the sky at night; solving puzzles; or looking at a beautiful painting. They can be anything that satisfies the senses and pleases the mind.

We also have the duty to perform what needs to be done. Here, there is inner growth and understanding. Actions born out of harmony and derived from friendship, sharing, helping others, charity work, education, and culture are all duties that give inner pleasure. For example, a doctor helping a patient in pain without financial gain is a noble duty. Pleasure that comes out of one's maturing process is a different type of joy.

As an example, for an infant, freedom means to get up and walk. For a prisoner, it's getting out of jail. For a person with crutches, it's walking without help. When you are forever displeased or dissatisfied with yourself, you constantly have to do something to please yourself. But the ultimate freedom does not mean always seeking freedom from something you do not want. The freedom I'm talking about is common to all, but only few people pursue it, and that is freedom from attachments and various forms of security.

If you are always seeking security and pleasure, when will you understand your life? When will you really be able to say, "I have made it"? It is possible only when you see yourself as secure and pleased with yourself. Then you are truly free, and no situation is going to change that. True freedom is freedom from seeking. You stop spending your entire life trying to manipulate the world in order to please yourself.

So the greatest secret, the secret concealed by yourself, is that "You are Happiness, Awareness, and Existence." You are well on your way if you make the effort to understand that "all exists within me," and "I am not different outside the universe or the Creator." If you have this mindset, the next step is to make the effort to know about yourself. Remember that the pleasures we seek last for only a while, no matter how great the pleasurable stimulus or situation is. People are many, and their tastes are different. So different people have different paths or pursuits toward knowledge. But it all comes down to the same thing: finding happiness *within*.

• Chapter 2 •

Money and Desire and Pleasure

Whether there is a heaven or hell in everyone's future, the bottom line is, "Are you happy now? Are you content here on earth?" Did you ever wonder what our basic human problem is? It is *desire*, the "I want" syndrome. If you look at a poor person, he may think that if he has two meals a day, he will be happy. Once this desire is satisfied, he will compare himself with someone who has more. This will then make him unhappy. On another level, suppose you have a million dollars. When you look at somebody who has *ten* million dollars, you may think he is happier than you are because he has "more." *More* is a relative term. There is no end to it.

Everyone wants to be happy, but often we do not realize that if we are happy because we own something of value (or even because we have enough food every day), this happiness is momentary until we start wanting something else. When we want, we are sorry for what we do not have. The feelings of sorrow can therefore penetrate us and destroy the happiness we thought we had. Human nature tells us that being sorrowful is not right or normal, so we try to console a sorrowful person in whatever way we can with either soothing words or kind actions. However, consolation, even if successful, can only be temporary. Therefore, trying to help someone else can sometimes leave us with the feeling of inadequacy. So we look for new ways to acquire happiness.

Nobody can come forward and say, "I am happy all the time and I remain the same all my life." Even if we are happy when we get up in the morning, by evening our mood may change. For example, when you look at the sunshine, you may be thrilled and excited. Yet on another day, depending on your feelings (such as that of inadequacy), the same sunshine may not give you the same thrill that it did once before. If you stop and think about it, it is not the sunshine that is different. It is your feeling of inadequacy or sorrow that made it different. To overcome inadequacy or sorrow we take vacations, attend events, and acquire objects, thinking that by changing the scenery, we will feel happier. Yet if the saddest or most sorrowful person hears a joke or sees something funny, he will usually laugh. What this tells us is that laugher is natural. Everybody is born with the ability to express it. But we all acquire and feel sorrow, even though we have the ability within to avoid doing so.

Look at the most powerful country in the world, the United States of America. She tries to help other countries that have poverty, political turmoil, or economic instability. Even though the United States is wealthy and, compared to many other countries, its inflation rate, unemployment rate, and poverty rate are very low, it feels the need to do something about other fellow human beings to make them happy. That is natural because we empathize with others who have less, particularly friends and family members.

But, how the United States, or an individual, helps another country or person is important in whether or not happiness is attained. As already discussed, the goal should be to acquire self-knowledge. With self-knowledge most individuals will be able to live happy lives without the need for government intervention.

You cannot control or kill desires because they keep changing. Desire is like a fire, it never says, "I have burned enough." It engulfs everything until its fuel is spent. Desire is a positive thing if you use it with wisdom and discriminative choices. To be able to choose is a great blessing of the Creator. How to channel your desires is very important, and the channeling of desire can uplift you if it is through a positive action. You can possess things without being possessed by them.

While needs change as we grow up, one thing that does not change is "desire" itself. The challenge is not to find out how to get a material thing or satisfy a carnal urge, but to satisfy desire itself so that we are content and blissful with or without the material thing, or the carnal urge.

There will always be struggles, whether you are poor or a billionaire, but in different forms. For example, struggle may be monetary or related to relationships. One person wants to get rid of something to make himself happy while another person needs to acquire something. If a homeowner needs money, he may try to sell his property. Another person wants to acquire a better house because she feels it will satisfy her desires and expectations. The same object will make both people feel happy. People's motives change, but the object remains the same.

An American tradition I've seen during my last twenty-four years living in America is the "garage sale." When you are out driving, during spring or summer, you see people with a lot of stuff for sale in their driveways, stuff that usually comes from a cleanup of their attics, garages, or basements. Junk piles up and some people may give it to the Salvation Army, but many people, instead of giving or throwing things away, want to make some money on it. I'm always surprised at how many people stop their cars, some of them driving Cadillacs and Mercedes, to look at and buy that second-hand stuff. So, one person wants to get rid of the junk from their basement and another person thinks it is valuable, and they feel happy because they bought it cheap. Thus, the one thing that does not change is the "desire" in the human beings. Like I said, the buyer was happy to acquire a "valuable" and the seller was happy to get rid of the "junk." So, as human beings, we always find ourselves to be "wanting persons." "I want this, I want that." It is a unique, unqualified desire every human being has.

If you look at the universe, plants want to survive, and animals want to survive, just like human beings want to survive. In fact, the urge to survive is common to every living thing. However, the difference is, if you look at plants or animals, they survive without much effort. They are able to survive without a government, without courts, without advocates, without police. They only struggle for food and shelter, which for them is a basic need. The other commonality is the biological urge, which animals have, but use only to propagate their species. Once an animal is content with food and shelter, it doesn't try to stockpile more food than its neighbor, or acquire a more *opulent* shelter. However, as human beings, we have the desire to *have more,* all the time. When we are content with, let us say food and shelter, we take a vacation. We wanted a car and we got it. After awhile we start to think, "What shall I buy or do next?" We're always trying to acquire or experience more. But for an animal, its life is fulfilled if it is able to survive and propagate. An animal is just living up to the expectations of nature.

Temporarily, an object, situation, emotion, place, or relationship can make you happy, but it is not forever. You eventually go through feelings of sorrow, no matter what. So the ultimate goal should be: "How can I achieve ongoing happiness?" Self-awareness is the answer because once you acquire this knowledge, there is no losing it or getting rid of it. It is yours, and it is what keeps you feeling content, full, and adequate.

You cannot attain self-knowledge if you think constantly about acquiring money or if you believe that material possessions will bring you security. We all know the power of money, and not having money can certainly make you feel insecure. But if you worry that people will not respect you because you are moneyless, you will be driven, in a negative way, to acquire it.

When we go to sleep we are all the same. We all have dreams, we live in those dreams for a while, and when we wake up we are back in the real world. For example, when a king sleeps in his palace and a beggar sleeps on the pavement outside the palace, both are sleeping. Until they fall asleep, the king was a king and he was conscious of his royal privileges, or his royal problems, whatever they were. Likewise, the beggar was a beggar, looking at the sky and figuring out that the stars conspired to put him on the road and not inside the palace. For the king inside the palace, given all comforts and luxuries, and for the beggar outside the compound on the ground, once they both fall asleep, time disappears, and space disappears. All their memories, their problems, everything disappears. By knowing "self," you realize that whether you are a king or a beggar, it doesn't make any difference for the physical body, which functions the "same" for all of us.

As human beings, we always want something, "I want this, and I want that." We always seem to have a sense of wanting, which is a very common human experience. However, we see ourselves most of the time incomplete, inadequate, insecure, and unfulfilled. We are always in the pursuit of pleasure, acquisition, and possession of material things and also trying to acquire wealth, power, influence, fame, and name. As a human being, there will be no end to our struggles to possess and acquire things. But no matter how much wealth you accumulate, it is never enough to satisfy your inner desire for the long term. Whatever pleasures we enjoy are not sufficient to bring everlasting fulfillment because we always forget a basic fundamental truth: *the gain of things, of any kind of wealth, also involves loss.* Gain always involves loss. Pleasure does not produce everlasting contentment, and the desire that brings the pleasure is always constantly changing.

So you can choose to act, but once you have acted you have no further choice but to experience the result occurring from that act. That result is in accordance with the laws of nature, and acts become problems when we refuse to accept outcomes that are different from what we expected. We rarely look at an experience as a good teacher because our minds are not clear of reactions; thus they are not attentive and not available to be taught. We as human beings enjoy our God-given free will all the time, and we can choose to act or not to act. But the results of our actions are not subjective or our choice. We are a society of people, and we constantly try to escape from ourselves because we are not satisfied with ourselves. We see ourselves as not being exactly the way we'd like to be, so we keep our minds continually busy; there is no time, place, or quiet in which we can be with ourselves. Even if we are on the telephone on hold, often music is provided so the mind can be occupied.

We take vacations to different places and we travel to different places to escape. For example, we go one time to the beach, one time to the mountains, from a sandy place to a snowy place and back again, to escape from ourselves. We have wanderlust, and we feel compelled to go to amusement parks, movies, sporting events, or parties or to stay home and watch TV. All these are a means of escape. Don't get me wrong. There is nothing wrong with travel or recreation. The point I am emphasizing here involves your thinking process. The problem is the *need* for escape. Some people look for other avenues of escape like drinking alcohol, gambling, or using street drugs. Always there is a compelling need to escape because we are reluctant to face our self. Without escape, which takes you from reality, you feel lost, sad, or incomplete.

Some kinds of recreation may or may not be escape. For example, a happy person while taking a shower will sing because he has nothing else to do. His mind is relaxed, so he sings, and that singing reflects his contentment. Singing or listening to music can either be an escape or nonescape. Sometimes we whistle, hum, or sing to shake ourselves from a reaction to an unwelcome thought. Here, this singing is not of happiness, but for escape. This tendency of the mind, wanting to escape, is universal.

Everywhere in the world, the inner workings of every human mind are the same. Whether you are American, African, European, Indian, Arab, or Jewish, the basic function of the mind is the same. The only differences you find are cultural because cultural differences are in response to the environment that molded you. So, from culture to culture, the avenues of escape will be different, and these avenues are determined by the nature of the society in which you find yourself growing up. Those social factors will determine the way of escape, *but the desire of the mind to escape is a universal phenomenon.*

If you enjoy staying by yourself in a quiet place, it doesn't necessarily mean you are a sad or introverted person. It may mean you are simply quiet and contemplative. It could very well mean you have the ability to face yourself happily. If you cannot face yourself happily, your mind will always require an escape. An escape is an occupation that engages the attention of the mind so that it does not have to be with itself. When you have learned to be with yourself, without friends or guests constantly inviting or being invited, and you still can enjoy yourself and feel happiness, that shows that you have come to terms with yourself and you have a clear knowledge of yourself. In no way does this advise you to be lonely, or an alone person, or an unsocial person. While it's a good thing when you do not have to have a "craving for company" to be happy, this doesn't mean company is bad, or that you should dislike being around people. But you are in a good place, mentally, when you do not *require* people around you to be happy. It is not that a quiet place in and of itself is intrinsically good or that the presence of company is something bad. You have to realize that a person who seeks seclusion out of hatred of people is not expressing a positive value. Such a person is afraid of people, and that is called social phobia. But the other extreme, where someone constantly needs the company of people all the time as an escape from one's self, is not any more desirable than the fear of people. The desirable attitude to develop is that when you are by yourself, you are content and happy and just as accepting of this situation as when you are surrounded by loved ones.

One time, during my fellowship training, my wife and I went to a friend's house for dinner. While we were talking, the host casually mentioned to me, "You know how my wife and I are, if we don't have at least $100,000 cash in the bank, we don't feel secure." I thought to myself, how on earth will that $100,000 give this person *real* security? What kind of security was he looking for? Is it health, happiness, or future? I truly didn't understand that. It raised many questions in my mind. Having money is only temporary happiness and security. Good health and a good state of mind probably give you more happiness. Then I realized how many people are so concerned about having a security blanket. If you make millions of dollars thinking that guarantees you and your children are going to be happy forever, you are fooling yourself. Throughout history we have seen, to verify this, many rich families becoming poor through an unexpected twist of fortune or a streak of bad luck.

When we face reality, we realize that money is not a cure-all and it does not bring happiness *all the time.* As I mentioned before, in taking a vacation or a cruise, happiness is going to be momentary in the sense it may last a week, two weeks, or a month, but if you don't have inner peace of mind, everything is temporary.

It amazes me that so many people think that having more money or more power is security, when it is actually inadequacy. There is no way of achieving adequacy through power or money or anything tangible because anything you gain is going to be temporary—because every individual feels he or she is not adequate and lacks something. Even if you had the whole earth or if you were the only occupant of the earth, still you could not solve the problem of inadequacy. It is not a social problem; rather it is an individual problem that is universal. You can say that you own the possessions you have gathered, but still you will feel inadequate. Even if you have excellent security in the form of money, assets, buildings, land, and other investments, it is actually insecurity because it lies in the realm of time. Anything within the realm of time is insecure.

I am not saying that you need to practice the complete suppression of your desires, or that you should be deprived of your possessions. Rather you should practice a sustaining state of mind whereby you are just as content with or without your prized possessions. And, by observation, inquiry, and analysis, you can achieve this. In our hectic world, we are so busy we don't stop to smell the roses or look at nature and enjoy the beautiful creation of God. Without self-knowledge, things can never be *always* bright and beautiful and perfect. Every one of us will have some kind of disease at one time or another. That disease can come at any time, any place, and it is not limited to a particular time or age. Likewise, pain is also a lifelong companion. This doesn't mean just physical pain; there is also mental pain. Pain, like disease, cannot be avoided. The various types of pain come in a variety of ways. But with self-knowledge, despite our pains, we can feel contentment and be fulfilled if we know the true meaning of ourselves. All this disease and pain, getting old, and losing our senses slowly, is not a negative experience. It is simply a fact and the nature of life. These "changes" are for a purpose, to direct our attention to see life objectively. So the time available for us during this life is very valuable, very precious, and we must make use of it with the right attitude and a positive mental state as we learn to know ourselves, and not fervently cling to materialistic pursuits and pleasures.

We should let go of the notion of "ownership" because when you analyze anything that you think you own, you'll find that there is nothing you can own forever in this world, in this universe. You come in with nothing and you leave the earth with nothing. You might say you are the owner of your own body, but if you understand the transitory nature of life, you'll realize that you are just the *managing trustee* of your body. With self-knowledge, you will not have an attachment or an attitude of ownership. Instead, you will develop a kind of nonattachment, dispassion, as you realize that there is no validity to "ownership" of anything. So, when you adopt an attitude of nonattachment to materials, possessions, or to people, when you experience a "loss," you don't crumble or fall apart. You will face the ups and downs of life with an easy-going attitude.

With self-knowledge, instead of keeping your vision fixated on your house or job, vacations, your marriage, or whatever represents a step toward completeness for you, you'll discover that all the achievements, accomplishments, or material gains do not bring forever-lasting satisfaction. This knowledge can change the definition and direction of your gains. And with this knowledge you will make your vision and thinking process clear. You will develop a new focus on the inner self, which will lead to contentment and satisfaction that can last throughout your remaining days on earth.

Purely knowing your self can lead to happiness. Self-knowledge, or self-awareness is the key to happiness because happiness is not something that can be created, produced, or purchased. You can't order it from a catalog or on the Internet. It is only incognizance or ignorance, which keeps you from knowing your self as you are. With self-awareness you are simply recognizing the underlying basic human need to be free. You are limited only by the incognizance of your true nature, and resolution of that incognizance through self-knowledge makes you feel limitless, complete, fulfilled, and contented.

You can take a path that is action oriented to gain self-knowledge, or you can take a path that is knowledge oriented to gain self-knowledge because all forms of self-awareness in various degrees of intensity lead toward happiness. We all work hard, look forward to retirement, and once we retire we try to enjoy the things we've acquired. Then what? Finally we look toward death. So all of our life, we've been looking for happiness, and finally we reconcile ourselves to our inevitable death. On the other hand, if you have a proper understanding of true happiness, you can achieve that happiness along the path of your life. Just having curiosity isn't enough. Self-knowledge is "knowing the truth about yourself." It is a lifelong pursuit. The means must be very clear. Not like a little bit of this, a little bit of that, let me do some yoga, some meditation, some healing, or let me change the methodology because the other one is not working. If you are clear in your mind that "I want freedom from all the problems centered on myself," you are headed in right direction to accomplish self-knowledge.

The seeking of happiness through material objects will continue until we find happiness and peace within our selves. We make many mistakes in our search for everlasting happiness and peace. This does not mean we have to dump the comforts the materialism provides you. It *does* mean you will have to give up your attachments to them. And when you do, you will pleasantly discover that you will be just as happy if they are suddenly gone. *That* is true peace of mind. That is truly being complete.

• Chapter 3 •
About Our Values

No one is ignorant of the importance of having values. However human beings seldom properly understand values. Almost every human being intrinsically knows what is universally right or wrong—it's just common sense. The problem lies in one's understanding of the value of the values.

As children growing up, we are all influenced by our parents, teachers, society, culture, and religion to name a few. Because we do not have a fully developed reasoning process, many times we just oblige our parents or teachers and follow their values, whether or not we understand their true meaning. However, as we become adults, we begin to think independently, and we assimilate the values that will guide us in deciding what is right and what is wrong.

Let's say you are hungry and can control your hunger for only a day or two. Even if there is food in the garbage, you won't jump in and eat like an animal. It is not because you are obliging the Health Department and adopting their principles of hygiene. It is because you have a very well assimilated value for eating only clean, fresh food. In the same way, some of us feel compelled to speak the truth, and not to intentionally hurt others. This is not so much the result of conditioning, but because such behavior is in one's nature.

How do we become like this? We followed or practiced the divine qualities, which are already within. We all have these divine "seeds" planted in our minds when we are born. The only thing we have to do in the pursuit of self-knowledge is to recognize and make use of them—that is, practice them.

There are many qualities already within each of us. To mention a few: purity of body and mind; absence of desire to harm anyone; absence of pride, inflated ego, greed, or jealousy; charitableness; truthfulness; controlled anger; compassion for all beings; and lack of desire for material objects to fulfill our happiness. These are all qualities everybody knows—but we don't always practice them.

People often forget a very simple, common-sense axiom that *whatever treatment you want from others, you should be willing to give the same.* If you want to be treated fairly, you simply have to treat others fairly. There is a high price to pay if you become a slave to your own greed, or become jealous and try to suppress another person who is adhering to those values, or try to interfere with someone's life or position in society. In practicing this one golden rule, one becomes sensitive to the needs of others, as to one's own needs. *One need not be a saint to have these virtues,* and anyone can cultivate them. And when you do, you oblige yourself, you become divine and you become a complete human being. Qualities that are the opposites of the divine qualities, like pretentiousness, vanity, conceit, anger, harshness, greed, jealousy, and the like are sooner or later going to bring unhappiness and sorrow to you. Temporarily you may feel that you are happy and that you are winning, but you cannot beat the laws of nature. Ultimately you will suffer sadness and sorrow because for every action there is a result. And if your actions are against the laws of nature, you are going to get the negative results—maybe not today, it may take several years, but you cannot escape from the consequences of negative actions toward others.

Many people do not realize that by being pretentious, they are setting themselves up for a fall. We all depend on so many others for what we are and what we accomplish in this world. If you forget that simple fundamental fact, you can boast however much you want, but with time others will see you for the pretentious person you are. People may not say it to your face, but in their minds they know. On the other hand, if you portray yourself exactly as you are, you don't have to keep track of your lies or your cover-ups. No matter what else, if you are honest and straightforward, people will have respect for you.

We often do not recognize the subtle gains we see in our lives by following and by practicing the positive values of life. If we put in the effort in the beginning and practice daily, later on it comes naturally and we don't have to make a conscious effort to do it. Practicing good values each day will make our lives simple and less confusing.

To become self-aware, it is important that you do not allow yourself to feel jealous of anybody or desire anybody's success, or feel that you must have what the other person has. Then you will know what feeling fulfilled and content means. It starts out with daily practice and soon becomes automatic behavior. Also, there is a saying that before you try to teach the world, or win in the world, you must win at home first. For myself, professionally, personally, socially, as a father, as a husband, and as a physician, I do my best to fulfill this obligation.

You should always speak the truth, but at the same time let it be "pleasant truth." I have seen some people who go overboard in speaking the hard truth. This will often result in alienating the people you are trying to help. Just being pleasant is a beautiful thing and it is a generous service to others that will be greatly appreciated by all. Speaking the truth kindly will not only have a positive impact on a person, but will also eliminate any possible resentment by that person.

Knowing and practicing positive values will improve your self-respect and self-esteem. It is fine to use the self-knowledge you gain to succeed in life, but you should be careful not to abuse your newly found power or inner strength—especially at the cost of other people (e.g., stepping on their shoulders to climb the success ladder). Unfortunately, I see this in my professional as well as my social life all the time. And sometimes when I point it out, people seem to have a phobia about upsetting a person in a place of power. They are often afraid that they might need that person one day, even though they know that the so-called "powerful person" is abusing the abilities accumulated over the years, just for the purpose of personal gain.

Whenever you accomplish something, it's important to be humble, just like a flowering bush toward its blossoms. Even though the flowers are colorful and fragrant, the bush simply blooms because it is its nature to bloom. And the bush makes no claim to glory. By just observing plants and animals, we can learn so much. All it takes is opening our eyes and minds to improve our self-knowledge.

One who is able to give is truly a rich person, not necessarily the one who has the most money. For example, a gift is truly a gift if it blesses the person who receives it, rather than making him or her feel obliged to the giver. Contrary to this, giving with a "cameraman" around or publicizing your charity for furthering your own ends is not a true charity. Giving without expecting to be rewarded for it is a noble quality to have.

You can be competitive for success, but you should not turn that competitiveness into personal jealousy. You should not use your abilities to knock the other person off the ladder to success or to create a hardship for them. Temporarily you may feel happy, but it will not be a long-lasting happiness. On the other hand, if while trying to succeed, you demonstrate respect for your competition, your own respect and glory will follow automatically, just like your shadow follows you wherever you go, and you don't have to take it along with you.

Once again, I want you to understand very clearly that self-confidence is different from exploiting your abilities. A simple person is one who does not have any complexities, and his mind does not have constant conflict with opposites like sadness and joy, hate and love, rich and poor, greed and generosity, or anger and equanimity. When you start identifying and glorifying the individualism, in other words the personal accomplishments, it creates an ego problem for that individual. Instead of glorifying an individual for his accomplishments or success it should be acknowledged that the whole society, or many individuals played a role. That used to be the philosophical thinking in the past, but with modernization in the Western world, the focus has shifted to the individual and worshipping a single person for his abilities in sports, movies, business, and other high-profile professions. This often makes the individuals feel inflated with ego, and they forget the friends and teachers who got them where they are until a catastrophe happens to them or they lose everything. Only then do they start realizing that they are no different from any other human being. Self-knowledge is the realization that nothing is accomplished alone—that others deserve credit for your victories or accomplishments. By giving this deserved credit to others, you will never develop an over-inflated ego. And you will gain the respect of your peers.

External cleanliness is a very well understood universal value: like taking a daily bath, brushing your teeth and wearing clean clothes. On the other hand, "internal cleanliness" is not always well recognized or appreciated. When I say *internal cleanliness,* I mean ridding the mind of jealousy, anger, selfishness, guilt, phoniness, possessiveness, hatred, and all the negative reactions, which ultimately lead to sorrow and unhappiness. There is no detergent to clean your mind, however. You have to think the opposite of unclean thoughts. If you practice this clean thinking, even though your negative attitude may seem to be justified, eventually, one day you will be able to completely "clean the mind." Also, the capacity to love all mankind will always keep the mind "clean."

Any person is capable of loving; even a serial killer has elements of love and sympathy. The people we worship, like Jesus or Buddha, have shown compassion, mercy, love and harmlessness, which made them divine. However, the seeds of those values are present in everyone. It is your responsibility to nurture them because God gave us this choice to make. The person who knows himself can recognize the unseemliness of mind, and for him the negative qualities like selfishness and jealousy are baseless. Just as we brush our teeth, take a bath, and wear clean clothes for external cleanliness, for internal cleanliness we need to exercise the mind with peacefulness, accommodation without pride, without phoniness and selfishness, and without inflated ego.

So a dedication to gaining self-knowledge is very important, we cannot negotiate with this, and we have to put forth full effort. It's just as if you want to be successful, or want to be "somebody," or with anything you want to achieve, you have to put the effort in, and there is no compromise to it. You have to do this wholeheartedly because a weak effort will amount to little or nothing for results. To see something, you need to use your eyes. To hear something, you need to use your ears. And to gain self-knowledge, you need to use your inner discipline. So please keep in mind that even though this book may look like a bunch of words, similes, and examples, it is a means to self-knowledge. Reading these words and sentences and paying close attention to the underlying meaning culminates in self-knowledge.

Too often we throw away values without understanding them, or they are lost because we have not assimilated them. Following positive values, not because your religion taught you, or your mother, father, or teacher taught you, not to oblige God or anyone else, but for yourself only, will make you a truly happy human being. By practicing and following these diving attributes, virtues, and values, people like Mahatma Gandhi, Martin Luther King, and Mother Theresa discovered the freedom of life. They were born with the same physical body as everybody else, but they understood the true meaning of these virtues. That is why they were able to become divine. You don't have to look for God elsewhere. He is within you as long as you possess these divine qualities.

We all face difficult situations with daily living in our society, with jobs, relationships, and family. A self-aware person may get angry and may make mistakes. However, with simplicity and straightforwardness, he is able to quickly get rid of his anger, and he also learns from his reactions, so as not to repeat the negative ones. The mind that is simple, factual, and without conflict is ready to discover the true nature and the truth of the self. When we say, "do no harm," it doesn't mean physical violence only. You can hurt people with your harsh words and sometimes even your thoughts unknowingly can hurt fellow human beings.

All living beings have value and the only difference is the relative level of awareness of life from plant to animal kingdom to human beings. You cannot condemn a person who is polite but is still eating meat by claiming that he is harming another life form. Because the Creator gave us the gift of "free will" and choices at the same time, the laws of nature also gave responsibility to the human beings. You must understand that you will never find in one person all the qualities you like or you dislike. Any given person is going to be a mixture of things, some of which you will find appealing and others that you do not find appealing. When you recognize these facts, you will automatically accommodate situations and people happily. I can safely challenge that you will never find a relationship that does not require some accommodation. It is always give and take, sometimes less, sometimes more. All relationships require a balance. And if you seek balance in all relationships (friends, lovers, business) there won't be big problems, and you'll have the best chance for happiness. You should always look at situations as mixed blessings. For example, sunshine is vital for all living beings, but the ultraviolet rays and radiation from the sun can harm your body. You can get skin cancer if you are lightly pigmented and exposed for a long period of time to the ultraviolet rays. But we cannot condemn the sun and declare that we should stop the sun from shining on us, for we would perish without it. As they come along, we should face our life situations as mixed blessings and avoid categorizing them as either good or bad.

You must remember that the world is wide and variety makes it more interesting. Accommodating other people's needs and other people in your life is a wonderful quality. By doing so you will find more happiness without the need for material gains. When you are nonjudgmental toward a fellow human being, forgiveness and mercifulness come naturally. With this understanding, you always have an alignment of your thoughts, words, and actions.

If you practice accommodation and being nonjudgmental on a daily basis, your thoughts, words, and actions will automatically become real and spontaneous. When you keep your mind "clean" in this way, it will be a quiet, alert mind, and a clean, quiet, alert mind is comfortable with itself and ready to learn.

Just by reading this book, a transformation can happen. You can be reading along and think it is just a series of words, followed by more words, but all of a sudden, you could have this incredible insight. *Something I've written will reach you with perfect clarity and you will have an experience of self-knowledge and an understanding of your inner self that you didn't have before.* Over time, these "insight experiences" add up to self-awareness. It may take one reading for some; it may take more readings or re-readings for others. But it can happen for everyone, so I hope you continue your journey of self-knowledge.

• Chapter 4 •
Actions and Their Results

When misfortune comes to a person we know or somebody we see on TV, the common reaction is to think that person must have done something wrong, and that is why this happened. Or people who don't like the person may say, "She deserves it." But how do we know? Who are we to judge another?

In the Hindu philosophy, everybody lives in what is called "maya," which means myth, the not knowing of what comes next, like a mystery. We don't know what will happen to us in the next minute, the next day, or the next year. Nobody knows when a person will die, and nobody knows who will be rich, who will be poor. Nobody knows if a rich person will soon become poor. Why did this happen, and how did that happen? Nobody has clear answers, but we try to rationalize the results of someone's actions by saying something like, "Oh, he invested badly in the stock market," or, "He's on a streak of bad luck." A person can be walking down the street, and as the result of a simple slip and fall, a seemingly inconsequential bump to the head can cause bleeding in the brain, and the person dies.

As a neurologist, or brain specialist, taking care of head injury patients for the last fifteen years, I have seen this all the time. I have also seen in my practice people you would think had no chance of surviving a severe head injury, who somehow came out of it beautifully, without any problems. On the other hand, because we do not have enough knowledge and perception about the mystery of life, if things don't turn out the way we expect them to, automatically we draw negative conclusions about them.

Most of us are conditioned to presume that almost all bad outcomes are failure. But if you think about it, almost all progress comes from failure. Sometimes failure can be our greatest teacher. The great inventor, Thomas Edison, realized this. Most of his successful inventions came out of learning "what didn't work." Sometimes it would take him over a thousand tries—or a thousand failures, before he would arrive at the solution he was seeking. Thomas Edison never took failure personally. When he failed, he did not consider himself to be a bad person. In fact, he considered himself to be a better person for having the learning experience. Failure simply said to him, "Now I know what *doesn't* work." You too can learn to look at something others would call a failure, but for yourself, you see it as merely a life lesson that is going to make you a better person.

One of the qualities that makes us different from the animal kingdom is our reasoning faculty, and hence we have choices. Animals are practically programmed by their instincts. Thus, when they get hungry they automatically eat; when they get thirsty they drink and quench their thirst. They lie down to sleep at the same time each day. When their stomachs are full, they are content, and they wait until they are hungry again to eat. On the other hand, we as human beings have many choices, but sometimes all these choices can cause grief, or a sense of inadequacy, or conflict within us.

A human being is a self-conscious, seemingly separate entity, who can choose his or her actions. A human being can choose to act or not to act in a different way at different times to the same stimulus. Wherever there is choice, there is free will. A man can even become a woman nowadays.

If you use a computer, you know that it can do many things, but it only does things that are programmed into it by a human being. It cannot make the choices on its own without a programmer first setting up certain commands. In a similar way, an animal's will is preset by its instincts.

Sometimes when we have a problem, we are not able to see things clearly, but everything seems clear if it is somebody else's problem. When the problem is somebody else's, we are all suddenly philosophers, and we try to counsel them. For example, if there is a death in a friend's or relative's family, we console the person, saying that, after all, death is inevitable and everyone who is born will have to die one day or anther. On the other hand, if it happens to ourselves or to our family members, we may try to blame somebody or something else. That, by the way, is what most of the malpractice lawsuits are about. We try to blame somebody else all the time instead of looking to ourselves and what we did that led to the problem. Usually, the person who is experiencing the problem is completely blind to the solution.

When someone who everybody regards as "a good person" dies, we wonder why. We say, "Why him (or her)? He (or she) had so much to live for!" But it is not for us to know the reason why. "God's will" seldom has a logical explanation. The reason is often *deeper* than we are equipped to understand. Consider this: there have been many positive things that have come out of a "good person's" death. When it's a so-called "bad person" who dies, often the reaction is, "Who cares! He deserved it," but when a "good person" dies, perhaps a law is enacted to protect thousands of others. Why did that one person have to be the "sacrificial lamb?" Perhaps in his subconscious mind he chose that role. Maybe that was his life's mission, to make that ultimate sacrifice for the good of others. Look at how many millions of soldiers have made the ultimate sacrifice. When a soldier dies for the good of his or her country, it is fully accepted because a soldier knows that any moment in a battle may be his or her last. Perhaps everyday people are *soldiers* of a sort, and once in a while make the ultimate sacrifice, albeit unconsciously, for the good of their country, or their fellow human beings.

Every action has a result. But the result of each action depends on the laws of nature—not particularly on the way you expect it to be. Sometimes we have a hurdle or situation where we feel we need help from God, so we go to the temple or church and pray for what we think we want. But the outcome may not be what we expected, and we get angry with God and say, "I prayed long and hard but God did not help me!" But prayer seldom works that way. The cause and effect of it are rarely direct. God *does* work miracles, but He works them His own way—which is almost always indirect and according to the laws of nature, created by Him.

There are three important things to remember. One is your effort, of which you may think you put in enough, but according to the laws of nature, it may be too little. The second thing is time. There is always a time factor involved when you are expecting a result, and this time factor runs on "God's watch," not yours. The third thing is the working of the laws of nature. God's help or His grace doe not depend on your expectations because the laws of nature are God in action, and they work independently of "human logic."

When there is an action there is always a result, but if you purify your mind by dedicating the action to God in an attitude of selfless service, you do not have to worry about the consequences of your action. When you do an action, the end result is taken care of by the laws of nature. Even if the result is not what you expect it to be, you should not be disappointed and think that you must have done something wrong. Even though you feel in your heart you did it right, you must not question (or curse) "Why did it happen *this* way?" As human beings, we have a choice over an action but we have no choice over a result. It's the laws of nature, and the laws of nature are the wisdom of God. He takes care of the result in His own time, in His own way. *This does not mean that you should not expect a result.* That is where there's a big misunderstanding in many religions about the action and the result. The result is hidden in the action. You have to remember that there are any number of factors that contribute to bringing about a particular result of an action, and we may not know all the various causes that led to that result because we expect only one type of result. Because it did not happen in a particular way, automatically we get disappointed, frustrated, or depressed. You have to realize that God, who is omniscient, created the laws of nature, which operate with a logic that is beyond our mortal minds to understand. Our interpretations may be different because we want something that suits us or brings us what we decided is supposed to be happiness.

If you expect one thing and the result is something different, it does not mean that you did something wrong. With self-knowledge, you'll realize that certain things are man-made and certain things are God-made. You have to accept your own personal responsibility for your actions. For example, you may be a churchgoer, or you go to temple, or a mosque, or a synagogue and pray to God regularly, perhaps even more than the average human being does. And you have faith in God and you believe that God is always going to save you. But one time you are driving after having a drink or two, and you're talking on your cell phone and not paying attention to the other cars, and you are involved in an accident. Immediately you blame God. You've been praying daily, so why did you have the accident? You do not consider that you have your own personal responsibility and that God gave you the ability to make choices—which can work for you or against you. Without this ability to choose one action over another, you would be no different from the animals, which are governed by instincts alone.

If two people are running for office in an election, or playing tennis, only one person can be the winner, but the person who loses the election or the game isn't necessarily a loser. From the point of view of the laws of nature, why he or she loses may have an explanation far beyond our limited thinking process. There may be a greater good yet to come, but the person who loses automatically feels disappointed, thinking that he or she put in a lot of effort and time and did so much practicing but still lost. But if the one who loses is able to keep an open mind and accept the laws of nature, he or she will see a positive outcome in due time.

We sometimes begrudge a successful person who we know to be cruel or greedy. We wonder, "Why does this person who is so mean have such a good life?" We are seeing only the exterior trappings of this person's life; we have no idea what is going on inside of them.

I have known very wealthy people who lived in mansions and owned yachts and luxury cars—yet they were miserable. In some cases, the wealthier they were, the unhappier they were. This is because they had it in their heads that the more they stockpiled wealth, the happier they would be. But life did not work out this way for them. More wealth created more problems and more responsibilities for them. For some, the more money they had, the more they feared they would one day lose it all. Some of them had ongoing personal or family problems. Others feared for their health and became hypochondriacs. Others feared that they would one day be found out, that some day the world would recognize that no matter how much money they had, they were still sadly unhappy. The point is, you can only see the exterior of a wealthy person. You may envy that exterior, but in many cases, if you knew the unhappy interior (troubled mind) that comes with it, you would not want their so-called luxurious life. I venture to assure you that if you could have a cruel or greedy person's wealth, but not without the price of also having internal torment, you would thank God for the simple life you have, no matter what your income level.

We sometimes see people who are very manipulative and we clearly know that they are selfish, greedy, money driven, and power driven, and they climb the social ladder and attain a lot of possessions at the expense of others. We know their hypocritical behavior and nature, which I have unfortunately seen in my own profession. We question why that person gets to enjoy those ill begotten possessions. Yes, they are enjoying them now, but for how long? Remember, nothing lasts forever. We come into this life with nothing and we leave with nothing.

You should seek to live the simple life. And when I say simple life, I do not mean a life that is without material objects. "Simple life" means a life free from conflicts. I am striving to lead a simple life myself in the sense of knowing the meaning of life and the truth of one's self.

The way the laws of nature work dictates that you have to make an effort, and you have to have a means, and a certain time is also required to produce the result. The final factor is the grace of God, which sometimes we call chance or pure luck. When you are doing something, you are conscious and aware of what you are doing, so you must realize that an action, whether it is right or wrong, has a result and the result may be fruitful or harmful. Or the result may only appear to be one or the other. Therefore, you need an abiding mind, which means to neutralize your likes and dislikes. This will lead to your acceptance that all results, whether they appear to be fruitful or harmful, are inevitably for your greater good.

Take the example of fire. You can use fire for cooking and for other useful things. By the same token, fire can also burn buildings and cause damage to thousands of acres of forest. Thus, we cannot automatically conclude that fire is either good or bad. While this is a very basic example, my point is that self-knowledge will give you the perception and understanding of the laws of nature concerning the inherent possibility for good and bad in all things. The only difference is how we choose to perceive it. Learning self-knowledge is like learning not to touch fire because it burns your skin. Similarly, the whole meaning of life lies in knowing that you are limitless, you are awareness, and you are always in a blissful state. Once you fully know or comprehend this, you will experience a big relief.

Desire is the basis of action, and as long as desire persists it creates a situation ideal for frustration if you have not prepared your mind—if you are not self-aware. All actions have a result, and you cannot avoid performing actions—you cannot become actionless. When you learn or gain self-awareness you will see that time, space, the planets, the air, the people, *all* move only in awareness. You come to realize that awareness is timeless, and you are that awareness in which all things exist, but which itself is free from time and space. By preparing your mind in the pursuit of self-knowledge, you can be actionless in action and take action in inaction. To be liberated you don't have to give up action as long as you are not attached to a particular result. Giving up is not an enunciation. Some people are happy eating tomatoes and some may be happy eating chicken or beef—it doesn't matter. So what is the key? What is the difference? The pursuit is the same, but the paths are different. In other words, the choice is yours to do or not to do a thing. But once you perform the action, once you make up your mind to do a certain action and you perform that action, the result is not in your hands, even though you may think it is, because you have no control over the result.

The result may fall into four categories. You may have a result *more* than you expected or *less* than you expected or *as* you have expected or an entirely *different* result. Then regardless, if you are disappointed in a result, you are misunderstanding the relationship between the action and the result. This is a most common misunderstanding because we do not realize that the result is governed by so many factors. But the ultimate one is the laws of nature that determine the result. For example, you are scheduled to take an exam. You worked very hard all year long, but just a few days before the exam you got deathly sick and you could not take the exam. Whom do you blame? Or do you take the attitude that your ultimate success in life does not depend on one exam?

How we can logically explain the negative results of our positive actions? A person may say, "I am always doing good deeds, why do I have this disease?" Or, "Why did I lose this or that?" So, "There must be no God!" and "This is all bologna!" Let's say you take a jar, and you fill it with water and then make an opening in the bottom so the water can leak out. But now let's say the jar is half-filled with dirty water, and you pour in pure water to fill the rest of the jar. The bottom hole will leak only the dirty water until it is all gone, and only then will the clear water start to leak. On the other hand, if the entire jar is filled with a mixture of clean and dirty water, half-clean water will leak from the bottom hole. This is how our actions and results work. People think, "Oh, I've changed and am behaving well now, why do I still have bad outcomes?" The jar of pure water mixed with dirty water easily explains this.

When you acquire self-knowledge, your attitude changes, and your thinking about actions and expected results changes. You get rid of your anxiety before, during, and after an action and while waiting for the result. That is one of the key elements in understanding self-knowledge. What makes human beings so special among all the living creatures? The fact that the self-conscious mind enjoys free will, which is a "choice." You have a choice to act or not to act, but once you act, the results are according to the laws of nature.

Roles You Play In Your Daily Life

Each human being plays a different role in relation to self, to family members, and to society. For example, you may be the son to your father, husband to your wife, father to your children, or an employer to an employee. By the same token, we all experience different emotions such as anger, jealousy, pride, and hate, to name a few. However, if you realize that all these emotions are really just your own reactions to events or situations, then you have self-knowledge.

Each reaction is different, yet it is your own. Regardless of the role you are fulfilling at the moment, it is simply a role. We all play different roles from the time we wake up until we go to bed—father, mother, student, teacher, employer, employee, husband, wife, sibling, friend—but this does not mean that you have to give up obligatory duties in pursuit of self-knowledge. Instead, as you perform your daily obligations, you will come to know and keep in mind what the self is about. This will make your life less strenuous and start you on the path toward happiness on a regular basis.

Awareness helps reveal the nature of the relationship between the timeless and the time bound, between the infinite and the finite, the absolute and the relative. The concept can be compared to an actor who plays a role. On the stage he may be a beggar or a king, but when the play is over his underlying self is not changed. He knows that he is not a king or a beggar. He is himself. And this is important to understand because with reference to these relative roles, you are the absolute and the one who plays all of your own roles. Each role has an existence.

Within yourself, you are independent of all the roles you play. While all of our actions relate to another as we assume our various roles—father, husband, son, uncle, aunt, mother, wife, sister, daughter, niece, master, or servant—each role is "I." But, the "I" is only the one assuming different roles, and each role exists only when there is a particular relationship to evoke it. The "I" is related to the universe, and as an individual, you are related to the Creator. This fundamental relationship exists for *every being in the world.*

Every creature in the world is related to the Lord or Creator. When you are with your father, you are his son, but when you are with your son, you become a father. Then the son that you were is gone. For another person, you are a friend, for someone else you are a boss. However, for the Creator, we are all the same, and the Creator has no role-playing. He is the sustainer, as well as the destroyer. We perform actions and He gives out the fruits of the actions—the results—according to the unwritten laws of nature that the Creator created.

Without understanding who or what the Creator is, you cannot fully understand yourself. You can transform from one role to another. For example, a cook who is fond of music can accept a cooking job in order to survive, but he still can practice singing. One day, though, he may become a professional musician, and cooking may then become a hobby. But underneath, the self is the same person. You must not forget that you are constantly "role playing," and no matter how deeply you are involved in that role playing, it is not who you truly are. The role you play is not your inner self.

• Chapter 5 •
How Is Self-Knowledge Acquired?

There are literally thousands of books that discuss the philosophical aspects of life based on different schools of thought. They discuss matters such as the existence of God and heaven, rebirth (aka reincarnation), and various metaphysical concepts. However, these areas fall outside the usual means of knowledge and, therefore, they are subject only to theory. To verify the means of knowledge, you do not require another means of knowledge. For example, to know that your eyes see, you only have to use your eyes and you have proof. This is a valid means of self-knowledge. In other words, you simply have to expose yourself to valid concepts to realize the truth of self-knowledge. Let us say you observed a person not talking at any given time. It doesn't mean you can conclude that, "I see this man, but he can't talk." Your perception and inference about various things in the world does not in any way contradict self-knowledge. Self-knowledge is purely a matter of understanding an equation in an implied way.

To give an example, I couldn't become a neurologist unless I first became a medical student and then specialized in neurology. I couldn't just walk in and say, "I want to practice neurology." The same is true for self-knowledge. You have to acquire it by practicing and self-learning. How do we gain knowledge of self? Is it through the sense organs? But the sense organs have limitations because with our eyes, we can see only so much. This is why we use telescopes and electron microscopes to see the things that cannot be seen with the naked eye. Some of us wear glasses because our eyesight is limited. And some of our other sense organs are also limited, though we may not be aware of it. So, gaining self-knowledge requires a degree of trust.

You have to use a different methodology or means to exercise and acquire self-knowledge. We need the mind for the rest of the senses to function. As long as we have the mind, our eyes can see, ears can hear, nose can smell, tongue can taste, and skin can feel. See how simple? The mind is the main thing we need for the utilization of all our sense organs. It is by operating our sense organs that we appreciate their function. Self-knowledge comes when we fully appreciate our sense organs instead of taking them for granted. For example, imagine you have a pot in front of you. If your eyes are closed, you cannot see the pot. However, when you open your eyes, you can cause your eyes to look at the pot and, through the brain, you can see the pot. Let us say that knowledge is a pot. For that, you have to use your eyes, through the mind, to see the pot. You need a valid means of knowledge to see the pot, and this is "pot knowledge." The same type of application applies to self-knowledge.

When the residents and interns are rotating in my neurology service, even though they've read textbooks about neurology, I have to show them the patients and demonstrate how to "think" when making a diagnosis. I have to demonstrate the fine points in the physical examination that give us the most important clues. Sometimes, tests like CT, MRI scanning of the brain, or an EEG may not be all that helpful to make the diagnosis. If the tests come back abnormal, it helps, but if they are normal, it does not help to determine what is wrong with the patient. This is where my experience and knowledge come into play. You may already have that self-knowledge, but you need a teacher to make a sense out of your existing knowledge to make it clear. It is like a lotus flower. In order for its beautiful petals open and blossom, it needs sunshine. The beautiful petals are there, but closed up and waiting. Not until the exposure to sunlight are they revealed.

As a physician, I can tell you that many times my patients come in with a lot of anxiety, nervousness, and fear, not knowing what is going on with their bodies when they are sick. After I explain to them in layman's terms what is going on, what is causing the neurological problems, and what the risk factors are, they feel great relief and satisfaction, and their minds are put at ease. It makes them feel much better instantly, and that is what self-knowledge is all about. Not knowing makes things worse and provokes unnecessary anxiety, tension, sorrow, and misery. It is like entering into an unfamiliar dark room. We fumble, we even feel anxious because we don't know what is in the room, especially if we've heard stories about ghosts and other things that may scare us. Naturally we imagine things and scare ourselves half to death, even if it is just a mouse or a cat making a noise we hear. The thought of a ghost or scary things distorts our thinking. On the other hand, if we enter the room with a lamp or candlelight, naturally the light is going to shed off the darkness, and then we can use our discriminative knowledge, thinking, vision, and hearing properly and realize that there is nothing to fear. This also is akin to self-knowledge.

Now, suppose you read something different, something that's against all that you have been holding as true for a long time. It will probably be very hard for you to accept this new explanation I am giving unless you have open-mindedness. On the other hand, if you already are totally open, then you can easily understand this, and you'll have no problem with it. Even if you have already been exposed to a number of teachings, as long as you have open-mindedness, you don't have to believe or disbelieve what I write here, as long as you stay open to the possibility, or at least keep a neutral attitude.

As human beings, we know we are limited, and we think that God is limitless, all-powerful, and that nothing is impossible to Him. But we see ourselves as limited by time, space, and other qualities, and we recognize that our sense organs are limited. For example, we think we can see so much, but we have to use a microscope to look at minute things that we cannot see with our naked eye. The same thing goes with looking at the galaxy. We have to use a powerful telescope to learn about the galaxies. When we recognize our limitations, we know that we are not perfect.

We think that we have "discovered" galaxies, as well as Mars, and other planets. But remember, they were already there; the only thing we acquired was the capacity or knowledge to acknowledge them. Similarly, even though some of what I am trying to explain may sound ridiculous or unbelievable, I am asking my readers to attempt to think beyond belief. As I've said before, it is reading with a neutral mind, and doing your own research. What we call "research" means searching over and over and over (which is why it is called *re*search). Through research, we are able to find things that already existed, and as we become aware, we achieve self-knowledge. The means is the research or the effort you must apply to realize for yourself that you and God are the same. What is the commonality between you and God? The answer is awareness. What is the difference between you and a rock? There is no life in the rock, and there is no awareness for a rock. However, if you close your eyes, everything is nonexistent, or when you are sleeping, everything is nonexisting from your point of view. But if you open your eyes, everything is there, daytime, or nighttime. For people who work night shifts, there is life throughout the night, even though most of the people who go to bed at night and get up in the morning think life starts in the morning. Life is always there. It is "you" and your awareness that makes it appear like there is a beginning and an end. If you look at everything globally and analytically and use your knowledge, you will see that it is always there. We all come and go, and we are born and die, but the world is always there, and the universe is always there.

To become something, you have to first have it as a goal. A pregnant woman has to wait nine months to have a baby. If you want to become a doctor you can't do it overnight. First you go to school and study mathematics, chemistry, science, literature, and various other required and elective courses, like everybody else. As you reach the higher classes, you begin to focus on the specialized subjects you have to take to achieve your goal. Even then, you have to put a lot of effort into it because many other people also want to become physicians and you have to show your ability, not just good test scores, to prove that you are eligible to study medicine and become a doctor. Then you have to go to medical school; there you have many students much like you. Again, you have to put in more effort to succeed. For example, if you want to go to Harvard or Yale University, you cannot just say, "I think I'll go to Yale." You have to show you have more qualifications than your peers to be eligible to be a student at Yale.

The same thing goes for me. I have a brain specialty, neurology, practice. I teach medical students, interns, and residents at a local university level, but I cannot say I am equal to a professor who is teaching in a university like Harvard or Yale because I know my limitations and the criteria that I did not meet to be a professor of an Ivy League university. In a similar way, to acquire self-knowledge and to know beyond, you have to have some qualifications also. Even if you don't have qualifications, you have to put effort into it, research, and acquire that knowledge. You need to always think beyond instead of just believing and following the religious rules and beliefs that were given to us centuries ago.

Success in attaining self-knowledge and awareness depends on your personal quest, basic knowledge, sophistication, your method of thinking about life, and your attitude. Do you see the glass as half full or half empty? Are you more positive or negative in your general attitude? Some people have strong beliefs and do not have an open mind for exploration, new logic, or advancement of thinking.

Belief can work for you, and sometimes it can work against you. Some people's beliefs have the unfortunate power to limit them. They fixate on something and conclude that there is no other way. They actually create no other way for themselves, and their life is confined by this limitation. A person who is fixed in his beliefs cannot be surprised, thus he cannot grow any further. He is stuck in time and space, so to speak. He will get no worse, but he will also get no better.

Other people have strong beliefs, but they allow themselves to be surprised. They allow themselves to learn something they didn't know. When you allow yourself to be surprised, you open yourself to a world of possibilities, which can cause quantum leaps in your spiritual growth—and in your self-awareness. That is what this book is about.

I urge you to maintain whatever religious beliefs you hold, and I invite you to read with an open mind, like a child, and allow yourself the gift of being surprised by new knowledge.

You may be wondering why I write on and on about self-knowledge, and I do not say *exactly* what self-knowledge is and how to acquire it. The reason I am not just coming out and giving you, in one or two sentences, a concrete definition of self-knowledge (or self-awareness) is that self-knowledge is not an instantaneous experience. It comes to you gradually, in stages. Gaining self-knowledge is like putting together a jigsaw puzzle. You can't assemble an entire puzzle in one or two motions. What I am doing in this book is giving you the little pieces of the puzzle one at a time. By the time you get to the end of the book, it is my hope that you will have enough pieces of the puzzle to see the big picture. However, with a difficult jigsaw puzzle, you don't always succeed on the first try. Likewise, it may take you another pass through the book, or two or three passes, to put it all together.

As another example, in kindergarten class, the teacher wouldn't start out by giving you four-syllable words. Instead, you are first taught the ABCs. Then you graduate to simple three letter words, then simple sentences like, "See Spot run." In more advanced classes you are taught the meaning of nouns, verbs, adverbs, adjectives, conjunctions, and the other parts of speech. The learning and repetition of these building blocks gradually lead you to an understanding of the English language (or French, Spanish, Italian, German). Similarly, I am giving you the building blocks that will lead you to self-knowledge, or self-awareness, which will then lead you to ongoing happiness. Thus, I am explaining logically and systematically using my thinking process, my experience, and what I have learned from the different scriptures of different religions. I am trying to write as if we are talking face-to-face and having a chitchat. All the while, I am introducing various clues (or pieces of the puzzle) in acquiring the self-knowledge that will lead to ongoing happiness. For this, I am giving different reasons and examples in hope of both holding your interest and creating a thought process in your own mind. It's a slow process, but once you learn, it will never go away and you will have this knowledge for the rest of your life. It will make you happier and less anxious, even in critical situations, losses, and sorrows.

As I mentioned before, to become a doctor, I had to go through many steps and stages of learning to get where I now am. I could not become a brain specialist overnight. Even a general practitioner, or internist, may know some neurology and how to handle simple neurological problems, but when it comes to complex issues or fine, thin-line judgments, a physician needs thorough knowledge to rely on, so that he won't harm the patient.

Similarly, to be free from all limitations, we have to get to a source of knowledge, and that source is acquired through learning, practice, enlightenment of our thinking process, and a positive attitude. As we acquire this knowledge, we slowly evolve into a state where we have freedom from all aches and desires. It's not that we don't face them in daily life, but our attitude and our reaction toward these become very different. If you accidentally get a very deep cut, you cannot change that. But what you do next, the decisions you make next, can make the difference between bleeding out and dying, or stopping the blood flow and recovering. The information in this book will not change the things that will happen to you in this life, but it can give you the knowledge to deal with the obstacles or bad situations that come up in your life in a different way, a way in which you continue to live more happily. And that also is what this book is about: experiencing more happiness in your life because you automatically put anything that comes up in a positive perspective. Thus, despite any negativity that comes your way, you can continue to live your life in ongoing happiness.

If it's self-knowledge you want to gain, you have to have a seeking or inquiring mind. For example, if you are thirsty and just sit in one place and say, "I am thirsty," you are not going to quench your thirst. For satisfaction you have to get up from the couch, go to the kitchen, open the refrigerator and get a cold drink in order to quench your thirst. Self-knowledge is accomplished by inquiry, looking into what it is. It requires a certain type of mind—a curious mind—and you need to prepare your curious mind to achieve that self-knowledge by looking at life differently—more openly—and be willing to make changes for your greater good.

If you realize that you are not perfect and that you are limited, and if you understand and accept that truth, then you can begin to feel content. In the beginning, it may be difficult to practice this notion as you dwell on your imperfections and limitations, but with practice you will reach the stage where happy acceptance of your imperfections and limitations becomes automatic behavior. Then you don't have to make an effort to think about it, and the majority of the time your life can be content, filled with bliss.

I will give you another example. Let's say a frog living in a small well looks up, sees the sky, and thinks that what it can see through the circumference of the well is the entire sky. Without any problems whatsoever, the frog hops around within that well and is content. That is, until another frog leaps into the well and tells the first frog how big the outside world and the universe are. Then that frog in the well hops outside and realizes how vast the universe really is and starts to feel discontent because it can't go all over the world. The frog was content until it went outside of the well to visit the whole world. Then it started to be dissatisfied, feeling unfulfilled and incomplete.

Similarly, we are given daily examples of how limited we are in every sense as human beings as we find limitations with our organs of smell, vision, hearing, taste, and touch. We can walk in only one direction; we cannot go in all directions at one time, and we can speak only one word at a time. Whatever we do we are limited, and because of our desire to be complete, it makes us discontented and unsatisfied.

That's why self-knowledge and understanding our *limitlessness* is important. You have to remember, and this is very crucial in my book, that *incognizance invites troubles, even though there are no real troubles as such. Incognizance or ignorance makes us desire material things, and when those things are unattained, the desire leads to unhappiness.* By putting forth the effort to gain self-knowledge, we can discover our inner tranquility and realize that a peaceful inner self is the true source of happiness. Having gained that inner peace and inner happiness, we will feel infinite and limitless.

I want you to understand this basic point I am emphasizing. In many places in this book, I emphasize the importance of self-knowledge, understanding ourselves, and how we are the source of our own happiness, rather than looking for something else or seeking happiness through our desires all the time. By attaining self-knowledge through learning and practice, we are shedding away our incognizance like a snake sheds away the old skin and gains new skin. In a similar fashion, we can shed our incognizance and gain the knowledge, *which is already there,* within ourselves, and which leads to happiness.

For example, let's say we are walking in the dark, we see what we think is a snake, and not knowing exactly what it is in the darkness (lets say the dark is our incognizance), then immediately we get scared, anxious, nervous, threatened; perhaps it's almost a fainting experience for some people. On the other hand, knowledge is like a flashlight you are carrying with you, and when you shine the light, you immediately realize that what you see is just a coiled rope and not a snake. That instantly eliminates all of your anxiety.

Here is another example. Let us say you are walking in the dark by a bush, and a thorn pricks you. Once again, if you are incognizant, at that moment you may get scared and imagine anything. You might fear that a spider, or bee, or perhaps a scorpion stung you. You could become anxious, nervous, fearful, start crying, and even faint. On the other hand, if you have the knowledge that you are in a thorn bush area and you are most likely to be pricked by the thorns, then you become less anguished, even though you have a little pain from the thorn prick. In a similar way, self-knowledge prevents you from automatically imagining the "worst case scenario," whenever obstacles or problems come up for you.

I am not saying that self-knowledge is all you need and you should not go to your temple, church, mosque, or synagogue. I am not saying that you must believe in this god or that god. Religion is also a type of guidance that provides self-assurance, and it gives inner strength. Nor am I saying that you should follow this god, or follow that religion, or follow this or that philosophy in order to understand what I am writing. All I am saying is that you should maintain a constant state of open-mindedness, and in doing so you will more quickly come to understand yourself. *You* are the source of your happiness; that is what I am trying to say.

If you wonder about my credibility, I can tell you that many of my personal experiences from birth until now, and the major events of my life have led me to realize that self-knowledge leads to happiness. Of course, I had exposure to the teachings of swamis, and I have read many books about the many religions and tried to learn what they are trying to say as well. However, my self-knowledge didn't happen overnight. For example, if you take my experience as a neurologist, in the beginning, when the subject was new to me, it took a longer time to listen to a patient, understand, and come to a conclusion about the problem (what we call a "clinical diagnosis"). After doing it for so many years and seeing thousands of patients, now when I start listening to a patient, ninety-nine out of a hundred times, I immediately know what is going on with the patient. When the interns and residents are making rounds with me, they always wonder because I look at the key points and come to a correct diagnosis, even though many physicians had already seen the patient. That is what practice is and applying your knowledge.

The same thing goes for life and the rules of happiness. In the beginning of my practice, when I was very young, I had to focus on exercising good bedside manners, listening to the patient, and trying not to make mistakes. However, now those things are second nature to me and I do them without thinking—even if it's an eighty or ninety-year-old patient; even at the end of a long and exhausting day. No matter what the situation is, I do not rush the patient, and I always listen patiently and in earnest. It doesn't matter to me if my office staff is waiting restlessly, or I have other pressing things to do. This is automatic for me now. This is the reason I can tell you with confidence, in my own experience, how to acquire self-knowledge and the means of happiness.

In some cases, I might have made an impression on a patient I had seen six or seven years ago, so he asks his physician to send him to me again. As you may know, in some towns, physicians have their own preferences when referring to a specialist based on personal, social, religious, cultural, racial, ethnic, or financial relationships. The physician may tell the patients that he cannot send him to me, but the patient insists that he wants to come to see me. Otherwise, he will drop his physician, even though that physician has been the patient's family physician for many, many years.

Can you see how it makes a difference? If you want to gain self-awareness, you cannot say, "Look, I don't have time to try to understand this," or, " This is too complex; maybe later." You have to put in the effort, but you do not need advanced schooling at a prestigious university, or postgraduate degrees. With the proper means like this book or a proper teacher, the proper place, and the proper mindset, you can learn self-awareness. I say proper teacher and place because if you want to be a scientist, you cannot sit home and say, "I am going to fly a spaceship." For that you have to learn space technology and train to be an engineer, and then you have to work at a "proper place" like NASA. You can't sit in a bar or nightclub to learn about flying a space ship, because you cannot concentrate there, and you cannot focus on the material you are working on. So, even though it may look simple and basic, "focus, study, and practice" are key elements of the learning process.

My goal or intention is not to make this a philosophical book, or to make myself look like some kind of a genius, creating all of these golden rules. I would like to clarify that my ambition is to share my knowledge in a simple way so that everybody, from all religions and all walks of life, can understand. In this book you may find the teachings of Hinduism, Buddhism, Jainism, Christianity, Islam, Judaism, Shinto, and Confucianism, but the bottom line is that every religion teaches the same essentially good things, and I am trying to compile all of them into simpler forms so that everybody can understand and make use of the common core teachings. In other words, "take what is good for you," and what is good for your self-improvement, knowledge, enlightenment, and happiness.

In no single religious or sacred book are you told what is good or bad in another religious book. Universally, the perception and understanding of good and bad, right and wrong is the same. That is why I would never emphasize one religion over another. If you learn, exercise your mind, and practice again and again, you will find happiness in every situation. You don't have to be an authority or master to be right about your choice of religion or philosophy, as long as you have the understanding of it, your intentions are good for mankind, and your message is beneficial for the universe.

For medical literature, medical magazines, and local medical society magazines, I have written articles about walking on fire, levitation, and alternative medicine, and I've tried to explain from a neurological standpoint certain things like the healing process through prayer. When you believe in a person, depending on his credibility, you develop faith that that person may cure you when he prays for you, or he may relieve your distress, sorrow, fear, or sadness. So with that faith, your mind becomes quieted and it develops hope. That hopeful mind itself may bring certain changes in the body, and thus a hopeful mind alone can be helpful in wiping out the distress. However, if you attribute your healing to the prayer or to the person who prayed for you, blindly for the rest of your life, you'll believe whatever that person says or does. When you go on a vacation or acquire some money or something nice, even though your efforts are the source of that happiness, you are likely to attribute it to external objects. The same goes for faith. Let us take "pain" as an example. The nervous system can release certain neurotransmitters, called endorphins, which are natural opiates that remove or lessen pain. Certain rituals or methods we use like praying, yoga, meditation, and holding hands in a circle promote the release of endorphins, which relieve pain, and we attribute the relief to those external objects or methodologies we've used.

Knowledge liberates, and it creates responsibility. Knowledge needs to be passed on from one human being to another and one generation to another, just as a teacher passes his knowledge to his students, and the students become the teachers, and the cycle continues. After you acquire self-awareness, or self-knowledge, you are obligated to bring that awareness to fellow human beings, but it is not difficult, and it is not unachievable. You have to realize that the awareness is for the whole world. Space retains its purity at all times; space is awareness, and space is a dress for the whole world. You have to realize that the knowledge you are acquiring here is not knowledge that you will be able to hide. You will feel compelled to share it.

Some of us have the false notion that we will be liberated after we die, and we will go to heaven or hell, whichever way our actions take us. But liberation can be gained while you are alive by acquiring self-knowledge. Even during the time you are gaining self-knowledge, by learning or realizing your existence, awareness, and fullness, you are also being liberated. In other words, as a wise person, you are being awakened to your limitless self, and this is the real self. After you acquire this knowledge, there is no going back, and it will be a lasting thing. As I've said before, knowledge has no beginning or end. When self-knowledge is gained, incognizance or ignorance goes and cannot come back. Incognizance has no beginning. It can go, but it cannot come back.

A person who is full of self-knowledge does not care or worry about the past. She keeps on working and keeps on putting her effort into the present. That will take care of the past and present, as well as the future. For example, take a student who got bad grades in the last semester. If the student starts dwelling on it, it is going to affect his present, and he will not be able to concentrate and improve. It will then affect his future performance and he may "psyche" himself into getting poor grades in the future as well. On the other hand, if he realizes that the past has already happened, and there is no possible benefit or advantage of dwelling on it, he can then focus on working harder in the present, and then he may improve his grades, which affect his future.

Once again, this is self-knowledge: taking what is good for you, for your self-improvement, knowledge, and enlightenment and discarding anything negative. This is like scratching your back by yourself. Here you are the subject and you are the object, hence, both subject and object are contained by reality.

Another point I would like to make is that there is nothing mystical or intellectual in knowing yourself. Everything you need to know is already inside you. It's just a process of discovery, of uncovering what is already there but remains hidden in a "fog" that you have the power to lift. It is being able to tell the difference between what is real and what is illusion. When we see magicians performing tricks or illusions, like bringing animals out of thin air or making people disappear, momentarily we believe everything is real. Everyone opens their mouths and eyes in awe because even though it is a trick, they believe it is true for a minute.

For self-knowledge, you need to see for yourself only what is true and what is not, and don't worry about other people and how they are trapped in negativity. When there is nothing to compare, there is no involvement of ego. To experience ego is to feel greater than another or feel different from another, so if you don't use another person for comparison, there is no room for ego in your mind. When you are everything, there is no ego. You cannot become everything but you can be everything you need to be. You are everything you need because you happen to be the truth, so you are not just making a statement. There is no ego involved here when you acknowledge that you are truth and you are awareness. When your ego is involved, you are retaining your isolated individuality, but you are learning here in this book that you are not isolated from the universe or from God. There is no comparison to others, and when you are happiness and bliss, when you are "being," there is no room for ego in your nature. Knowing the fact that "I am everything," is a matter of knowledge.

When you see the fact that God is the body, sense organs, mind, and all else, there is no ego, and you are not separate from awareness, which is the truth and self-knowledge.

You should not let your experiences pass by without making you wiser. As you understand those experiences and assimilate them, they will make you feel humble. With that humbleness, you quickly grow into knowledge and eventually get rid of confusion and the false ego. Any person who keeps an open mind with reference to any topic will learn that is the law of nature and everybody's experience. Also, you have to have the desire to know until the assimilation of knowledge takes place. You must practice, and you have to keep up with that desire until you find the knowledge. Then everything else comes to you naturally. To simplify this statement for you, I will give you another example from my own profession. I don't have my name in the yellow pages and I don't advertise my practice, but when I started my practice in 1988, I worked very hard; I was available for every physician and showed my extensive knowledge in the field of neurology. After awhile, automatically the patients came to me, the referrals came, and I didn't have to make any extra effort to maintain my business. Other physicians were aware of my practice, knowledge, ethics, morality, how I care for patients, and my "bedside manner" and felt very comfortable referring their patients to me when the need arose. Similarly, once you put your effort in, self-knowledge comes automatically.

With simple effort and a prepared mind (open-mindedness), you can achieve self- knowledge very easily. This is what I am hoping you will ascertain. *This is not a goal merely to improve your mind.* Please understand that. It is to recognize your "self."

I have always thought it odd that we are born with crying, and if we don't cry the pediatrician will slap our bottoms until we do. Thus we are born crying and we continue to cry, moving from sorrow to sorrow, until the day we die. But that is not the case after we attain self-knowledge because God did not create us to be unhappy, sorrowful, sad, or full of misery. We created these ourselves. Seeking this knowledge is just like a person looking all over for his head. Why do we have to look everywhere, when it is there all the time within ourselves?

There is a big difference between self-knowledge and self-realization. You have to realize the basic concept that self-knowledge is not a bodily experience. It is purely an intellectual analysis of one's self so that we can get rid of the incognizance which we are born with and acquire the meaning, which is the knowledge about our own self, which is existence, fullness, and awareness. On the other hand, self-realization is experiential like a bodily experience. For example, a person taking a street drug has a bodily experience of feeling happy or the experience of hallucinations. Studying books and our inner nature in pursuit of meaning is knowledge, and pursuit of bodily experience is self-realization. That is why I keep using the word "self-knowledge." It means you are trying to pursue the knowledge, not by a bodily experience, but by trying to recognize the self who is always there; it is always present, and you are trying to unfold it by shedding your incognizance. It is just enlightenment of your own self and learning the meaning of the self. Preparing your mind is the commitment to the pursuit of that self-knowledge. In this pursuit, you don't have to give up any obligatory duties of daily living.

However, to understand self-knowledge, you have to be free from prejudice in the sense that you have to have open-mindedness, and readiness to put aside any prior conclusions if they do not serve your growth or better good.

You have to have that curiosity; you have to have the goal that you want to be happy in a true manner, not just by material wealth or with the fulfillment of one desire after another. Instead, if you prepare your mind to search for the true meaning of life and happiness, this book can help bring some light into your life by shedding away the darkness and incognizance. With self-knowledge, you see the world as it is, as real as it is, not colored by your likes and dislikes. You will come to see that any unhappiness is your own creation, and it is only a projection of your mind. The world does not produce sorrow; it only produces *experiences* for you. If you derive sorrow and sadness from these experiences, the problem lies within you and not with the world. When you point a finger of accusation at the world, the other fingers point at you.

This book lays the groundwork for the self-awareness that can lead to ongoing happiness. It gives you a solid starting point and can get you well on your way. The rest, dedication and practice, is up to you. But the fact that you are reading this book demonstrates that you have the necessary curiosity and drive to get started.

We all have questions like, "Why are all people not in the same category, even though we are all human beings?" The answer is because some of our thinking processes are different, our outlook on the world is different, and our objectives and desires are not the same. Then the question comes, "How can we clump all human beings into one category?" Obviously, we cannot, even though we all have the same awareness, which is common with the universe and the Creator. Therefore, we may not fit into one category because we all have different interests, and we are not equally interested in the same things. However, we all have a common goal, which is happiness. Nobody says, "I want to be miserable," but we all take different paths in pursuit of that happiness. If your mind is emotionally free, you gain clarity. The desire to know one's self is not an ordinary desire; it might even sound crazy to some pragmatic people.

When you read this book, the question might pop into your mind that after acquiring the knowledge of happiness, do you still have to take action to perpetuate it? Remember, darkness cannot meet light. Because when the light comes, darkness goes. In the same way, incognizance and knowledge are opposed to each other, and as you are acquiring self-knowledge, incognizance goes away automatically. You don't have to make any special effort to get rid of that incognizance, it becomes automatic for you on a daily basis, and the problems or miseries we create ourselves on a day-to-day basis become less stressful for us.

Knowing one's self takes its own time, you can't push it too much. It is like the opening of a rose bud. You can't push or force a rose bud to blossom. If you forcibly open it petal by petal, it is not the same as when the bud blossoms naturally, taking its own time in becoming a beautiful rose. Self-knowledge is purely a "fact-revealing statement." Making "aware" to you that which was not known to you before. Knowledge does not come to you automatically. You always see what your mind is ready for, and there is no accidental knowledge. Alexander Fleming, the scientist who discovered penicillin, was experimenting and observing what was happening as a fungus-like substance clothed a bacteria culture he was growing. In that moment, his mind was ready for new knowledge. He put the data together, and penicillin was born, even though he was somewhat lucky in a sense. Similarly, for gaining knowledge you have to be ready.

I am not saying that we can reach a point where we do not face problems of daily living. We all feel hungry, we have to eat, and we need shelter, protection, and other creature comforts. Those are the basic needs we'll always have, not unlike animals. But because we have the faculty of reasoning, we have the means of acquiring self-awareness, facing the unavoidable situations and using our self-knowledge at least to minimize our suffering, unhappiness, and discontent. This is like teaching children not to touch fire. Very young children don't know that when they touch fire they'll burn their hands. But the parents or some other elder teaches them and protects them from doing so, and later on, children automatically know that when they see fire they should not touch it, even though they did not have the experience of getting burned.

After you acquire self-knowledge, you do not have to practice it every day, it becomes automatic in your life. For example, when you learn how to ride a bicycle, you never forget how to ride it. Self-knowledge is like that. It requires a special effort to realize who you are, how to make yourself happy, and what happiness is all about. When you learn that, it becomes your automatic behavior.

• Chapter 6 •

How Does Self-Knowledge Work?

If we can understand our inner selves, we will become content, and when we are content in this life, any situation we face does not shake us up, does not make us unhappy, and we experience less sorrow, depression, anger, frustration, jealousy, and other negative emotions. As you know, life has no guarantees, but with self-knowledge, you can feel fulfilled, which is the experience of happiness. According to all the religious scriptures, God did not create anybody with sorrow or unhappiness, nor did He create a cause to have grief. Having self-knowledge makes us react differently because we understand the underlying human problems, which are common for all of us. Self-knowledge makes us feel adequate and content, which naturally solves the problems. If we realize that we are all created equal and every human being is adequate and complete, then there is no problem at all. It is like darkness going away when the sun shines. Then, every situation we face becomes effortless, and happiness becomes natural for us as we look at all the situations in life from a different angle with a sense of knowing we already have the solutions within.

Of course, we all have likes and dislikes toward people, relatives, family members, our jobs, material objects, and even the food we eat because of the choices we have made with our thinking and reasoning faculties. Naturally, when we possess the things we like, they bring happiness, and how long the happiness lasts is individual and situational. Our dislikes bring unhappiness, grief, and sorrow. As we have discussed before, when you get up in the morning, depending on your state of mind, the sunrise may look beautiful one day and will not make an impact on you on another day.

As human beings, because of our desires, our multitude of choices, and our tendency to make comparisons with others, we are always trying to get what we don't have. For example, even though we have the greatest thinking faculty, which makes us superior in the animal kingdom, we may wish we could fly like birds. Look at the simple animal kingdom. Birds can fly, and even insects can fly. If we think in those terms, we realize how we are limited physically. Thus, whatever we acquire to feel good and happy, we realize that these things do not give us happiness all the time in all states of our minds.

With self-knowledge, our minds and attitude change. Self-awareness neutralizes the dislikes we have in everyday life, and we face the challenges of daily living like a sport. There is minimal room for sorrow, grief, and unhappiness because self-knowledge provides tranquility, stability, peace, and open-mindedness in our thinking process.

Initially, you may not be enthusiastic about acquiring self-knowledge, but in the long run you will see the benefit as you achieve more and more happiness. In this modern era, we are used to getting our coffee warmed up in fifteen to thirty seconds, or having a TV dinner ready to eat in five minutes. In the olden days, our grandparents used to prepare the meal for the whole day to have a good dinner. Now we are so used to instant gratification, we expect a quick fix for everything—but life does not work that way. That is where the frustration, depression, anger, violence, greed, and jealousy can come into play.

When you go to a doctor, he cannot make a diagnosis without your telling him your history, and then he will do the examination and, with his knowledge and experience, come to a reasonable conclusion of what your problem might be. There are multiple steps involved in making a diagnosis, and for the doctor to come to that diagnosis, he has to have knowledge of medicine. Then, by the process of elimination, he comes to a *reasonable* diagnosis.

In a similar way, to gain self-knowledge, you have to prepare your mind, make an effort, learn step-by-step, and try to understand and acquire this knowledge by inquiry. You have to understand the fundamental principle that new knowledge is not created or earned.

It is always there, and you are only shedding your incognizance. Over a period of time, and with practice, this becomes a reality; it becomes automatic behavior and attitude. You begin to look at even the most catastrophic things objectively, and you maintain your happiness in spite of them. Just like riding a bicycle or learning to swim, repetition is necessary for this. Along the way, you also gain self-worth and emotional maturity. Even though in life you pursue many things, the way you look at those pursuits and their results will be entirely different when you have this objective knowledge. The past does not have a hold over you. Once again, your effort and practice are very essential for this pursuit because you cannot simply sit there and expect your mind to take care of itself.

With self-knowledge, you can have thoughts like anybody else. You can have a daily life like anybody else, with sorrows, grief, sadness, losses, gains, happiness, pleasures, and material things. You don't stop anything. You don't stop living. Self-awareness doesn't teach you to be a saint or a person dispassionate for material things, and you don't just sit in a corner all day and meditate. Maybe you can't have it all, but by gaining inner knowledge about one's self makes a whole world of difference in your attitude, approach, and the meaning of happiness.

With self-knowledge, you develop the right attitude and you face all the challenges in life without getting excited or dejected by them. A person with self-knowledge can face all challenges with patience and peace, without complaining, without trying to waste energies by being too defensive or offensive. A person without the knowledge of one's true nature gets entangled with the physical body and all the bodily ailments that come along. A person with self-knowledge realizes that the body is a creation of God, and the body is an objective thing in the Lord's creation. Self-awareness leads to freedom from certain wants and desires, but this does not mean that self-knowledge will lead to a total freedom from physical desires and wants. To say "I want this" and "I want that" does not mean you haven't attained self-knowledge. You still have desires, but the difference is that with self-knowledge, even though you want a certain thing, that thing is not the source of your happiness. Thus, it is not going to be a binding desire. That is, you know you will be just as happy with or without the thing you desire.

The concept here is that you are not bound to any of your desires. This means that even though from now until the day you die you will still have desires, with self-knowledge, you will be able to put each desire into the proper perspective. You will know that you can be just as happy with or without the objects of your desire. Thus, if you attain a particular desire, you are happy, or if you don't attain it, you are still happy. Or, you are no less happy for not attaining it—so you do not blame yourself (or anyone or anything else for that matter). You develop a constant "easy come, easy go" state of mind. It will be a common experience for you that if you do not get something specific you desire, you know that there is something even better that is coming your way, and you will enjoy this new discovery even more than your original desire.

With self-knowledge you lose your attachments to physical objects and sensations of pleasure. You may not get the precise thing you desire today, but you do not mind because you know that the next day, or the next week, will bring you something equal or greater.

With self-knowledge, you happily accept whatever result comes. In other words, you are not unhappy, even if you don't get what you want. Then you have what is called "freedom from want." It does not mean you don't have the desire to have whatever you want. I want you to understand this point very clearly. Some people, after reading this book, might think that having self-knowledge means they have no desires. That is not so. After you gain self-knowledge, you are still a normal person like anybody else. You don't look like a saint or a sannyasi, but you will have no need to harm others, or to be envious of others, because your thoughts and vision become pure. Your emotions become much more real, and your mind does not have constant conflict, does not have constant confusion, and does not continue on a roller coaster of opposites like extremely high positives and extremely low negatives, or deep sorrow one day and spine-tingling happiness the next. A person with self-knowledge becomes concerned with helping other people, as did Martin Luther King, Mahatma Gandhi, Dalai Lama, Mother Theresa, Jesus Christ, the prophet Mohammed, and others. Usually the fulfillment of a desire makes us happy, and nonfulfillment makes us unhappy. But with self-knowledge if you don't have fulfillment of a desire it does not matter to you at all. You don't feel the sense of loss; you don't miss the objects of your desire because they have become nonbinding desires to you.

You should not mistake this attitude toward fulfillment of desires with the main goals in your life, your objectives in life, or their accomplishment. The desire to accomplish something worthwhile is different from the desire to get something that is material. When you acquire self-knowledge, you are happy, not for any particular reason, but because you know that happiness is part of your nature, and you know you are the fullness, you don't spend all your life consumed with desires to be happy and secure. This self-knowledge will help you realize that you are free from feelings of smallness and incompleteness. You realize that you are already full and complete just as you are.

While you are gaining self-knowledge, performing and practicing, your attitude will change, and you will no longer be swayed by your likes and dislikes. You will look at everything objectively, and you will be able to see things clearly that before may have baffled you. You can continue to perform your daily actions with a dutiful attitude while you are pursuing your self-knowledge, or you can have a more contemplative life dedicated to the pursuit of the knowledge. The choice is up to you, and there is no right or wrong way. Even if the temple or church has labeled you a sinner, self-knowledge is a way out of this ignominy. Once you are on the path of self-knowledge, your problems will become solved. You will be like a dreamer who has committed multiple murders in his dream but is innocent when he wakes up.

Similarly, you are free from all sins when you wake up to the knowledge that you are actionless awareness; there is nothing as purifying as knowledge. *The fire of self-knowledge consumes every sin.* I am not referring to sin in a legal sense. Nor am I in any way suggesting that you can commit a heinous crime such as murder, thinking that you are absolved if you suddenly choose the path of self-knowledge. I am strictly referring to the mental state of sin—such as self-condemnation. You cannot escape from the results of negative actions, which are against the laws of nature. You cannot take these statements and try to escape from an unlawful action using a spiritual loophole. This book is meant for you to be happy without limitations, but by no means can you use this book as a scapegoat for your unlawful actions or for actions that go against the laws of nature.

I will give you another simple example to explain how self-knowledge leads to freedom from desires. Let us say that as a child you are very fond of playing marbles. However, when you enter young adulthood, even though you still like to play marbles, your father tells you that you have to give up playing marbles and start playing other games like baseball, basketball, and football. You may respect your father's wishes and give up playing marbles. You give the marble collection to your younger brother, but you feel unfulfilled, there is no change in your attitude, and you have an ongoing sense of loss for the marbles. On the other hand, let us say you have grown up and have become a father. You take joy in seeing your child playing marbles, but looking at the marbles does not arouse any kind of desire in you to play marbles again. Instead you find just as much happiness seeing your child playing marbles as if you were a kid again, playing marbles, because the marbles are no longer important for your happiness. You don't have desire for the marbles, and that is a real change in your attitude, because you are free from the pairs of opposites like joy and sorrow, pleasure and pain. That is the attitude you will develop with self-knowledge. That is the basic foundation of self-knowledge, which I am repeating over and over with different examples throughout the book, and in all the *Five Golden Rules for Happiness* at the end. Thus, when you achieve self-awareness, your heart will automatically find fullness and maturity.

As you are reading this book and acquiring self-knowledge, you should be aware of your new status. I suggest that you meditate for a few minutes each day, visualizing yourself as unlimited, full, and complete, and make this a part of your day-to-day life. Constantly condition yourself that you are coming to understand that you are the limitless fullness that you long for. It is important to remind yourself that you have to practice, just like you would practice a sport such as tennis or basketball, and make it a daily habit. Otherwise, over a period of time, complacency will take over and you may slowly level off and remain a "beginner."

I will give you another example for this. Let us say there is a poor fellow in a third-world country who won a million dollars in a lottery. Now he has a lot of money and he can have material belongings, his own car, an expensive house, and every comfort that money can buy. Because he has been poor all his life and all of a sudden he has this new status, it takes a very long time for his new status to sink into his mind, even though the material things are there to make him aware of this. And, if the rich status he's acquired didn't sink into his head, if he's walking down the street and sees somebody distributing food, with his age-old habit, he will automatically run to see what is being given out. He might even stretch his hand out to receive his share, totally forgetting that he won the lotto and he is a millionaire now. This is what his old habit makes him do, unless he constantly reminds himself that he won the lottery and he is rich now. Similarly, as you are acquiring self-knowledge, you must realize that your self is limitless, and full, and if you don't exercise that realization, automatically you will go into your old habits of living for your desires.

It is easy for an objective person to get along in the world. When one discovers in one's self a dispassion with reference to the various material objects in this world, that person is able to be objective, and he or she doesn't project on a material object anything more than what it is. It's like seeing through a clear glass rather than a prism or a colored glass. A person with self-knowledge is always happy because a particular situation is not required for him to be happy—he is happy by himself, independent of a required stimulus. Because of self-knowledge, you can accommodate other people as they are, because it is very natural to you. Stress, self-induced, or as a reaction to others, becomes a thing of the past.

• Chapter 7 •
The Meaning of "I"

You are the universe, you are the world, and you are happiness, just like gold is gold whether it is a solid brick or it is within different ornaments in various degrees of purity. If you question yourself, "What is self, and what is "I?" the answer is, it is the nature of being one who is abiding in the self, or "you." In other words, by nature, the self is pure, eternal, and free. Because of our incognizance, we identify our self with our physical body, which is limited, bounded, and perishable. This is a fundamental error. If you look at the whole world, this entire creation is subject to change and modification. The entire universe keeps going, and it keeps changing.

If you say, "I am tall, I am short, I am brown, I am white, I am black, I am *this*, I am *that*," you are just describing your physical body, which is perishable. But if you look at "self," you don't make a distinction between yourself and your physical body. The reality is that the self is full, complete and lacks nothing, and it is also pure, free from all attributes, limitless, and it cannot be modified.

If you identify the self with your body, mind, or emotions, then you are making yourself limited, incomplete, and lacking. If you look at your gross body, it has five fundamental elements that are subject to modification. For example, bones grow, change, exist, decay, and die. The six forms of modifications are birth, growth, existence, change, decay, and death. Every human gross body goes through these modifications.

The five fundamental elements that compose the body (as well as the universe) are space, air, fire, water, and earth. I will give you two simple examples relating to our own bodies. For instance, take hair and nails. Hair grows, and when you cut it, it becomes dead hair; the same thing with your fingernails. They become dead matter after they are cut. The body, starting from one cell becomes many cells, which become a grown human body. Even after death, after the body disintegrates whether you cremate it or bury it, it still goes into the earth, which is again composed of the five main elements.

We are born from the five gross elements and maintained by food. We are born from the earth and return to earth. We are born of the earth from which the food comes and return to the earth. The earth itself is made of the five basic elements, food comes from those five basic elements, and the body itself is created from those five elements. The body needs those five elements to maintain and sustain itself until it dies. In other words, the five elements will always remain the same, but the bodies vary from individual to individual—each person is a unique entity. Take fingerprints, for example. Even in the case of identical twins, the fingerprints are entirely different, even though the appearance of the external physical bodies is nearly identical.

We all experience such feelings as happiness, sorrow, grief, joy, anger, love, jealousy, and pleasure. Actually, your body is the source of happiness or unhappiness because you are not able to separate yourself from the physical body, which is "I." If we look at the entire cycle—birth to death—the body has to go through several changes, a metamorphosis from existence, birth, growth, change, and decay to death. Even the sense organs are the same from newborn to old age. They probably peak when we are young adults, and they start decaying when we get older. The moment we are born, our cells start to decay and die slowly, until they completely die away. When the physical body dies, the "tenant" vacates the premises, and the body turns to dust.

The "I" is the experiencing part of the human body. For example, when you say, "I am thirsty" or "I am hungry," this is an experience of which you are aware. That means, experience is not self, but the physical body. The physical body is kept alive by those physiological systems I mentioned. If you make a distinction between that physiological system and the self, you realize that you are thirsty, which is an experience, but you are not "thirst." Or when you say, "I am hungry," it is an experience that you have for hunger, but you are not "hunger." If you can make that distinction, then you are able to make a distinction between "I," which is the physical body, and self, which is knowledge.

With the five senses of perception, we have the bodily functions or physiological functions, which we are born with. These functions are respiration (or breathing), blood circulation, digestion, elimination, which is the evacuation of waste matter, and finally, reaction to a "touch." These five aspects of bodily functions are connected to the five sense organs, which are connected to the five sense objects, which are connected to the five basic elements. These are the fundamental functions of the human being, which is not connected to the self but is connected to the "I," "I am," "me," "mine," "myself," and so forth.

As we pay attention to our own body, the physical body, we find ourselves saying, "this is mine," or "I want this, and I want that." Over time, this body has pain after pain. The body is always subjected to pain of one type or another; it always aches. There is no physical body that is free of, or without, an ache. We deal with it. If it is not your body, you have aches from the outside; somebody is always giving you an ache, such as a "pain in the neck." If it is your own body, you have a toothache, headache, backache, *this* ache, and *that* ache. You go to a doctor to get rid of your bodily aches, but it is self-knowledge that eliminates your mental aches like sorrow, grief, anger, and jealousy.

You cannot change the past, but you can change your attitude, your actions at present, your personal habits, your thinking, and your behavior, all of which actually cause recurrent problems. You can change those in the present so that your future can be experienced with few problems. With daily practice of the *Five Golden Rules*, putting them into action in your daily life, you can make yourself free from any limitation—but I don't mean physical.

You are the subject and you are real and you cannot give up this status of realness at any given time. You are like a crystal assuming a color in the presence of a colored object. When we are in deep sleep, we are not awake, and we are not dreaming; when we are dreaming, we are not awake, and we are not in deep sleep. When you are awake and aware of your surroundings, you have all kinds of feelings, happiness to sorrow to anger, and reactions to the external world as you live day by day, or minute by minute, irrespective of religion and culture of Eastern world or Western world. It doesn't matter because we all believe that the physical body is mortal and we all have the perception that whether one is tall or short or male or female, all these notions are universal on the planet with reference to the physical body. That is the "being," and it is universal.

When we say "I am hungry, I am thirsty, I am sad, I am happy, I am agitated," we are referring to the physical body. But the soul itself is free from all of these feelings.

When you are looking at me, what do you really look at? You are only looking at my physical body, and similarly I am also looking at your physical body only. We only know the physical body. When I ask you the question, "Who are you?" Your answer is "I am so and so, or I am the son of so and so," and that answer reveals the nature of "I."

You can wear a shirt and you can say this is your shirt but you cannot say you are the cloth, even though the cloth is on your body, and you can feel it, and you can touch it, and it is covering your body. You can say, "This is my shirt," but you cannot say the shirt is you. You are quite aware that your clothes are not you.

When I touch your body, you don't feel your body is touched. Instead you feel *you* are being touched. When I touch your left ring finger without your permission you say, "Don't touch *me*." You don't say, "Don't touch my *left ring finger*." If I touch your left hand, you know that I am touching you and your whole body perceives that I have touched you, and you feel that you are being touched. It's that simple. When your body is walking somewhere, it is not that somebody else is walking, but you are walking. If the body is tall, you are tall. If it is fair, you are fair. If it is dark, you are dark. If fat, you are fat; if lean, you are lean. If the body is here, you are here. It is not like the body remains here and you walk away. So, you don't leave the body. Where the body is, you are there. Therefore, when the body sleeps, you sleep. When the body stands, you stand. When the body walks, you walk. When the body is lying down, you are lying down. Whatever the body is, you are. Whatever the body does, you claim, "I did" because you perceive yourself as the physical body.

The same goes for the mind. When the mind is restless, you say that you're restless or when the mind is quiet, then you say you're quiet.

When the mind is angry, you say you are angry. If the mind is sad, you are also sad. Thus you may draw the conclusion that the mind and you are identical, but once again this is not true. It is only your experience, and experience is not knowledge. In a similar way, when your mind is restless or agitated or angry, you say, "I am very angry" or "restless" or "agitated." It is your mind, not you, the "I." When you have a memory, you cannot say you are the memory because you are only the one recollecting the memory.

What I am trying to say is that you do not know the dimension of yourself, and you do not know the truth of yourself—that you are dimensionless. This knowledge is not an experience that you have to go through by perception or inference or bodily experience. This knowledge is not an experience to be gained.

This knowledge is always there, and it is not going to change, and if you acquire it you will not be shaken. You are never away from yourself. You are not something to be gained as a new experience. You are already there. You can never go out of the experience of yourself. You are there experiencing yourself in every experience. You are never outside of yourself. You never get lost. Everything else, any object you take, may get lost, but not you, the subject. You never get lost. Therefore, there is no question of lack of experience. In fact, you are the essence of every experience. Therefore, there is no question about gaining an experience of self. You see what you are. You are seeing, hearing, walking, talking, thinking, doubting. In all those experiences, there is only you.

What I am trying to say is that self-knowledge is not about bodily experiences. If I ask you, "Who are you?" your immediate answer is, "I am John" or "Mary" or "Abraham." Or, if I ask you further, you say you are the son or daughter of so and so and you start giving answers only related to the "I" and to your physical body. You do not give the direct answer that you are *awareness*. So, to conduct day-to-day business, we have a name, a personal identity, and in some countries a Social Security number. If you are a businessperson, you have a tax ID number. You may also have a driver's license with a picture. All of these things are to make your physical body identifiable. That is all right because we all cannot say, "I am awareness." It confuses the world and confuses everybody. So when I am explaining the true nature of yourself, I am not saying that you should not have your personal identity. However, I want you to understand the true meaning of yourself, and that will come with self-knowledge.

If I ask you, "How do you know you are John or Mary?" you show me your ID or birth certificate. Your family, friends, and everybody recognize you with that name. Even in a big crowd, if somebody calls your name, you immediately answer. And if you are next to the calling person, if it is not your name, you do not respond. So we are being, in a sense, "brainwashed," and made aware, from birth onwards, of whom we are. You are constantly being reminded and confirmed in society all the time, by your family members, your friends, society. People recognize your given name and identify you with that name. Indirectly they are telling you, "This is you."

If I ask a friend of yours about you, she will give your description: your height and weight, your physical appearance, color of your hair, color of your eyes. She will identify you with your physical body. But knowing one's self is not knowing the physical body, even though the mind and the senses are connected to your physical body, and through the mind you feel happy or unhappy. These are only transient feelings, and they do not give you the total awareness of your self and the ultimate happiness.

With reference to your body, if I ask you, "do you feel your age?" you may not quickly answer me (but you do realize that your answer is "no") because the age we talk about is the chronological age since your birth. We all have the same experience. We feel that we really don't have "age" other than physical age, and we don't feel our actual age. Even my patients tell me, "I don't feel I am so and so age." For example, some patients feel very happy, and even if they are in their 80s, they don't feel that old. And vice versa. Some patients in their twenties and thirties have so many physical problems like diabetes, hypertension, kidney failure requiring dialysis, severe back pain, or migraine headaches that they don't feel that young. This itself gives us the knowledge that we never feel our actual age, exactly how old we are (other than the chronological age). Our real "age" depends on our self-perception.

The "I" is the one doing things, enjoying things, having feelings and emotions like love or anger. As long as you have attachment to the physical body and say that "I am the body, I am the individual, I am this, I am that," you will not acquire self-knowledge. On the other hand, self-knowledge comes to you when you realize that your physical body is *not* the self, and you are *unattached,* and you are the nature of existence, awareness, fullness, abiding in all beings in the form of awareness, limitless like space. You are the individual with immediate knowledge and not knowledge mediated by the sense organs. When you fully understand this, the knowledge of truth has been born and you are liberated while living.

Finally, the day will come with this understanding when you'll realize that the individual "I" is the self, and self is not an individual. Understanding the nondifferentiation between the world, yourself, and God is a very important matter for self-knowledge. When you recognize that truth, the apparent, the unreal, will shut off automatically.

If I take a garland, show it to you, and ask you what it is, immediately your answer will be, "a garland." If I ask you what is it made of, you answer "flowers," and you might name the flowers like rose, lilac, or jasmine, and you may describe the colors. But unless you are totally aware you don't answer, "there is the thread also in the garland." The garland looks beautiful because of the colorful flowers that were put together nicely, but we don't see the thread, and without thread, there is no garland, and the flowers fall apart. In the garland, the thread is like awareness or God. We are all like flowers in the garland, and God is like the thread.

The difference between you, the limitless awareness, and you, the limited individual, is the difference between the real and the apparent. The gold is real and the gold chain is apparent. Similarly, you shine independently; everything else is dependent on your existence, *so, you are not what you think you are.* In fact, you are the opposite. You think you are limited, but in you the whole creation exists. This is the greatest secret of you.

This is just like a person searching for a wallet, which is always there in his coat pocket; or a person who is searching for his head, which is always there on his shoulders. For a person who has been regarding himself or herself as limited, the truth of this awareness is a secret. In reality, you are the center of the creation, and the creation is because of you. When a pot is made, the space enclosed by the pot does not have to elbow out an area in space to make room for it. The space is in and throughout the pot; walls do not restrict it. It will accommodate everything and still remain one limitless space. Similarly, "I," or "awareness," sustains everything. A pot filled with water and submerged in the water of the ocean is full inside and outside.

This awareness has no gender, form, or quality. Just like electricity, which is in fans, lights, refrigerators, generators, TV, radio, everywhere, but at the same time electricity is free from all of them. In a similar way, space pervades everything and at the same time, it is free from everything. Awareness comes through the sense organs, as they perceive all objects, yet awareness is free from all sense organs. Thus, the one who is able to be free from all can be all. Because "I" is all pervasive, "I" is not attached to any particular thing, but "I" is the one from whom everything is born, by whom everything is sustained, and in whom everything resolves. Therefore, the "I" is the witness of all, the one who permits all, and the supreme God.

For another example, let us take a street lamp that illuminates a street corner. Under that light, nothing you do bothers the lamp, which is shining the light. It is neither happy nor miserable on account of good or bad things that happen under it. In a similar way, "I," or "awareness," witnesses and permits all; *awareness* does not interfere in your affairs. It allows your mind to do whatever it likes. That is why one person is wise and another is not wise. Wisdom is once again the thinking faculty, the result of choices you make. Like the shining street lamp, awareness does not react to the differences, disparities, or discrepancies in our thinking process. Thus we cannot blame the Creator for our unhappiness. He provided that knowledge for you, and it is for you to understand and choose to utilize it properly or improperly. Free from qualities, awareness sustains all qualities.

Again, awareness is everything, but it is free from everything. Just like space, which is undivided but appears divided because of walls. When thoughts move it may appear like awareness moves, but awareness is motionless. This awareness is what you really are. A human being has a mind potentially capable of knowing, analyzing, and assimilating experiences, and a human being is endowed with the ability to reason and to know independently, unlike animals.

Animals are programmed by their instincts and subject to further programming. For example, a chimpanzee can be trained to drive a motorcycle, but it will not get down and ask for a drink or count change. The capacity to think and analyze, to conclude, is unique to the human being. However, a person may be programmed, but the reasoning faculty is definitely not programmed. Otherwise, learning would not be possible for human beings. However, a human being can subject himself to programming voluntarily.

Physical body is subject to growth, decline, and death. If you pay too much attention to your body, then it will not let you pay attention to anything else. This doesn't mean you have to neglect your body. You should have a proper healthy attitude toward your body. With self-knowledge, you realize this and you have no big attachment to it and you will be objective about it because you realize this body is subject to disintegration. This attitude comes only with self-knowledge.

• Chapter 8 •
Life, Mind, Soul, and Self

No one wants to die. We all want to survive as long as possible. That is why there is so much research going on in the field of geriatrics (aging) with a focus on how to slow the aging process, and also how to be youthful again and live for as many years as possible. For many of us, there is a mortal fear of dying, even though we all know that we have to eventually die. It is a law of nature that the physical body, composed of the five basic elements has to die one day or another.

We all have the experience of what death is because we have seen it in the external world, in our own family members, relatives, and friends. Yet we always hope for "freedom from death." We also want to leave something behind when we do die. That is why we have children, and we see ourselves in our own children. Having self-knowledge will help us in dealing with the facts of aging and death.

Water and iron both can take on the heat of fire, but between those two, only iron when heated to certain degrees can show the brilliance of fire. If you take a red-hot iron ball, the fire and iron are together and fire is all over the iron ball. The fire blesses every atom of iron, and it glows with heat and brilliance. Let us take our own physical body: When it is alive, it is capable of experiences, and it is sentient (capable of feeling). The same body when dead and ready to bury or cremate, then is insentient like any other gross matter.

What really happens at death then? You cannot say that the soul has gone away because that is like saying space has gone away from Russia to America. In fact, the limitless awareness cannot go anywhere.

Whatever makes the body sentient must have gone away. That is the subtle body, which is the matter, but the subtle body is capable of reflecting that awareness, just like iron is capable of taking all the heat and glow of red, hot fire. Our mind, which is blessed by awareness, is conscious. In turn, the mind makes the sense organs shine and each sense organ illuminates its corresponding object. For example, the forms of sight, taste, smell, sound, and touch are reflected by the eyes, tongue, nose, ears, and skin respectively.

When you say, "I am sentient," that "I" is a subtle body, which is identified with the gross physical body. This gross body is inert body, just as fire is identified with the iron ball. The differences between the insentient objects, which are the gross objects, and the living beings, which are the subtle body, are basically due to the presence or absence of the subtle body. In a living being, we have the subtle body, and we are sentient. The insentient objects have no subtle body and they are all gross form. There is no subtle body in a table. If the table has a subtle body, then it would be aware of you sitting on it, or putting a lot of weight on it, and it would protest whenever you bang on it. So to the self, all-pervasive awareness is present in the table, but it is not manifested as consciousness because there is no subtle body in it to reflect that. In a living being, consciousness is manifest because the subtle body is there. When the subtle body leaves, we call the body a "dead body," and we have to dispose of it. No matter how much we love a person, when the subtle body is gone, we rush to cremate or bury the remains. So the combination of subtle body and gross physical body is what makes a living being. Calcium, carbonate, oxygen, hydrogen, phosphorus, and other chemicals that make up the gross body, nor the five elements we talked about, cannot make a vivified being.

Awareness, which is reflected in the subtle body, is what glorifies the physical body. In other words, making the inert body into a wakeful one. Let us say a person is in deep sleep, when you touch her or shake her, if the subtle body is still there, she wakes up. On the other hand, if there is no subtle body, she doesn't respond when you try to wake her because there is no pulse, no breathing, and then the doctor pronounces, "This person is dead." On the other hand, for a person who is in deep sleep, there is no difference between that person and a dead person, except for the pulse and the breathing—and when you shake him, he wakes up. That is due to the subtle body only. In a dead person, the subtle body has left, so there is no illumination to vivify the physical body. That means the tenant has left the guesthouse.

So many friends and colleagues have asked this question of me when I talk about awareness, depending on their religious beliefs, and how they were brought up, their culture, and other factors: "What happens after death?" Possibly, this will help us to understand the difference between the gross body and the subtle body. At death, it is not the self that leaves, but consciousness conditioned by the subtle body leaves the gross body. That conditioned consciousness is the one that is called life. That is the one that occupies the different bodies.

There will be many obstacles in the mind that prevent the acquiring of self-knowledge, but you can remove those obstacles with inquiry, reasoning, logic, understanding, and, finally, mastering the mind. Many people believe that only saints, gurus, monks, swamis, and the like can master the mind, but with clear understanding of what the mind can do, we can also master the mind. Just by realizing that the mind is restless and always subject to change, and with that recognition, we win half the battle with the mind. We cannot just tell someone when they are agitated, "Don't get agitated, it's not going to solve the problem" because it is the nature of the mind to get agitated.

The mind is a dynamic thing and it doesn't stay still. It wanders all the time. If you close your eyes, instantly you may think of being in another country, other places; there is nothing faster than the mind. It never has a constant thought all the time. Imagine how it would be if you did have only one constant thought. It would make you go crazy with one perpetual idea presenting itself over and over. That is what we see in psychiatric patients who have repeated thought processes. Also, you have to realize that the mind has its own logic, and the thoughts in the mind do not come out of nowhere. That is the reason why the mind has logic. Whatever thoughts you have, even in dreams, even though they seem random, there is always a reason for them. We must understand that is the mind's nature. By understanding that, you can learn to discover the difference between the mind and yourself, and then you don't react to each and every thought that comes into your mind. This ability also helps a great deal to resolve the conflicts in the mind that we constantly have in daily life.

What I am saying here is nothing revolutionary, nothing secret, and nothing that is newly discovered. Self-knowledge is a combination of knowing, learning about, and recognizing your true "self." You look at yourself and understand yourself. If you practice and look at it objectively, the mind can be mastered to some extent. You can gain certain distance between yourself and the mind that helps you to look at yourself positively and makes you "realize" yourself exactly as you are. Even though every thought that pops up into your mind is you, you can be free from negative thoughts if you look at them objectively, and with practice you will be able to instantly dismiss them from your mind.

As I explained before, you cannot eliminate all thoughts from the mind, and you cannot have only one thought all the time. Neither of these is normal for human beings. However, making your thoughts into useful forms happens with self-awareness. It's a common belief that a mind without thought is a well-trained mind or a meditative mind. Even if there is a split second of absence of thought between two thought processes by meditation, yoga, or some other means, this is not necessarily an enlightenment of mind. On the other hand, a mind without *conflict* is a peaceful mind.

Every human being has the capacity to concentrate, learn, develop, nurture, and foster his interests. Unfortunately, almost all of us look on material objects as our source of security, happiness, and comfort. That is why our mind goes toward objects as sources of our happiness, without realizing that *we, ourselves,* are the source of happiness. The extraordinary thing about human beings is that we have the ability to love anything under the sun.

When you are looking ideally for peace of mind, you do not realize that the mind is always vibrant, constantly thinking. But if you realize that fact, it is easy to put the mind at peace rather than trying to control it. When you understand the mind, you realize that the world can disturb you only to the extent you let it do so. A peaceful mind doesn't mean that it has to be inactive or thoughtless. It is not true that the mind is peaceful only when it is not thinking.

As a neurologist, I can tell you that *a peaceful mind means you, as* the *"self," do not enter into conflict with the mind when thought processes are constantly occurring. Rather, when you understand the nature of the mind and accept the mind as being peaceful at all times, then there will be no conflict at all.* Understanding this truth leads to happiness. If you are thoughtless, it means you are in a deep coma, or a deep sleep. Thoughtlessness is not possible when you are awake. Hence, you have to understand the mind rather than trying to control it. And you also have to understand that thinking is your prerogative and that a peaceful mind is not necessarily an enlightened mind. It's not like all of a sudden you became a genius or attained sainthood, that you got "peace of mind."

Happiness or peace of mind is not about control, but about acceptance. Thus, self-knowledge is not a technique where you learn to control your mind; it is a "path" by which you learn to accept and appreciate everything just the way it is—and to accept yourself exactly the way you are, and to accept the world the way it is.

I am not going to give you a technique whereby you "train" your mind to have happiness. I *am* going to give you the knowledge, which, if you comprehend it and apply it to your life, will free your mind from disappointment when you don't get the material things or the physical pleasures you say you want. Thus, with this knowledge, when pain or loss comes your way, you will acknowledge the pain or loss, and you will not begrudge the source of the pain or loss. Rather, you will fully understand that pain and loss have just as much validity in your life as pleasure and gain. And when you reach this state of mind you are truly free, and ongoing happiness is yours.

However, it is important to understand that self-awareness does not take place just because your mind is peaceful, even though a peaceful mind is more readily open to knowledge, and for this you do not require a university education. You do not require a master's degree or a PhD in philosophy, psychology, or theology. Even if you spend all your life loading up scholarly degrees, self-knowledge will not take place this way. Self-knowledge is self-driven, self-motivated, and as long as you have a curious mind to understand yourself, achieving self-knowledge is not a difficult task. It is just like practicing how to ride a bike or to swim.

Self-knowledge causes you to look at things objectively and to have a dispassionate unbiased outlook on life. For example, the world cannot really touch you unless you desire it to. Let us say I am a bald-headed man. If I go to the shopping center, two things that will never interest me are hair oil or shampoo. Perhaps the sight of them will cause me to feel envy toward men with full heads of hair, but if I am not self-conscious about my baldness; I can look at hair oil or shampoo dispassionately. Conversely, if I am self-conscious about my baldness and I notice somebody is looking at me, I automatically perceive that they are looking at my bald head (which might well be a misconception). You have to realize that the world is like a supermarket. It has a lot of things, some of which are meant for you and some that are meant for others. You cannot take everything you see or hear and project it onto yourself. You should not let the world pass judgment on you or have control over you. The world cannot do anything to you; much less can someone's eyes do anything to you. Eyes, themselves do not cause any harm, and ears do not cause any harm; they are all just instruments. Equally, the thoughts in another person's mind do not cause any harm to you.

The mind is an ever-changing pool of thoughts in motion. You have some thoughts that are beautiful, some that are not beautiful; some are useful, and some are not useful. The mind is only a process that performs as a useful instrument. The soul is the thing that illumines the mind. Self is the thing that is boundless, timeless, form-free, action-free, and full of awareness.

When we look at the mind, we think of the brain with gray matter, white matter, neurons, which are the nerve cells, the electrical impulses, the memory process, and other aspects of the brain with different roles and functions. You can master the mind through your way of thinking, the way with which you shape your collection of deliberate thoughts, mechanical thoughts, impulsive thoughts, and spontaneous thinking. However, spontaneous thinking manifests only in one who has self-knowledge.

To have complete mastery of the mind requires knowledge of the self, which can eliminate the power of the likes and dislikes that govern our everyday lives. That complete mastery is evidenced by spontaneity. With a "clean" mind, with choice, you can hold your commitments, even in the face of distraction. Good choices require alertness, which makes it possible to master your mind over the ways of your thinking. With mastery of mind, you don't have to suppress your desires; however, you will have a dispassion toward them. You can gain the dispassion by clearly seeing the objects for what they are. For example, a new bronze statue can be made to look like an antique, and automatically a normal person might think, "Wow, it must have very high value!" But a person with dispassion for objects, with clear thinking, can look at it and appreciate it all the same as just a beautiful piece of metal.

Some religions think that the soul is like water in a sponge. That is, a soul needs the friction of this earthly existence in order to move forward on the road to enlightenment. Irrespective of religious beliefs, race, and culture, most human beings understand that the soul and mind are not the same, and the soul is not easily understood. I will try to explain the soul in a metaphor. The nature of the soul is that it has existence, awareness, and fullness. If you take a pot (human), which is made of clay (soul), you realize that clay existed before the pot was made. The existence aspect of pot is clay, and clay is in the pot, and the clay remains after the pot is destroyed. The timelessness of the soul is eternity or existence.

Everything that is perishable has to be made of a substance that is fundamental and permanent. That is the root of understanding self-knowledge, which makes us happy at all times, irrespective of ups and downs. The soul was before, and is now, and it will be with or without the body. You cannot produce the soul. The best example is that you are existence, and you find yourself in this world, just like the supervisor who goes to the factory for the first time must find out how he fits into the scheme of things. In a similar way, we have to fit into the scheme of the world, even the universe. When someone says "this world," you are also included because you are related to this planet, this universe. Self-knowledge involves "appreciation of the universe."

Another aspect of the soul is awareness, which is also the nature of absolute knowledge and is also the nature of existence. This nature of awareness cannot be changed in the past, present, or future. The final aspect of the soul is the nature of happiness. It is also absolute happiness, and it is not dependent on any object. It is the experience of being happy and being full and complete always, not just now and again. This happiness is our fundamental nature and the Supreme created everybody to be happy. He did not create sorrow. When you have a desire and it is fulfilled, you gain a momentary happiness, but it is just an experience within yourself for that moment. However, with self-knowledge, knowing you are awareness, existence, and happiness of the soul, you can be happy at all times, as long as your human physical body lives. So, in simple terms, self-knowledge is nothing but realizing that your physical body is not the self, rather the self is the existence, the awareness, and fullness. Remember those three golden words: *existence, awareness, and fullness.* That is the nature of our soul and the *self,* which is not the "I," which is a physical body. Comprehending and applying this is what self-knowledge is all about.

Truth is the cause of the entire universe. In everything we look at, the truth is what we experience, but the experience is only as good as the one who interprets that experience. If you look at the interpretation, it is only as good as one's knowledge. As you are trying to unfold this, it is not going to be like a special kind of body experience like people claim with "near-death," or like swamijis with their "suspended animation." It is not a bodily experience such as when you take a hallucinogenic drug or have an "out-of body experience." For example, drug abusers who take street drugs experience hallucinations, misperceptions, or delusions. A typical example is an alcoholic who feels elation and the sense of false happiness as a bodily experience. That is not what we are trying to achieve or gain with self-knowledge. It is merely unfolding "the truth of one's self." When you are experiencing this special bliss, it is part of the truth that it is your birthright to be happy and joyful. It is not going to announce itself and say, "I am the soul, I am self-bliss," so that it can be recognized. Instead, it will be a subtle and almost imperceptible shift in your consciousness.

As you unfold this truth, through self-knowledge, you'll discover that you are the limitlessness and fullness that you experience as happiness in a conducive state of mind. When you recognize this fact you automatically remove the error of seeing yourself as unhappy, incognizant, and mortal. So when you understand the meaning of this awareness, existence, "being," and your inherent blissful nature (happiness), it helps you to recognize the self as free from all the daily struggles of living.

As for illness and health, both are equally real. Does thought deny the self, or is there a thinker without self? Is there a thought without the self? In fact, thought is the self, but self is not just a thought. Self is real, being present in all situations. That is the logical concept you have to understand for self-knowledge. The self is timeless. However, the concept of time dissolves the very moment you understand the character or the nature of one's self, which is awareness, without leaving any misconception in the mind.

Even the meaning of awareness has to be clear in one's mind. For example, if you hear the word "apple," you are aware of the meaning of the word, apple. On the other hand, if you hear the word "awareness," unless you really know the deeper meaning that awareness is one's self, you may have different interpretations or misconceptions about this word. That is a problem with popular modern philosophy. There is often confusion when we say, "Self-awareness is an independent means of knowledge; it is not another state of experience."

I repeat: Self-knowledge is not another state of experience. It is the correction of an error about one's self and the recognition of the invariable self as the truth or basis of all experiences. It is nothing but a correction of our own incognizance or ignorance and error about our selves. It is not a state of experience, but purely the gaining of knowledge. The problem for us is that the mind is restless and vagrant, but we like to have very quiet, peaceful, restful, or tranquil minds. If you understand the true nature of the mind and accept it as being natural, then awareness becomes a little easier.

As a neurologist, I can explain that the mind's nature is to feel and think, like feeling the emotions and thinking in terms of desiring, resolving, inquiring, discovering, recollecting, and other such activities. *This is common to every human being.* Even though we all have the capacity to apply the mind, the hard part is to apply it in a chosen, always beneficial direction.

Because concentration requires interest in the object on which the mind has to concentrate, the lack of interest is the thing that often prevents learning. In a similar way, to gain self-knowledge, you have to have certain preparation of the mind, which I said earlier, and it is nothing but to create some interest in learning and understanding the concept. If you keep on practicing this, finally you start liking the experience. Take the example of a musical instrument. If you keep on practicing, not only do you master it, you also come to enjoy it.

One of the obstacles to self-awareness and ongoing happiness is the problem of self-judgment. That is, being critical of yourself and seeing yourself as unworthy—or any other type of self-condemnation. You have to have a firm belief in yourself, that whatever may happen, cannot be shaken.

Without self-knowledge, we feel our limitations, such as the time limitation of our life span and the limitation of our learning capacity. With self-knowledge, we realize that the self is indestructible, immortal, unborn, and limitless. The self is the source of all happiness. Many people, after hearing this, do not understand and they cannot imagine that there is happiness that is limitless beyond time and space. One reason is because when we go to the temple or the church, we are constantly reminded that we have sins. The mistaken conviction many people accept is that humankind, by nature, is sinful and limited, and the religions generally make promises of redemption, saying that if you do this or that, you will be saved.

With misinformation, we accept and believe everything that binds us to a life of limitations. We do not think logically that we need not do anything; we are already existence, knowledge, and fullness. Truth is not a private thing. Knowledge of one's self, of the world, of God is not the personal property of anyone. It is an ancient creation and knowledge from the Creator Himself.

By this knowledge you gain fullness, total freedom from limitation, and there is nothing equal to this knowledge in releasing you forever from the notion that you are limited. The more you know, the more you realize how much you do not know. This analysis is not in any way a criticism of modern science, but rather an illustration of the indefinite qualified relative nature of all objective knowledge. Truth has no compromise. Truth is like fire: It does not discriminate—it simply burns. Acquiring the knowledge of the self can forever release us from our limitations. When we realize the fact that the self is limitless awareness and we are free from all notions of limitation, there is nothing equal to this knowledge.

To appreciate this awareness, you need an abiding mind, and you can prepare that kind of mind very easily with a little effort and concentration. Even though this development of the mind takes some time, there is no reason for despair or frustration. *You must learn that you should never look down on yourself or conclude that you are not fit for self-knowledge.* That type of attitude and that type of self-condemnation will seriously work against you. I also emphasize here that if others condemn you, never accept their judgment. It is common for a person to be criticized by others. It often starts in our childhood, and the attempt to make you feel that you are inadequate continues throughout our lives, at home, at school, in society, at the work place, anywhere. You should never let those incidences or experiences cause you to conclude that you are hopeless or helpless.

Often the perceived limitations of our physical bodies and minds overwhelm us. This is due to the habit of taking ourselves wrongly. Our existence, consciousness, and fullness is the truth of each individual, and that which pervades everything is called "self," who is limitless, changeless, and depthless. The Lord is the whole creation, while "you" and "I" are only "limited beings." Because of our "costumes" we appear to be different. However, the Lord's existence is all pervasive. It is all the power, all the knowledge. *However, in our role as human beings, we are limited in power, knowledge, and other aspects, but these do not represent the real differences.* The limitations belong to the *body*, not to the *self* that is the nature of self-awareness.

Therefore, for self-knowledge, you have to understand that you are awareness, that you are not limited. Your physical body is only an *apparent* limitation, and one whose mind is awake to this fact is identical to God.

This knowledge of awareness is "what it is" and it is not "what it appears to be." When you look at yourself in a concave or convex mirror, you don't become alarmed at the distortion that you see because you know that your distorted form or figure exists only in that mirror. It is only apparent, and you have clear knowledge of what you really are. Similarly, you can play the role of a beggar on a stage, but you don't suffer as a beggar when the play is over because that role is over. Therefore, you have to develop this clear vision that even though your physical body is limited by knowledge, or by power, or by other aspects of time and space, it does not make your self limited. If you do not understand the true knowledge of your self, or if your knowledge is partial, it can be shaken, and because of that, people can criticize and reshape your mind.

This is an amazing phenomenon, and you have to follow it very carefully: *You are limitless awareness, therefore, the world is of your own making, whether it is proper or not.* All things exist in the Lord alone, and this is the greatest secret. So the Lord is the 'I.' With that, you can say all things exist in you alone. This vision is not from the standpoint of your body, but from the standpoint of pure awareness, which is your nature.

We have the *self*, which is changing, as well as the *self* that is changeless. All beings are subject to change. However, the most exalted self is the unchanging Lord who sustains all, and He is the world of changing, as well as changeless. So the entire creation, including our physical bodies, is subject to change. The cause, from which the changing world is born, is called changeless. This is with reference to the Lord who is beyond the changing and the changeless.

The Body-Mind-Sense Complex

You stand apart from your self because of the body-mind-sense complex, which began when you were born. This complex is a combination of your physical body (gross body), think tank (the mind), and sensory functions such as sense of smell, sense of taste, sense of touch, sense of vision, and sense of hearing.

The physical body is the place where all the experiences take place. It is a recorder of experience. The sense organs, organs of action, and the mind are the instruments for gaining various types of experiences. However, experience is not knowledge. What self-knowledge does is create a change in your attitude and the way you look at things. When you gain that attitude, which is born out of wisdom, then you are not overly elated when there is a desirable situation, and you are not deeply depressed when there is an undesirable situation.

A misconception for many people, even for great psychologists and philosophers, is that "one's innermost self" is buried somewhere deep inside of us. Thus, one has to dive deep within to discover it. If this were the case, then one's self could not be all pervasive or eternal.

The common misunderstanding many have is that the "body-mind-sense complex" is generally taken to be the soul. You can say that the soul is distinct from the physical body; therefore it survives death and goes to "heaven" after the body dies. Most of the religions stop here because they consider heaven as the very end. There are other notions, such as the mind being the house of the soul, but in actuality the mind has only the characteristics of the duality of the soul. Without the mind, it is not possible to distinguish one object from another. The whole world enters only through the mind. Therefore, whatever you see is only what is there in your mind, and the mind moves very fast, so rules do not work for the mind. It is the mind that rules and not the rules. All the emotions are very powerful, which is why emotion is more powerful than your will.

It is my contention that knowledge of the inner self can be gained without deep analysis. It can be gained by practice and self-inquiry. All the qualities of the body-mind-sense complex are taken as the qualities of the soul. You become limited because of the fact that your fullness is completely missed by the superimposition of the attributes of the body-mind-sense complex. If you have a strong desire to be free, limitless, happy, and blissful, the desire itself is already converted into a driving force to know, and with that force, you acquire self-knowledge.

The body-mind-sense complex is you, but you are not the body-mind-sense complex. Just like the example I gave earlier that the pot is clay, but the clay may not be the pot; the clay can be anything. A shirt is fabric, but the fabric need not be the shirt. Any role you play is you, but you are not the role. You are born with incognizance, and you start your life with incognizance of both the world and yourself. Incognizance of the self is destroyed by the fire of knowledge that is the burning of the discrimination between the soul and the self. Knowledge is often linked to fire. As the fire reduces a wooden log to ashes, so, too, the fire of knowledge reduces bondage, the effect of incognizance, to ashes. Knowledge does not come without effort, and it does not flash suddenly when you are sitting under a tree. The self is nothing but you; therefore, it cannot flash any more than what it is doing now. Again, as the self is all pervasive, you don't have to "dive deep" to see it.

There are two types of perception. The body-mind-sense complex is the one where perception continues even after you have accurate knowledge. The other perception is like the rope/snake example, when the false perception disappears in the wake of knowledge. Actually it does not go away; rather, your confusion is resolved. When you see a movie, you know that it is not real, but still you respond to what is happening in the movie. Even as you respond, in the back of your mind, you know that this is not real. That kind of knowledge is very natural for a person who understands that the soul is limitless. A similar example would be a person who dreams he or she won a lottery. It may have seemed all too real, but the dream is not going to benefit her when she wakes up. Knowing one's own self makes you free from any association with the body-mind-sense complex.

The only thing that goes away with gaining self-knowledge is the body-mind-sense complex. A person who has this knowledge of self is free from any sense of limitation. However, you can accomplish this only when there is firmness in that knowledge. That is, there is no doubt or vagueness in that self-knowledge. With self-knowledge you will gain a new vision of life guiding you to your self-improvement and happiness. The truth is the real nature of all creation. Even in a stone, truth exhibits itself as existence, but awareness may be lacking, which is a little bit more present in the plant kingdom. There is more awareness in the animal kingdom, and ultimately, the human being has not only awareness but also has choice. More specifically, that is "the freedom of choice."

Why Am I the Way I Am?

Before a thought arises, you are existent, and after the thought has gone, you still remain. This self-existence does not require any kind of proof or validity. On the other hand, if you go into a coma, you are not responding, and you are not conscious, then all kinds of tests are necessary to prove or disprove that you are existent. Before I studied neurology, I studied psychiatry, and I have learned that there are three kinds of people in the universe. Some are positive thinkers, some are negative thinkers, and some are neutral thinkers. Because of the positive thinkers, progress is made. And because of the negative thinkers, a lot of problems are created because their belief is weak.

They are usually very unhappy and they don't look at tomorrow with hope or anticipation. The neutral thinkers are neither positive nor negative, or they flip-flop between the two. Basically, they just exist, and they don't want to take a chance either way.

Similarly, if we have to classify the human beings in the universe according to their relationship to God, there are three types of people. One type looks for God for some gains. When their lives are in shambles, only then do they throw up their arms and accept the Lord's power and seek His help. The next type has curiosity about God and wants to know about God, and they put in some effort. To get whatever they want, they do not depend solely on God, but they also appreciate the necessity of God. The third type has partial knowledge that God exists, but they do not view God as separate from themselves. In other words, they may not understand God very well, but they always seek God's help in gaining knowledge. With all these three groups, each one knows that the Lord exists. One wants the Lord to help them, the other wants the Lord to give them something, and the third one wants to gain knowledge of the Lord. Of these three, the one who wants to gain knowledge is the most fortunate because they know that accumulating vast wealth and possessions in life only solves small problems, and the basic problem of limitation cannot be solved by any amount of gain. Therefore, they know that freedom from limitation can be gained only by knowing one's self, so they want to know or understand their relationship to God.

• Chapter 9 •
Being and Awareness

Human beings and animals drink, eat, and breathe to live. In a lot of ways, we both are alike. But our thinking process makes us different from the lower animals. Animals don't change significantly over a period of time, and the members of a particular category of animals or species are exactly the same in their behavior and habits. You cannot cause a goat to act like a cow, even though they both give milk. However, human beings from childhood to adulthood make drastic changes in their thinking process. Even though we all have our basic needs to survive (like eating, drinking, and breathing) human beings have far more options than do animals. A cow eats only grass and a lion eats only raw meat. However, human beings not only have a wide variety of foods, even with one specific food, they can prepare it in several different ways. We don't just drink water to quench our thirst. Some of us drink various beverages like soda pop, beer, wine, and juices. Why? Our advanced thinking process desires variety. When its stomach is full, an animal is satisfied, and it doesn't hunt or look for food. On the other hand, we human beings are seldom satisfied or content with eating just enough to survive. We constantly seek more for contentment. For example, if we are hungry, we eat to satisfy our stomachs, but soon we start looking for various foods to prepare for the next meal, or for dessert, whether we are still hungry or not.

The point is that both animals and humans are beings. However, humans not only have the highest level of awareness but ability to choose. Humans don't just act by instinct; they make calculated decisions for innumerable reasons.

The whole understanding of self-knowledge is based on three things. One is awareness, two is existence, and three is happiness. Even as a brain specialist, after years of learning how the brain functions, there is still very little one can know about exactly how it works. Even renowned scientists are faced with an enigma about precisely how the brain functions. As for myself, a brain specialist, it still is a huge puzzle to me in the sense that even if one were able to understand intellect, that understanding would not explain the "self." There are no magic pills available, no magic diets or natural atmospheres to make you always feel good. There are no special audiotapes to make you aware of the "self."

Let's say one pound of gold represents truth—or existence. If you make different chains with the pound of gold, different forms, shapes, and designs, each chain is only a name and a form, and each chain itself is unreal because it has no existence apart from the gold. In all the gold ornaments such as bangles, rings, and necklaces, the gold keeps changing its shape, but the gold remains the same. In other words, gold is always one, ornaments are many, but the ornaments don't exist without the gold. The ornaments are not "in" the gold, but the gold is in the ornaments. This metaphor also explains the relationship between God and humans.

When I say you are God and God is you, this is because the common thing we both have is "awareness" and "existence."

Self-knowledge is nothing but EXISTENCE (the state of being fully in the present moment), AWARENESS (the state of knowing you are not separate from God), and FULLNESS (the state of having freedom from wanting). Existence is "being," which is constant like "I," and this existence abides in all three periods of time: the past, the present, and the future. Again, it is like a pot made of clay. Clay existed before the pot was made, and clay is in the pot, and it remains after the pot has been destroyed.

Certain values or attitudes are necessary for the development of a mind that can see the truth of the self. Those values are actually a means of gaining that knowledge, like helpful tools you use to make a table or a computer. Similarly, those values help as a means in gaining self-knowledge.

When you see the truth, beauty, profundity, and limitlessness are perceived as "you." Keep this vision and appreciate it in contemplation. These are the values, the means of gaining knowledge of the self. And if you acquire these, you have everything. You will discover yourself to be what you are seeking. You will know what you are, and that is the essential nature of the individual.

Ego is a big obstacle in the learning process. It is a main source of our daily problems—and pride goes along with ego. Absence of pride assists us in being humble and makes it easier to achieve self-knowledge. Also, if you are keenly aware of the inevitability of death, old age, disease, and sorrow, you can attain freedom from "ownership." Thus, you are able to care without attachment, say, for a son, a wife, your home, and other people or property.

A proud or conceited person demands respect, and when he is respected only because of his power, that respect will disappear when his power is gone. Respect should be commanded but not demanded. Presenting yourself as other than what you are will only invite problems. Then, if you keep on telling one lie after another, you must remember each and every one of them to avoid being caught. On the other hand, if you always speak the truth, you don't have to remember anything. Because you are always telling the truth, there is never the fear of being caught contradicting yourself. You don't expect fire to be cold or a snake not to be poisonous; you just accept their nature and handle them properly, or keep away from them.

Being truthful also brings straightforwardness because when the thought, the word, and the action are all in alignment, naturally there is no discrepancy, and it achieves positive results. We should maintain cleanliness not only outside but also inside, and that inside cleanliness is what gives you happiness. You should not become a slave to the sense organs. You should have a dispassion toward the sense objects. You should never think that you have achieved everything all by yourself. As I discussed before, throughout every minute of our lives, from birth to death, we owe much to so many people, living and deceased, who are part of our daily living, or who have had an influence on us in our past. Accepting these realities and appreciating the universe gives you the true meaning of life. By holding these and other values as sacred, the resulting knowledge will make us much wiser and give us a special attitude.

Our problems relating to other people can be solved very easily if we understand that everyone is governed by their perception about their abilities, and the change that you want may not be possible for them. The world is wide enough to accommodate the other person. Until we accept this, there will always be wars, fights, killing, or ways of trying to harm another person. It will continue because of the lack of self-knowledge in the majority of the people—and especially a lack of self-knowledge in the people in charge of passing the laws or making the rules we all have to live by. (But that is another book. In this one we shall focus on you, the individual.)

Also, the desire to own everything we can will get us into trouble and lead to grief and frustration. As you learn through self-awareness, we don't own anything in this world, and we are not the authors of anything here. Self-knowledge gives us a certain attitude where material gains don't cause us to get carried away. It is true, when it comes to your family, children, wife and other relatives, you should think of yourself as the managing trustee of them (and the same with your own physical body), but not as the owner. This gives you less grief, sorrow, and sadness. The right attitude gives you tranquility of mind, whether you are faced with good or bad, success or failure, and whatever happens, your mind doesn't go to extremes.

This is not to say you should not try to acquire things. Rather, you should not become *attached* to the things you acquire. The attitude I am describing is, "I am very happy with my possessions, but I would be just as happy if I did not have them." When you have this kind of detachment, you are free from worry. You do not worry that you might lose any of your possessions. This is because it is not your possessions that make you happy. You may greatly appreciate your possessions, but you do not view them as the source of your happiness. You fully understand that happiness comes from within, and as such, your happiness is always there. This is because your source of happiness is an unwavering *positive attitude*, which is nonmaterial. Thus, there is no way it can ever be taken away from you. Only you can give up your happiness, but why would you?

Another thing I have observed in society is that a lot of people crave company. They constantly look forward to going to a social dinner or look forward to event gatherings or parties. Otherwise they feel lonely.

In excess, this tells that they are not secure in themselves and they do not enjoy being with themselves, or they do not enjoy the presence of their family or their children. The *need* to spend time in the company of others can be a form of escape, and every escape is a postponement of seeing who you are. When you understand the true nature of your self, you don't mind being all by yourself, and actually you can be very happy by yourself without craving for company. This does not mean you should be antisocial or you should live alone. Rather, if you are comfortable in yourself, the company of others is always an option and not an overwhelming need, making you anxious when alone. Also, I have seen in my own social life various people who actually suppress their egos and are submissive to a certain group of people or persons. This is so they will be accepted in that community or society and so they will be invited to the dinners and be part of the company.

In many cases, these submissive persons are actually afraid of the people they want to socialize with. Often, they do not respect the person they want to socialize with. For example, they may feel he or she is a hypocrite. They are afraid to say what they really think to that person because of that person's social circle. They fear that they may not be invited to the parties, functions, or the dinners if they don't "kiss up" to the host. I feel sorry for those people, for in their inner minds, inner hearts, they know that they are in their own way pretentious, too, because of how much importance they put on being accepted. As you gain self-awareness, you realize that you have no need to gain acceptance or approval by others.

Awareness is free from time. Awareness is timeless because it is eternal. When you understand this you will have no fear of mortality or death. It's easier to grasp this when you understand that time is relative and it differs from one mind to another. For example, if your mind is preoccupied and you are busy doing something you enjoy, an hour of time seems to go by very quickly. On the other hand, when you have nothing to do and you are not preoccupied, or even bored, and you keep looking at the clock, an hour of time seems to go slowly. But it's the same sixty minutes of time. Therefore, the mind is the maker of time, and your "awareness" is free from time. This awareness is self-knowledge. When you reach this point of understanding, then your desires are complete and fulfilled, and your hope of freedom from death is achieved, even though the physical body dies and disintegrates into the five basic elements.

Awareness is nothing more than self-knowledge and truth. Fullness is nothing but happiness and joy. Awareness is the nature of absolute knowledge, and it cannot be changed. The nature of happiness is not dependent on any object. The experience of being happy, being full and complete always, is our fundamental nature. Awareness is the key to self-knowledge, and if you can help somebody else be aware of this, your goal is fulfilled, and you have made another person happy. Initially, sometimes the interaction or the understanding between two persons when one is trying to make the other person aware may not be a fruitful, pleasant situation, but in the long run, the other person will realize the good you are trying to do for him or her. Do not be quick to give up if you meet with a little resistance, but by the same token, you cannot force knowledge on someone who is not ready or open to receive it. It's equally important to know when to take "No" as an answer.

Detachment and dispassion come through self-knowledge. That is the goal to be reached for true happiness. The persons who make use of this book can be free from pride, ego, delusion, and desires, free from the pairs of opposites like misery and happiness. These people will reach an end that is limitlessness, which is awareness, which is the knowledge of your inner self. And our minds shine because "I," the awareness, shines. Consciousness, through which everything is known, need not be illumined by any other source of light. Once you know yourself to be that awareness, self-knowledge takes place, and you cannot remain incognizant. And that incognizant state does not come back. All creation is born of this awareness alone, and everything is awareness.

• Chapter 10 •

Who is God? Where is God?

Everybody has a curiosity about God. Who is He and what does He look like? If we don't have a clear understanding of the universe and who God is, it is hard for believers to logically explain to others who don't believe. However, to one who has a logical understanding of the universe, all is very clear.

We all know there is a sun in our solar system. If you look up in the sky and you see the sun, you believe there is a sun. If you close your eyes, everything is dark, and you won't see anything, and it will be as if nothing exists except your mind, which realizes you exist. You know you need oxygen to live; you breathe in oxygen every second, and even though you cannot see oxygen with your eyes, you don't doubt the existence of oxygen for a moment. We may not able to see God, but we feel His presence in every atom of this universe.

The concept of God always seems to bring up questions. Where is He? What does He look like? How can we reach Him? It is a very complex issue and depending on your intellectualization and knowledge and personal experience, reaching your inner soul is touching God. Many books have been written about the concept of God and the mystery of life. I have visited temples and had discussions with pundits, scholars, saints, and swamis about God. The quest for information about God has been going on for centuries. Almost everybody likes to believe in something, and if anybody else contradicts or tries to disprove a belief we hold, we usually get upset because we don't want to be proved that we are wrong. Nobody wants to have questioned beliefs they have held for most of their lives. This is a natural human tendency.

The way I came to understand God, and to get answers to the questions I raised, was through countless discussions with hundreds of knowledgeable people. I would ask: If there is a God, why is there suffering? Why are there poverty, sickness, and wars? Why is it a mixed up world where people are born with blindness? Why do some people have cancer? Why are some people rich and others poor? These questions of "Why?" have raised curiosity, anxiety, apprehension, whatever you want to call it, in many thinkers and philosophers. Even some of the greatest minds cannot come up with a definitive answer. Thus, the feeling pervades: if only we knew for sure!! I've come to the conclusion that there is not one single answer that could satisfy *everyone*.

There are so many ways we can look at the universe and the things around us to get some answers for ourselves. Take, for example, a particular brand of car sold by one car company. For one person, regardless of how much or how little care is given, the car will run without any problems for a long period of time. Yet, for another person who takes very good care of the car, cleans it every day, and checks the oil regularly, still some part can malfunction with maddening frequency. This happened to my car within a few months after I bought it. In midsummer, a small part in the air conditioning blew and I had to wait for two months to get that part replaced. Because it was a brand new car and a brand new model, the dealer didn't even have the parts (they probably figured they wouldn't need replacement parts for at least a year or more), and it is a very expensive car, too. Some cars sit in the repair shop all the time. Some run very smoothly. Some become useless and cannot function after a few thousand miles. The same process goes into building each car. At the factory, as cars go down the assembly line, each is constructed in the same way, one right after the other. The process does not differ from one car to the next. So why does one come off the assembly line and perform beautifully (virtually trouble free) for years, and another ends up in the repair shop week after week? In other words, it's a "lemon," and there is no logical explanation for it.

When you apply the car example to the various people and countries in the world, it helps explain why some are well off and some are poverty stricken. Again, there is no logical reason. It is simply the random nature of nature, itself, but it is this disparity that makes some skeptics question the existence of God.

We all may look different in our shape, height, skin color, facial features, the language we speak, the culture we have adopted from our ancestors, or the material possessions we have. Taken globally, each country is different from other countries. But none of this really matters. These are all material differences, social and cultural differences. In essence, the laws of nature are the same and apply the same to all human beings and all countries. That is the fundamental premise of this book. If you understand this, you'll have no problem understanding the *Five Golden Rules for Happiness* later in the book. To understand the concept of God, we have to follow a certain methodology, and at the end, it should become very clear and make complete sense.

Almost everybody comes to an understanding that there is only one God. Then, whose God is the real God? When you think about when the universe started and how far back we can go, which God is the first God? For example, who was before Jesus Christ for Christians, before Jehovah for Jews, and before Allah for Islam? How far can we go back and how far do we want to go back? The question repeats, who was before whom? We can go on like this infinitely.

Even if you look at scientific dating of objects and events, you find that scientists have arrived at some answers using mathematical calculations. If you ask them if they are one hundred percent sure, their answer is "No, it is just a logical calculation." They cannot give the exact time in years, months, and a specific date. Once again, time is a relative thing. They can approximate the age of a tree by analyzing the rings, or the age of a stone by analyzing the carbon, so they can tell *approximately* how old, how many millions or billions of years old, but not exactly. Once again, years are for our human concept of time. It may be different for another galaxy, if there is another life form, or another universe. Everything becomes apparent, but there is no universal kind of understanding or knowledge that is not contradictory.

We can take our imaginations as far as we can and draw pictures or paintings or write concepts, depending on our beliefs and notions, how we were brought up in our own religion, and how the previous generations or the ancestors taught us about our God. However, that does not make us knowledgeable. That only makes us believe and develop faith in one aspect of God. When I say this, I, too, attempt to provide a logical explanation with my own limited thinking process or thinking faculty, which the Creator gave to each of us. With that, I will try to make sense out of the Supreme, why He is universal, and why He is everywhere.

When Hindus visit a temple to pray to the Lord, they light camphor, which they believe stands for the light of knowledge. If you know camphor, which is used in some of the food products we eat, and medicinally, it is a peculiar substance because when you light it, it completely burns itself up and does not leave any trace behind. When Hindus light the camphor and offer it to their God, they compare it with the light of knowledge. When you light the camphor, it's just like you are lighting your knowledge, and all ignorance or incognizance is burned up. Even though it is just an analogy, if you look deeply into the meaning of it, it carries an important understanding of life. Burning the camphor has a double effect. It provides the "light of knowledge" and at the same time it "burns away the ignorance" (or incognizance). Camphor does not leave any trace behind. That means the ignorance is totally burned away.

Even the richest person on the planet at this time, with his money, can build a palace or a "heaven" just like Disneyland, but he cannot build or create a universe. As human beings, we have limitations, and we look up to somebody. We are calling him God, which is the name we gave Him, or the Lord, and He did not ask for that, nor did He tell you that was His name. That is what we gave Him. Therefore, you can invoke the Lord with *any* name, any form, because *He, She, or It* is not limited, physically, spatially, or temporally. If you look at the Islam, likewise the Muslims did not give a form to Allah. But the limitation (and the problems) comes when you say that Allah is the only God, or Jesus is the only God, and only by worshipping Him can you go to heaven.

The teaching of self-knowledge, about the existence of God, is also like starting with the basics. To first explain an idea, you need to give a reference point. Then explain what you know, and then you can expand your knowledge about the pervasiveness, the existence of

God. The Supreme, the Lord we call God, permeates everywhere and everything. He is undivided. He is a huge mass of structure, and you cannot give Him a form or shape. This is because He is pervasive in existence, and He is awareness in both the moving and nonmoving, the living and nonliving material or objects.

Of those materials I mentioned before, the basic five elements, one of them is the space within which we are living and in which we exist. If we acknowledge that the space itself is created by God, that means the space is a tiny fraction of God and that space is within Him, within the Creator. Otherwise, you cannot say that He created something from outside and the space and everything came of its own and exists outside of God. This would not make sense. That would mean you are pushing Him into one corner. In that corner there is a space, and He is also there. So, if space is accommodating us and we are in the space, we are like stardust. If I ask the question, "Can you divide space?" Obviously, the answer is that you cannot. Your power or strength is not capable of doing that. If, as small stardust, you cannot see the whole universe, and if you cannot see the whole creation, which was created by the Creator, the Lord Himself, how can you see God? How can you give Him a shape? With the knowledge we have, which is not one hundred percent sure of the universe, black holes, dark energy, and other cosmic forces, if we cannot see the whole entire creation, how can we understand God and how can we visualize Him? How can we visualize God in a particular shape or form with all the limitations we have? He is everywhere and everything, which is why it is useless to try to give a shape or form to God.

So, in our quest for self-awareness, I am saying that all 6.5 billion human beings do not have to be unified with one religion, one God, one culture, or one belief system. Whatever the religion, whatever form you invoke God, if you have self-knowledge and if you understand the meaning of "one's self" you should not have any problem accepting God the way He is, which is *all* ways. And then you will realize that God has created everything and He loves everybody, He takes care of everybody, and He looks after every part of His creation, whatever form, shape, color, social status, whether it is animate or inanimate, whatever it is. It doesn't make a difference for the Lord.

There are hundreds of different religions, but there is only one

God. The only difference is how people choose to worship that one God. There can be an abstract painting in a museum, and each person will have a different interpretation of what that painting "means," or whether it is a good or bad painting. Some people may say it is beautiful, others may say it is ugly, and some people will have no opinion whatsoever about it. It doesn't particularly catch their eye one way or another, and they will walk by as if it isn't even there. Some will say the artist is a genius; some will say, "My three-year-old can paint better!" There are all these different opinions about an abstract painting—but it's the *same* painting. It doesn't change from one day to the next. How people *view* the painting is what differs. This painting makes some people happy when they see it. It makes other people angry when they see it. Perhaps they think the artist was grossly overpaid!

The same can be said of a movie. Ten people can go to a movie and come out with ten totally different experiences, or maybe they liked only one part of the movie and hated the rest. But the movie or painting does not change. The plot of the movie and the colors of the painting do not change from one day to the next. A person can hate a painting or a movie one day and then see it a year later and completely change his or her mind about it.

The point is, God is just God. God is everywhere and in everything, but how people perceive God is what differs. One person could have mostly bad luck and blame God. Thus, he sees God as unfair or vengeful. Another person could have mostly good luck and credit God. Thus, she sees God as loving and giving.

To give you another example, almost no one would argue against the statement that a tree is created by God, and therefore trees are "of God." Let's say one particular tree sits right on the border between two neighboring yards. In autumn, many leaves fall from this tree. One neighbor likes doing yard work and happily rakes up the leaves. He loves the tree. He uses the dried leaves for compost in his garden and sees them as "a little gift from God." For the other neighbor, raking leaves is an exasperating chore. He hates the tree. Every week he has to pay a gardening service to rake up the leaves and haul them away. He sees the leaves as "a big blight from God." Over time, the two neighbors fight over this tree. The one sees only its beauty and wants to keep it, and the other sees only its ugliness and wants to cut it down. All the while, it's the *same* tree, made by, or of *one* God. This is how different people, different countries, or different religions see the *same*, *one* God differently.

God just goes about His business of being God. A person could win a million dollars in the lottery one day and think that God is great. A week later that person could be in a bad traffic accident, perhaps become paralyzed. *Then* how does that person view God? God is considered loving and benevolent when things are going great and is considered vengeful and cruel when things are going badly. But God does not change. *Only your perception (of which you are in control) changes.* Knowing and understanding this leads to self-awareness, which leads to happiness.

Mankind has not really *created* anything. We only rearrange, making combinations of what the Lord has already created. We naturally feel obliged to offer our thanks, but we find that the object of our prayers is beyond our comprehension. When you appreciate that God is the material cause of the creation, you will realize that you need not go anywhere to look for Him. God is everywhere. He is the space, He is the air, He is the water, the earth; whatever there is in the universe, He is there. Anything that exists in time and space, including your physical body, sense organs, and mind, anything that is created is the Lord. He is the cause of origin of the entire universe and so, too, of its dissolution. You can cleverly state that because the Lord is the material cause of the creation and "I know the creation, therefore, I know the Lord," but the Lord cannot be an object of your knowledge. For an object has to be different from you; it has to be a subject. God is not different from you. If everything were different from the Lord, what would be left of the Lord would be precious little. If you can imagine that you can look on the Lord as an object, you are making yourself superior to Him. If God were an object from your thought, He is then separate from you, and you could dismiss him very easily from your thought. But this is impossible because God exists even as your "thoughts." Your thoughts are inseparable from God.

If you could go to "heaven" and see the Lord, then the Lord would fall into the category of something that comes and goes depending on your thoughts. Then God would be no different from any other limited being. If you analyze this example, even if you were in heaven sitting in front of God and you saw His front portion, and then you might want to see His back portion, but suddenly you turned and saw somebody else. At that time, the thought of God, even though He is right in front of you, the thought temporarily can be dismissed by your mind by your acknowledging somebody else. That means you have the power to dismiss God. This belief of a God in a place called "heaven" arises out of the wrong understanding of what God is. On the other hand, if you understand the pervasiveness of God and the omniscient and omnipotent nature of God, then you realize that you cannot give Him a form or shape, and He is everywhere, even within you. If you don't appreciate that you and the Lord are identical, you have only partial knowledge about God.

Waves are born out of the ocean, and by the ocean, they are sustained, and into the ocean they resolve. Just as a wave is related to the ocean, as an individual, you are related to God. The ocean inherits every wave, yet the wave looks on the ocean as different from itself because it thinks that the timeless, limitless ocean created him, a limited wave. Of course, this wave's interpretation of the existence of its creator, the ocean, is a big leap in thinking as compared to that of the "naive wave" that thinks it came from heaven or that there is nothing beyond itself. If you acquire this knowledge, you automatically become humble to God and you realize that you don't have to see God to know He is existent, and He is within you. As an example, you know that you had a great, great, great, great grandfather, and even though you haven't seen his picture, you are here, in existence. This means he had to have been here before you were, even though he is not present in front of you now.

Let's say you have the question in your mind, "how big is God?" or, "How can He be in a single atom and throughout the entire universe at the same time?" Suppose you look at a small ant—and let us presume hypothetically that the ant has a thinking process and can question you—and the ant asks you how big you are. Your immediate thinking processes would probably cause you to ask, "In relation to what?" An ant is a tiny insect, and if you look at yourself through an ant's eyes you look huge, but you are not the whole world. There are 6.5 billion people like you, plus all the other living organisms, so can an ant think that because you are huge, you represent God? On the other hand, if you look at an ant, there is one common thing between both of you. Aside from differences such as physical features, size, thinking faculty, and the choices God gave you, the one common thing you share is *awareness*. You and the ant both have awareness. In a similar way, between you and God the common factor is existence and awareness. However, we are limited by our sense organs, and our sense organs are limited, as when our eyes have limited vision. However, God's vision is unlimited.

In one aspect of learning, our sense organs actually *limit* us to what we know or what we can know. We know what things smell, taste, sound, feel, or look like. But our sense organs do not help us with that which we do not know, such as the pervasiveness of God in all things. We cannot smell, taste, hear, feel, or see God to verify His existence, but with self-knowledge, we achieve the awareness of God's existence in everything we smell, taste, hear, feel, or see.

With self-awareness, you see an order in the laws of nature, which is the world, and you or I or our ancestors did not create it. We are born into this order and we are part of this order. In this order, you find yourself as an integral part, because you or I, or anyone like us, does not author this order. We have to appreciate its authorship in a being that is all knowing; in a being we call God, or the Lord. That Lord cannot be outside of this world because there is no place outside the world. Nor can that Lord be only in a corner of this world like you and I. If that Lord is the author of the world, the world is not separate from that Lord. The Lord is the maker, as well as the material of this world. The Lord Himself is the material because the world is not separate from the Lord. Thus, the Lord's form includes our physical bodies, our minds, and our senses. His knowledge includes our knowledge; the power He wields includes our power. So the Lord is all, and He is all pervasive. Having this power of knowledge about yourself, about the self, the universe, and the Creator (the Lord/God) makes you free from any limitation.

The nondifference between the Lord and yourself is a matter of self-knowledge. The difference is apparent in the external realm, and you also recognize that. Gaining that knowledge makes you realize the truth about existence, awareness, and happiness. Whatever religion you choose to follow—Christianity, Islam, Hinduism, Judaism—we all become believers in a God. If you take the 2000 census, the percentages of the religions in the world are Christians thirty-three percent, Muslims twenty-six percent, Hindus thirteen percent, others like Judaism, Jainism, Confucianism, Shinto, Taoism, Buddhism, and tribal religions eighteen percent, and no religion at all ten percent. This means ten percent of human beings don't believe in God. But for those ninety percent of human beings who do believe in God, what *makes* us believe that there is a God? We have to take God on pure faith, without solid physical evidence or proof. We do not know *where* the Lord is. We do not know *who* the Lord is, or whether God is a He or a She, but when we acknowledge the glories of God, we see the sun, we see the moon, we see the order in the creation, and they are all His or Her or Its glories. And with this acceptance of a Supreme Intelligence that operates far beyond our logical capability to explain or understand, we can become a believer that there is a Lord, a Creator, or a God.

Again you do not question the existence of your great, great, great, great-grandfather, even though you cannot have possibly seen him. But the very fact that you exist proves his existence. In a similar way, the existence of all that encompasses the universe guarantees the existence of the Creator, the Lord. Because you exist, your great, great, great, great-grandfather had to have lived, existed. It is not just a matter of belief, but it is a fact. Elements of your great, great, great, great grandfather still exist and remain alive, and are expressed in you. So, too, the universe and its Creator always exist in and of themselves. That is the type of logic you have to use to attain self-knowledge. This knowledge is ancient, it is directly from the Creator Himself, and we are trying to learn and understand this knowledge through a method that defies the type of thinking process most of us were taught in schools. For this world to exist there must be a Creator who has both the knowledge of the entire creation and the power to create it.

If I show you a watch and ask you if there is a watchmaker behind this, you automatically realize there is one. Even though you don't see the watchmaker yourself, you know that somewhere there is a watchmaker existing. In a similar way, the Creator exists also. You don't have to see Him but you see the creation, so there has to be a Creator. We are constantly reminded that we have to believe in something, even though that belief is nothing but a judgment before we gain the knowledge. Whenever it is just a belief, it is always subject to verification by inquiry. If somebody you trust says, "so and so is a good person," even though you did not meet that person, you believe it because a reliable person is saying so. On the other hand, if you actually met that person, and he turned out to be not so good, then it is no longer a belief you hold. Then it is knowledge you have gained about that person. In other words, belief is not based on knowledge, so it can always be shaken up. It cannot be shaken if it is not a belief, when it becomes knowledge. Even if a million people say that fire is cold, you will not accept that because you know for a fact that fire is hot. It is proven knowledge and a truth that cannot be shaken by anyone, even if a million people say it's so. It's the same with the watch and watchmaker, where you have knowledge of the watchmaker from the existence of the watch, and it is not just a belief.

By understanding this, if someone were to ask you, "Where should one search for God?" the answer would be, "He is the material of which we are all made and everything else. All the natural things like fire, air, water, everything is God." Therefore, remember, there is nothing that is apart from the God. So, how can you search for God unless you have concluded that God is away from you? As I mentioned before, a man never searches for his head because it is always on his shoulders. You cannot find your head separate from your body. If someone has the confusion that his head is separate from his body, he could look for his head everywhere and he would never find it until he looked on his own body. Similarly, if you are seeking God and you want to *see* God, obviously He is not going to be *seen* because you are making an inherent error that God is different from you. In gaining self-knowledge, conclusions are unnecessary because the knowledge itself is conclusive and not subject to interpretation or negation.

As we discussed earlier, a small wave in the ocean is nothing but water, just like the whole ocean itself is also water. And the small waves should "realize" that the water is the unchanging truth of this whole ocean that created a small wave. The comparison for us is that the ocean is the Lord that has created you, me, and countless other human beings, just like countless other waves are created by the ocean.

So the Lord pervades us all, and in time, we will resolve into Him again, just as the wave hits the shore and resolves back into the ocean. In this metaphor, you are not different from the ocean; you are water, and the entire ocean is water. If you understand this concept, you will see that you are not mortal. There can be no destruction for you. As both the ocean and the wave are the same water, the Lord and you are one. That is "the limitless awareness."

If I ask you now, with all this explanation and logic behind you, "which form is God?" I am sure now you know the answer, "Which form or which symbol *is not* God?" If I touch your little finger, immediately you know that I have touched you. I don't have to do a whole body massage to get your attention that I touched you. I don't think you'll disagree with me on this logic. Whether you touch my forehead or my little finger or my back, with a simple touch, you can easily get my attention, and I can appreciate and realize that you have touched me because every part of my body is "I." I am equally present everywhere in my body. Correct? Similarly, any form is God's form, and so you can see the Lord in any form.

If you still do not understand this, if it still does not make sense to you, please read the book one more time, and I can assure you that you will come to understand. Just as I tell my interns, read the book the first time for pleasure. That will create some kind of curiosity, and it will provoke a thought process in your mind. The second time when you are reading, pay a little bit more attention and try to understand more deeply what I am trying to say. If you have a little bit more time, or if you are more curious and your mind is prepared for this, read it a third time, and I'm confident that you will understand the essence of this book. You don't have to be a Mensa-level genius to understand. If you still don't understand, you can always discuss it with another person who also has read this book. Between the two of you it should be easier, by comparing your understandings and interpretations, to determine what is logical and what does not make sense. A discussion of this book by two people is an excellent way to increase self-awareness in each of you.

If the question of whether or not it was God who created the universe still hasn't been satisfied for you, consider this: For the universe to exist, you know that there must be a Creator behind it.

That Creator would need to be omniscient, omnipotent, all pervasive, and powerful. Just like a potter must have the knowledge of the pot and the skill to make it, or a goldsmith must have the knowledge to make an ornament from gold, the Creator of the universe must have all the knowledge, all the skill, and all the power to create this enormous universe. If you can't imagine such a being here on the earth, you imagine that He or She resides in another place, which we call heaven, and which is unknown to us. Some people say that God is in heaven and He created this world from heaven. However, this simplistic statement will not satisfy our intellect for long because the problem here then becomes, *who* created heaven, where God supposedly sat when he was creating this world? If God created heaven, where was God seated before the creation of the heaven? This endless chain of questioning comes up if you try to intellectualize existence. This is because we fail to recognize another important quality for the cause of creation, which is that for anything to be created, not only is there a creator who has the intelligence to make it, but also there needs to be the material with which to create.

Without clay, a potter cannot make a pot. So, for the potter to make a pot, the clay is the material cause. For the creation of this universe, God must have needed material to create it. If that material was different from God, then you have to ask, "Who made that material for God to create this universe?" If you cannot say that someone else made the material to create this universe, then you must say that God Himself is the material cause of the creation, and God finds the material within himself, and from it he creates the world. It's like a spider that spreads out and draws in the thread that it spins from within the spider itself. Thus, the spider is both the material of the web and the spider is the one who weaves it.

Similarly, when you dream, you are the author of your dream creation, and you are also the material of it. You create all that you see in your dreams out of yourself, so in your dream world, you are both the material and the intelligent cause, which is the effective cause. This is the same as when I talk about the universe or the world, which is authored by someone who must be efficient (intelligent) and material cause. If God is the material cause, He does not stand apart from the creation. When you pick up a pot, you also pick up the material of the pot that is the clay. When you hold a gold chain, you hold the gold. Wherever an object goes, its material cause accompanies it. The material of which it is made sustains the object. An effect is never separate from its material cause. If the Lord is the material and He is the intelligent (efficient) cause of the creation, then what is the distance between the Lord and the creation? There is no distance, so the Lord is the creation. Because the Lord is the author and the material cause of the creation—space, time, stars, sun, moon, earth, trees, seeds, man, woman—all within the creation are within God. All of these came from the Creator, and they will get resolved in the Creator. Because God is not separate from His creation, it is not possible that He is separate and seated in heaven watching us. The Lord pervades whatever moves on the earth.

So God indeed is the one from whom all creations are born, and what is born from Him is sustained by Him and resolves into Him alone. God is not merely the efficient cause of the creation (the intelligence behind it), but the material cause as well. At the end of its existence, the object resolves not into its efficient cause, but into its material cause. The pot does not resolve into the potter, but only into the clay. There is nothing beyond the Lord or other than God in the creation. No object stands apart from God because He is the very cause of the time-space continuum and everything that exists in it.

Consider an atomic bomb. A tiny atom can destroy the whole earth, and that tiny atom was created by the Supreme. The atom is extremely powerful. If I ask you, "Have you ever seen an atom?" The answer is, "Of course not." It's far too small to be seen, but just because you haven't seen it, can you discard it and say the atom is not powerful? I believe the same thing applies to someone asking, "If you haven't seen God, how you can know for sure He exists?" But if you can accept the existence of an atom, which you cannot see, which has the power to destroy the earth, how can you not accept the existence of God, which you also cannot see?

You can look at *reaching* God or feeling the experience of God in two ways. One, that it is very easy to reach or experience God, or two, that God is most difficult to experience and reach. If you are looking for Him, you cannot find Him. But for a person whose mind is ready, God is very easy to know.

Perhaps the most fundamental mistake many of us make is that we try to give a *form* to God. Almost every religion has its own interpretation of God, how He looks or how He should look, in all varieties of forms. But let us say that God were to appear before us in a given form; it would be an error to conclude that He has *only* that form. This would be making God limited, which is the opposite of God. God is the entire creation, and therefore, *all* forms are His forms. Therefore, one can invoke God in any kind of form you want because He is the author of the creation, and in and out of the Lord everything merges.

So the Lord is space, the Lord is time. God is the moon, and He is the earth, the galaxies, the Milky Way, the solar system, the black holes, the wind, the trees, the foliage, flowers, bees, anything you want to give as an example, the Lord is. The Lord is the thought behind our eyes, and the Lord is the conscience behind all these creatures, the universe, behind the creation, space, time, stars, and galaxies, behind everything. And the Lord Himself is everything. So, to answer the question, "Where is God?" He is everywhere, and He is pervasive in every material cause there is. Or if somebody asks you where is God, you can simply say to them, "Where is He not?"

Allah, Krishna, Jesus, and others have tried to put God in a form that is easier to relate to. It is very difficult, if not impossible, to simultaneously visualize God as everything and as nothingness. How would you make a symbol or an icon that is both everything (all objects) and nothing (the space surrounding all objects), both visible and invisible, at the same time?

The true symbol or representation of God could not be one thing on earth, it would need to be everything you see on earth and in the universe, plus everything you do not, or cannot see. In addition, God is feelings and emotions, such as love. How could you create a symbol or icon that for every single human being evokes the feelings of love? It would be impossible to create one representative object that everyone would have the exact same response to. This is why there are different religions with different symbols, icons, and figureheads. The symbol is not God Himself, but God is within the symbol, and this is why certain religious symbols can evoke the feeling of worship in a follower of that particular religion.

When I say this, I am not disputing or disagreeing with anyone that Jesus is not God, or that Allah is not God, or for Hindus that Rama or Krishna is not God. All I am saying is that you can believe or worship your God in any form you want, and He is there in that form because He is everywhere. The only problem comes when individuals blindly say, or say with fanaticism, "my God is the *only* God," or "He is the *only* Son of God," or "we are the *only* chosen ones!" Claiming a monopoly on God is like saying, "The sun only rises in New York and sets over Honolulu beaches."

With this type of attitude, you are seeing the Supreme with tunnel vision. Like the example of the frog in the well, you are making God limited and you are limiting yourself. Unfortunately, the majority of us already have a certain concept of God as a person sitting somewhere far away and running the world. We end up justifying our own notions because they are preconceived notions, and there is some prejudice involved depending on our race, culture, religion, likes, and dislikes. On the other hand, if we enter into a discussion of God or an attempt to understand God with an open and attentive mind, we can come to understand the world a little bit better.

And finally, to know God, while you can, you do not necessarily have to seek the knowledge of persons wiser than yourself who have made a career of studying their particular religion. The understanding of God is already within you and can be attained or revealed through self-awareness.

• Chapter 11 •

Theometry: Is God Understandable, Testable, and Predictable?

A Logical Journey on the Path of Self-Knowledge with an Analytical Mind

The title of this chapter poses a zillion dollar question. As a knowledgeable and experienced brain specialist, I use logic and common sense to arrive at a particular diagnosis. Using the same analytical mind and thought processes, I will take you on a logical journey to find the answers. Science deals with secular knowledge, which is important for human progress, and the validation of science occurs when its findings are understandable, testable, and predictable. Much of the breach between science and religion stems from the claim of scientists that neither spiritual knowledge nor anything to do with God can be validated in a scientific way. In this chapter I will show you that such validation is possible.

Remember that incognizance (ignorance) is the root cause of all the evils in the world, and the events such as the following recurring topics in recent news reports provide evidence of continuing widespread incognizance in the world today:

1) What curriculum should schools teach children to span the gap between creationism and evolution? Or should they teach intelligent design, the theory that takes a middle path?

2) War on terrorism, suicide bombers, Middle East cultural and religious clash with Western society and Christianity. There are ongoing killings between Jews and Muslims, between Muslims and Christians, between Hindus and Muslims. These events occur purely on the basis of lack of understanding about God. Historically, bigotry, secularism, fanaticism, greed for power, and greed for material wealth are the root causes of human bloodshed on the earth's soil.

3) There is no single day that goes by in which numerous television shows do not mention obesity, diets, various studies and products that claim to burn fat without effort, and the recent bankruptcy of the owners of the Atkins' diet plan. We spend billions of dollars every year for useless diet products because, once again, common sense is lacking in the general public.

True knowledge is covered by ignorance, just as a shining mirror is covered by dust. You can shine the mirror by simply dusting it, and similarly, you can achieve true knowledge by shedding your ignorance. Because of incognizance, we are bombarded with hatred, unhappiness, terrorism, wars, and killing. We live in a planet of extremes:

1) On one end of the spectrum, people are starving to death, while other extreme people are markedly obese.

2) One side in a war promotes suicide bombing by fanatics in the name of religion, and the other side, in the name of war on terrorism, kills many innocent people, while at another extreme, millions of lawsuits are argued with double standards and hypocrisy toward humanity at large.

3) On one end of the world children don't have food, while people in the wealthy nations feel unhappy and depressed despite abundant material possessions.

To obtain truth, we can't have a preconceived notion or colored vision. Doing so would degrade us to the level of the Romans who accused Jesus Christ of blasphemy. What a shame! When we do not use our free will, we easily become victim to our own emotions.

Knowledge is always with us, and to access it, we need only to shed our ignorance little by little as the snake sheds its old skin in order to gain new skin. It took millions of years for humans to reach the level of understanding we have today.

Theories of Creation

School boards throughout the United States are involved in heated debate about which science curriculum to teach. In the following sections, I will try to shed light on the three major theories of creation that are at the heart of all the controversy.

Creationism

The Christian version of creation is based on the book Genesis in the Old Testament of the Bible, which says that in the beginning God created heaven and earth and that He created all the living beings in six days. This was 6,000 years ago. Then came Adam and Eve and their sins and the crucifixion of Jesus Christ to redeem our sins.

Different religions have different stories of creation. In Hinduism, Shakti is the primal energy and pure consciousness, and manifestation is from unmanifestation. Hinduism also has Trimurtis (three Lords manifested out of Shakti), analogous to the Christian Trinity, with Brahma being the Lord of Creation, Vishnu the Lord of Preservation, and Shiva the Lord of Annihilation.

We can go on and on with different religious beliefs and different creation stories. This disparity among different creation stories contributes to scientists' skepticism about God and creationism. Examination of dinosaur fossils and study of the stars and galaxies make it undeniable that the universe is more than 6,000 years old as the book of Genesis claims. However, Christians view time as linear, with a definite beginning and a definite end, whereas Hindus believe that time is cyclic, an endless repetition of events.

Critics of creationism argue against the reason and purpose for the mass extinction of dinosaurs if they were, indeed, created by God. What unwritten law of nature explains such a phenomenon? Logical thinkers wonder that if God created Adam and Eve who had two sons and three daughters, then what are the relationships of the rest of the human beings to each other?

There is instrumentality even in Genesis, which tells that Elohim was transformed into Jehovah and created the universe in six days. But unluckily, no scripture clearly answers the "why" and "what" questions about creation, which has neither beginning nor end. It is a continuous process. Millions of galaxies take birth every day, and millions of galaxies destroy themselves every day. Energy can neither be created nor destroyed. Manifestation is created out of unmanifestation. It is part of nature to create and procreate.

Evolution

Darwin's theory of evolution, Neo-Darwinism and the survival of the fittest, evolution of the human race from apes, trying to find the missing link, Lucy, fossils found recently in South Africa—all this hard work has been invested in determining our evolutionary origin. But the theory of evolution has its own caveats, including the genetic leap of the fruit fly, which is still a missing link.

Scientists can only dissect and try to explain how a simple flagellum works in a complex way. To restore function to a body part—a finger, for example—scientists have invented complicated, elaborate, computerized gadgets to make the finger move. A normally functioning brain can make the same move in a fraction of a second.

Why can no one create something from nothing, from a material that does not already exist in the universe? We have the Big Bang theory of creation (the only logical theory to have won the Nobel Prize); Einstein's theory of relativity; ten-dimensional (later eleven-dimensional) vibrating theory of an elegant universe; and, recently, the M theory (the fabric theory of vibrating strings of energy that make up the universe). Despite all these theories, there is no definite scientific understanding of the universe. The theories keep changing, and these elegant theories are neither testable nor reproducible in a lab.

Scientists spring a theory of an ever-expanding universe one day and then talk about the rubber-band squeeze and the big crunch another day. Would that mean the end of the universe? The more we know about the world around us nowadays, the more we realize how little we know about creation and annihilation of the universe. What was there before nothing—what was before and before and before? There is no answer.

If humans evolved from apes, why are apes still wandering around in abundance? Can scientists create life out of nothing? Can they explain how the very first spark of life came out of water, and the very first unicellular organism came out of no life? They have the answers only for the observations they make from dissecting something that already exists in the universe. We still don't have an answer for what was before the widely accepted Big Bang (no other theory seems logical), and until we have definitive answers and we know for sure, logical explanations using the available knowledge seem to make sense to me. You need both of your eyes for proper vision and depth perception; monocular vision (tunnel vision) only limits your perception.

At the dawn of the twenty-first century, modern science is still groping in the dark. It still has only theories about the beginning of the universe; it still can't define death; its inventions are creating more and more greed, anger, deceit, and stress among us. At the end of the twentieth century, science may have touched only the tip of the great iceberg of knowledge. There are billions of galaxies in the universe, and each of them consists of billions of stars. We may never see a signboard saying, "Stop! The universe ends here."

Modern science is still in the state of a blind person. I am not asking you to abandon the comforts science has provided, but science can't solve all riddles in life. The most important aspect of life is being truthful to yourself. If you lack that quality, you will be able to grasp neither religion nor science. Each time science discovers something new, it opens up another thousand questions.

Intelligent Design

Intelligent design is the middle path between the creationism and evolution (just as Buddhism is known as The Middle Path). Let's have an open mind and look at this theory logically.

Because the human body is so complex, and the odds are so slim of having the precise proteins and DNA to be what we are today simply by chance, the theory of intelligent design was developed from the two extremes of creationism and evolution. Something as complex as the human brain has to be the work of an intelligent designer. However, the scientific world argues that the so-called "God" is not testable, predictable, or understandable. It takes nine and half years to read aloud one person's entire DNA (genetic map) information. Is this complex DNA just a coincidence and the result of a random act? The Discovery Institute showed a video in which researchers tested the probability that a group of Scrabble letters, when dropped to the floor, will spell out Shakespeare's famous line, "To be or not to be? That is the question." It could not be done. The Big Bang took only 10^{-43} seconds to occur.

Scientists, with their insatiable curiosity to search for purpose and earth's significance in the universe, have learned that our planet is a privileged planet in that it has all the right ingredients to support a life form as complex as human beings. They were astonished to understand the consistency in the laws of physics and chemistry. Even the location of the earth (which is a speck in the cosmic dust) is just right in our solar system for creating a habitable zone. It is estimated that the probability of combination of every element in the exact amount necessary to sustain life is 10^{-50}. The list of necessary factors for complex life to be sustained on planet earth keeps increasing and making scientists drop their jaws by looking at the odds and comparing them with data for the other planets in our solar system.

We cannot discover or invent anything that is already in nature. To understand the complex human body and to become a brain specialist, I had to show my intelligence with my grades, and I had to work hard and spend years in medical school and further studies. To understand theology and religion, I had to read the history of all the known religions and belief systems so I could grasp the essential nature of every religion. I've also studied philosophy, psychology, and psychiatry in order to understand human normal and abnormal behavior. A person's understanding of God depends on the capability to understand the rhythmic and orderly nature of the universe.

To understand the universe, one has to engage in serious study, and to see stars and galaxies, we need powerful instruments like the Hubble telescope. The unassisted power of our eyes is not enough for us to see complex human genetic material, so we make use of electron microscopes. Without putting a lot of effort into studying the meaning of $E=MC^2$, one cannot say that it is not understandable.

So, You Want To Understand God?

In order to acquire knowledge, understand a subject, or obtain a degree, you have to study hard and go to a college or university. You cannot become a PhD in astrophysics or a medical doctor by sitting in a bar and wishing. To understand God, you need to put in the same effort to acquire knowledge and shed your incognizance. It is like a pinch of salt trying to find the depth of the mighty ocean; the moment it touches the surface of the water it dissolves, implying the God realization. If you cannot see or feel the edge of the universe, how can you understand the mighty God?

If you can create something out of nothing that belongs to the universe, and if you can create nature without sun, moon, or water, if you can create a living cell, you definitely understand God. Everything that is born in this universe must perish, and if you can create an imperishable object, you understand God.

How do we know God is male? Why not female or an "it"? One religion calls God by the name of Allah; another, Yahweh; some, Jesus, Son of God; others, Krishna; still others, Buddha. Nearly everyone refers to God in the male gender. Why? How do we know God's form, shape, or gender? My given name is Devakinanda Vithal Raja Pasupuleti. For my parents, I am their son, and I am sibling to my brothers. I am also husband to my wife, father to my children, doctor to my patients. I am also a friend, teacher, colleague, truth seeker, and so on. Whatever name I am called, I respond. What do you think God will do when you call Him with whatever name you please?

The understanding of God in theology has varied according to the times and current social problems. God asked Abraham to sacrifice his son, whereas Isaac wrestled with God and had lunches with Him. God asked Moses to take his sandals off in front of Him and talked to Moses from behind the burning bush saying, "I am that I am" and declaring Himself to be the only God, establishing the revolutionary concept of monotheism and eradicating the practice of polytheism by the Jews. Every religion on earth claims divine inspiration for its scriptures, and every religion has its own dark side (no exceptions). The famous question, "What was God doing before He created heaven and earth?" was answered by St. Augustine, the theologian, that God created hell for those who ask questions like that one.

Every religion provides us with many suggestions on how to tackle our day-to-day problems, but a true religion should give us only suggestions on how to solve our problems, and it should never order us what to do. There is no true salvation but peace and harmony in life and in a way to have a stress-free life. Ignorance is the root of all evils, and knowledge is the answer to all problems.

In a true religion, tolerance is not simply a matter of policy, but an article of faith. It accepts the truth behind all religions. A true religion should teach its devotees both tolerance and universal acceptance and should encourage a devotee to seek truth from all religions. Just as a honeybee gathers nectar from different flowers, a true devotee of any religion accepts the essence of different scriptures and sees only the good in all religions Contradictions are seen in every scripture in the world, and it is wrong to judge any scripture by quoting lines from it here and there. We have to look at the summation of ideas of the whole scripture and not the literal meaning of specific quotations.

To be a nonbeliever in God is quite easy from a state of incognizance or ignorance. One has to think and explore all realms of thought in order to understand. Doubts come out of ignorance and should be destroyed by the sword of knowledge. Just have an open mind and be ready to explore new realms of thought. Ideas are unwritten laws of the universe; they are open to all who are in the relentless pursuit of truth.

Ego is ego, in whatever form it manifests. You should be able to worship in a Christian church, a Jewish synagogue, a Muslim mosque, a Hindu temple, or a Buddhist vihara and see your personal God in all those places of worship. By doing so, you will be able to establish the oneness of God, as well as eradicate your ego, which is a stumbling block in your spiritual progress.

Without individual effort, without changing consciousness, God cannot come to anyone, even though God is already a part of every one of us. Who sincerely seeks the absolute truth will finally realize it and will know that all religious scriptures are only aids in the pursuit of truth, not a "must" for attaining the ultimate truth. All methods of God-realizations are equally important.

Testability of God

If you take a tiny, tiny seed from a banyan tree and plant it in nature's soil, that tiny seed will grow into a huge, mighty tree. Can you put another banyan seed in a glass jar and make it grow into a huge tree? If your answer is "Yes, I can," then by all means you can test God. We know the story of blind men and their perceptions of an elephant, one describing the tail as a snake, another one describing the trunk as a tree, another one describing a leg as a pillar, and none of the blind men perceiving the magnitude of the mighty elephant.

You cannot search for an object in the darkness; you need a source of light like the sun or a flashlight to see things clearly and to describe an object. You cannot see oxygen, but you know you breathe oxygen to survive. You can test for the presence of oxygen simply by closing your nostrils. The powers of observation also apply to testing the existence of God. You don't see oxygen, but you know you need oxygen to live. You don't see galaxies, but when you look at the night sky, the stars you see are testimonials to their existence. Everything you understand is not necessarily what you can see. Even if you don't understand the whole equation of $E=MC^2$, the theory of relativity that revolutionized the world, you realize the essence of it, and you accept it.

For a skeptic who likes to see tangible proof of validity, the questions will remain unanswered. Why did the almighty, omniscient, omnipotent, and benevolent God need six days for creation and one day to rest? Can creation occur with the snap of a finger?

Predictability of God

You can predict that when spring comes, flowers will blossom. The tree that looks like it is dead in autumn is lively with green leaves and colorful flowers in springtime. This is predictability of unwritten laws of the universe. The sun rising, the sun setting, seasons, and recycling of the universe are unwritten laws of nature. These are predictable.

Soon after they are hatched from the eggs, baby turtles crawl toward water; this is predictable.

Unwritten laws of nature are universal and predictable, and these laws act in a similar manner in similar circumstances. For instance, if you put your hand into a fire, you will automatically burn your fingers. This happens at all times and at all places, to the baby who accidentally touches the fire without knowing the nature of the fire, as well as to a physicist who might have done years of research on fire.

If I deprive you of water (the source of origin of the first living cell, which is the fundamental unit of our existence) and oxygen, then it is predictable with certainty that you will die. It is the unwritten law of nature that anything born out of the five elements must perish, and that is predictable. You can bet your life on it.

Now, can you see how logical, common sense clears away one's incognizance about God, creation, and evolution? All you have to do is take all the information that is provided to you and use your own brain to draw conclusions. There is no middle person for salvation; you are your own salvation. Once again, there is no more powerful tool in the entire universe than knowledge. Knowledge is gold, and your brain is your own gold mine for extracting it. Doubts come out of incognizance and should be destroyed by the light of knowledge.

God neither hates nor loves anyone, though He may appear to do so. God has given us free will, and our fate is decided by our own actions and our own thoughts, according to our knowledge that we acquire about our own self. Logicians who have God realization through knowledge perceive God as an entity without any feelings or consciousness, as a power source just like the electricity we use in our daily lives.

True knowledge is covered by incognizance, just as the sun is covered by clouds. Thought is the best medium for realizing true knowledge. The subtle truths are indeed difficult to express in words because words tend to limit the magnitude of the truths. For example, $E=MC^2$ may be just a few letters for common folks, but to students of science these few letters speak volumes. It will be correct to conclude that the human mind can never conceive the ultimate truths of the universe. As Einstein once said, "We are like a little child entering a huge library." Only by transcending human existence can one understand the supreme reality. The ultimate truths are beyond mind and beyond duality perception.

Today, all great religions of the world are a mixture of contradictory ideas and thoughts. St. Augustine said, "True religion always existed and became Christianity after the appearance of Jesus Christ." The same truth can be found out by anyone who is in relentless pursuit of it.

Why don't the world's preachers, popes, imams, clerics, priests, vicars, and bishops preach that God will respond to whatever name, form, or shape one worships? More important, why don't they preach that all religions and faiths are personal, started by humans; that all scriptures are similar in all essential aspects of doctrine; that you don't need a middle person for salvation? No religion should claim a monopoly on God or the path to salvation. Instead, the teachings of the world's religious leaders are biased, politically motivated, and driven by power and greed.

I can guarantee you that terrorism will fade away over a period of time if we teach children at home and in school that all religions are the same in their essential teachings and differ only in nonessential aspects and that no single religion is superior to another religion or has a monopoly on God or one's personal salvation. We don't need a middle person for salvation; all religions lead to mighty God, just as all the rivers join the mighty ocean.

After all, who knows, and who can say, from where it all came and how creation takes place? Almost all scriptures in the world are part and parcel of history and tradition. Metaphor is part and parcel of all religious scriptures. The poet within the saint has taken off and written things in almost all the religious scriptures in the world. Therefore, religious scriptures should be scanned to get proper meanings rather than considered as true in every written word. We will make grave errors if we try to analyze the literal meaning of the scriptures. The essential message of a scripture is lost in interpretations that are strictly based on observable facts. There is a poet in every saint, and all writings can consist of truth as well as figments of the saint's imagination. This is true for all the religions in the world.

At the same time, an atheist or an agnostic has no right to insult the beliefs of billions of devotees (theists) around the globe. Another fact of the matter is that agnosticism is the starting point of a relentless pursuit after truth. Just as a pinch of salt goes to find out the depth of the mighty ocean and then becomes part and parcel of the ocean, an agnostic will finally realize eternal truths if he or she persists in the search of truth. However, the agnostic won't be able to explain the truth to the world because that truth is beyond description or comparison.

You can see with one eye, but you lack depth perception; you need both eyes to perceive a three-dimensional picture. In the same way, you need secular knowledge for human progress and spiritual knowledge to bring fulfillment and meaning to life. These two are like your two eyes. If I ask you to choose only one eye, which one would it be? Spiritual knowledge and secular knowledge of science are two eyes, and arguing that one is more valid, important, and real than the other is like blind men describing the mighty elephant.

God is beyond any comparison to anything known to mankind. God is indeed a timeless and formless entity. God is beyond existence, has no attributes, and is beyond all definitions. No word or image can express or describe the magnitude of God. To try to do so would be like saying that if you can analyze one drop of sea water, then you know everything about the entire sea, or that if you know the properties of electricity within the light bulb, then you know all about the electricity in the entire network.

We don't have to run away from our earthly belongings and duties to achieve God-realization. We can possess things without being possessed by them. Change of consciousness is more important than change of outward appearance or change of lifestyle. The seeking of happiness in material objects will continue until we find happiness and peace within ourselves with self-knowledge, which is the true knowledge. Every person has the right to the pursuit of happiness. Unwritten laws of nature provide the opportunity for self-growth, and you can accomplish that self-knowledge. Can you measure, test, or predict happiness? The meaning of happiness varies from person to person. Happiness is fortune, pleasure, joy, contentment, acceleration, delight, bliss, fulfillment, gratification, enrichment, and much more.

Now, you tell me! Is God (the absolute truth, which is timeless, formless, unborn, imperishable, indescribable, and shapeless) understandable, testable, and predictable? On one side, we are all just an amalgamation of chemicals, no more than an array of DNA molecules. On the other side, we are conscious entities. We are all part and parcel of nature. Neither science nor religion has all the answers for the riddles of the universe. The lack of proper answers should make us humble people. As of today, we know for sure that we know very little about ourselves and about the universe. We also know that anyone who seeks the absolute truth will ultimately realize God!

• Chapter 12 •
The Creation of the Universe

Nearly all religions have had creation stories to explain the origin of life. These stories often have a mystical explanation of how the world and living things came into existence. There are religious explanations like the Book of Genesis in the Bible, and there are the modern scientific theories like the theory of chemical evolution, Darwinism, creationism, and the theory of natural selection.

Creation has neither a beginning nor an end—it is a continuous process. Energy can neither be created nor destroyed. Creation is just manifestation. The microcosmic picture of the infinite is the universe. Creation is beyond human capabilities to fathom, nobody has a precise answer, and there's no perfect answer in any scripture. Likewise, there's no perfect answer to the question of why is this world imperfect and problematic? Why is the Creator evolving the great web of illusion from its own essence? This is the twenty-first century and still science has only theories about the beginning of the universe. Science still cannot define death or explain the process of aging. Modern science has only touched the tip of the great icebergs of knowledge. Stars and planets are said to have evolved from huge clouds of gases. Single forms of life lived three and half billion years ago from which all species evolved (speciation). There are thousands of species now extinct. Today more than two million species inhabit the earth. There are several theories like speciation, gradualism, and natural selection (survival of the fittest). There is much evidence and many scientific facts about evolution, like mutation, genetic drift, fossil records, geographic distribution of species, embryology, vestigial organs, and direct observation of evolution and artificial selection, which have been largely rejected by many religious beliefs. The opposing view of creationism by religious leaders is that the earth is only few thousand years old, and God created human beings in six days in His image.

The universe is space, matter, and energy. The universe is infinite, and we may never find a signboard saying, "Stop, the universe ends here." Theoretically, the universe began with a huge explosion—as a "Big Bang" of radiation fifteen to twenty billion years ago, which later changed to matter. There are 4,000 species of mammals, and more than 3 million species of life exist now. Human beings' existence goes back 4 million years with gradual civilization from developing and using tools, hunting, making fire, to farming and building cities. The earth has more than 3,000 minerals, including precious gemstones like diamonds, rubies, emeralds, and sapphires. Laws of the universe are so precise that we have no difficulty building a spaceship to fly to the moon, and we can time the flight with the precision of a fraction of a second.

If the force between nucleons were only a few percent stronger, the universe would be devoid of hydrogen, the stars, including the sun and water could not exist, and then life would be impossible. There are other factors whose values must be fixed precisely for the universe to exist. Minute subatomic particles, galaxies, and all known natural phenomena appear to follow certain basic laws. There is logic and order in everything that is taking place in the universe. These laws have unreasonable simplicity and elegance. Even minute variations in the values of some of Newton's universal law of gravitation, or in the electric charge on the proton, would drastically alter the appearance of the universe.

It makes sense to think logically that:

1) The universe is governed by unwritten laws.
2) There is an intelligent Lawmaker who formulated and established these laws, such as "Energy can neither be created nor destroyed."
3) In the anticipation of life and conditions favorable to its sustenance, the laws governing the operation of the universe

appear to have been "made." (Actually there is no such thing as "invention." We cannot find out something which is not actually there in nature, and hence we really only "discover.")

The geological time chart outlines the development of the earth and of life on the earth. For example, it is estimated that bacteria started four and a half billion years ago. Modern human beings developed from a primitive form of human being more than one million years ago. The first human beings lived about 2,600,000 BC, Homo sapiens appeared about 300,000 BC, and modern human beings appeared about 90,000 BC. The invention of writing occurred about 3,000 BC in China and southeastern Iraq, which used to be Babylonia. Hence, the recorded study of world history began around 3,000 BC. The universe consists of everything known to exist: all matter, as well as light and other forms of energy and radiation. The earth and the sun and the rest of the solar system form just a tiny part of the universe; the stars, huge glowing balls of gas, are the basic units of universe. The sun itself is a star and it is one of more than a hundred billion stars in the galaxy called the Milky Way. The Milky Way, in turn, is just one of countless other galaxies that exist in the universe. Even though various theories have tried to explain the universe, the one most scientists accept is called the Big Bang Theory. According to this theory, the universe began ten to twenty billion years ago with a huge explosion.

We are so used to being inundated with scientific knowledge that for many of us everything has to be *proved*. That is the only way we will believe something new. But I want to start another discussion regarding the universe. Let us say we take the whole world, its objects, human beings, or whatever—animate or inanimate—and we give names to them and we describe their forms or their shapes, and we describe the qualities of each object or that being. The human beings gave all of these names. And if you want to think that something was created, or that something existed before the creation, logically that something should not have a name, or a form, or a quality because human beings gave those things to animate and inanimate objects. The nameless, formless and quality less existence or entity is what we call God in religion, or truth in philosophy.

When I say, "Who created the Big Bang?" there has to be something in reference to the "Big." Logically, can we say that the universe was created from nothing? If I ask you how the letter Z was created, we keep on going back and back and finally we say, well, the beginning of the alphabet is A. Then if I ask you how the A was created, you keep on going thousands of centuries back, even before Christ, there has to be something. So if we keep on tracing back, that is where we eventually get stuck. Even for language or anything that is has to be from the Creator Itself.

Therefore, the Supreme has to be omniscient, all powerful, all knowledgeable, and all mighty. I don't think anybody would disagree with this, even if you take the ten percent of human beings who don't believe in God and if you discuss with them logically, they are stuck with the point that when we talk about the creation, the universe, even for the Big Bang, where did the "Big" come from? So there has to be some kind of almighty supreme control to have everything happen or function orderly. Otherwise, there would be disasters every second in the universe, like collisions between asteroids or stars, and planets flying out of orbit.

The creation could not have come from anywhere outside, because there is nothing outside the Lord Itself. As I explained before, if He is almighty, omniscient, and He is pervasive everywhere and the universe itself is part of Him, then there is nothing outside of the Lord. Let us say we don't believe in God or the Supreme or the Creator. Even if you want to argue that everything came from outside, then the question becomes, who created that outside? Again we are stuck until we acknowledge that it has to be from the Lord within Himself and He is in existence everywhere.

When we talk about the creation of the universe, and the Big Bang Theory, it boils down to the formation of the basic five elements. Then the question always comes, "Who created those five basic elements from which was created everything else?" For scientists, it is a given fact and truth that matter can neither be created nor destroyed. Even if you split an atom, still you cannot make it invisible. On this the whole scientific world agrees. You cannot separate the material cause and the efficient cause because they are inseparable. You cannot make a creation without material, and for that material, you need a creator.

The creation of chains or ornaments from gold has two causes: one the material cause, which is the gold and two the efficient cause, which is the goldsmith who made it. Similarly, any creation involves a material cause, as well as an efficient cause. So, with creation, the material cause is the universe and the human beings, living and nonliving material. And the efficient cause has to be the Creator, or God. He is the only one who has the skill and the capability to create this universe. Because, just like the goldsmith or the pot maker having the skill, the creator of anything has to have the knowledge of what it creates and also the power and the skill to create it. If you look at the entirety of the universe, there has to be a Supreme Being to have the power, the knowledge, and the skill to create such a phenomenon—to create the radiation or the tremendous power to have that Big Bang occur? Otherwise, who has the power and ability to keep everything orderly—the solar system, the galaxies, the Milky Way? If we ask the scientists, the generally accepted theory is the "Inflationary Big Bang." But this does not explain how energy in *any* form could have come into being to cause this monumental explosion leading to the formation of the universe. Therefore to come to a meaningful conclusion, what is left but the rationale that there has to be a Supreme, the Creator?

In other words, how did *that* which exploded to form all the galaxies in the universe come into being? Who created *it?* How far back can you go until there was *absolute nothingness?* But how could there ever have been nothingness since nothing comes from nothing? Do you see the dilemma? At some point you have to look past the implausible explanation of "random happenstance" and realize that some Supreme Intelligence was at work.

You may ask, "If God is all powerful, why didn't He create everything on earth in an instant? Why did it take Him several million years?" But I ask you, "How do you know it wasn't an instant?" Time, as they say, is relative (to each individual). An instant for you may be a second. But an instant for God may be a million or a billion years. Think of it this way: how long does it take to build a house? Let's say a particular type of house is generally built in one year. One person may look at that span of time and say, "I can't believe it took a whole year to build that house. I could have done it in six months!" However, another person with a different perspective might say, "I can't believe it took only one year to build that house. I couldn't have done it in less than two years!" Another way to look at it is when you're having fun, an hour seems to pass too quickly, but when you're bored, an hour can seem like forever. In both cases, the hour is the same sixty minutes. The point is that time is a matter of perception. Thus, perhaps what human beings call a "million years," God calls a "second."

Physicists are in a better position to give us a *partly satisfying* explanation of the world, although they won't be able to explain why the laws of nature are what they are and not something completely different. Scientists explain the physical forces of the universe acting under impersonal laws. They have proposed a natural scenario of the universe with pure vacuum (nothing) and universe tunneled by means of random quantum fluctuations to a false vacuum bubble (no matter, no radiation). This bubble had energy stored like a strung bow, and as the bubble expanded, it transformed into radiation and matter. Then there is formation of hydrogen, deuterium, and helium, and fine-tuning of the carbon atom evolving into life forms. Of course, oxygen and water followed this.

The probability of the right atoms and molecules falling into place to form just one simple protein molecule is 1 in 10^{113}, and mathematicians dismiss as having never taken place anything that has a probability of occurring of less than 1 in 10^{50}. Just for one cell to maintain activity, we need two thousand different protein molecules, and the chance that all of them will occur at random is 1 in 10^{40000}. The subatomic particles in vast galaxies follow law and order in everything that takes place in the universe. Even if there were a minute variation in that law and order, stars like the sun, or even water, couldn't exist and life would be impossible. If the universe is governed by laws, then there must be an intelligent Lawmaker who formulated or established the laws and the sustenance of them (outstanding intelligent design). The design and purpose are not mere blind coincidence. The more we know the world around us, the more evidence we have for the existence of an intelligent Creator. I remind you that some scientists dismiss this concept with the mere speculation that the events of creation are just coincidences, like a person winning a lottery.

Even a common man can realize that everything is quite orderly and everything in creation is useful creation. Even if you feel that something has no use for you, it may well be useful for somebody else; so there is no such thing as waste. Your eyes are a useful creation because with them you can see the beautiful world and its colors and forms. Your ears are a beautiful creation, allowing you to hear beautiful sounds or music. Your taste buds on your tongue are a beautiful creation because you can savor so many varieties of food. The nose is a beautiful creation. You can smell various pleasurable aromas. So everything is a beautiful creation, and the Lord is the Creator who has that power and skill. You can see that, even for a scientist or a genius, it's impossible to create an organ and make it function properly. For example, if you lost your leg or a hand in an accident, they can fit you with an artificial limb, but you won't have those fine motor skills of your real hand or leg. You can see how complicated and complex machines such as computers are, but to design an artificial finger that moves skillfully is humanly impossible. But God created us with such a skill that, unless damaged, every organ functions with an uncanny precision. Sometimes we tend to forget this—or take it for granted.

You know for sure that man cannot claim the authorship of this creation. Even if a man says he can make bricks or cement, he did not create the material used. He did not create the fire that makes the bricks. The law of nature that "fire shall be hot" was not created by man. Your house is standing still and not flying away. The gravity that causes this was not created by man. So, if you take a few moments to think about these things, and you realize the beautiful creations, then you can appreciate, "Oh my God, what did humans create then?" Nothing that we know of. Everything was created by the Supreme, so man cannot boast of these creations. Human beings come and go. Anything that has creation, that was born, has to die—material and immaterial objects—everything has to go into the five basic elements we discussed before. If you understand this, then you realize that the Creator must have the knowledge of what He is creating, just like the creator of chains, (the goldsmith) knows about gold and ornaments. To create this vast universe, the Creator must be very powerful and skillful, and He must have tremendous knowledge of everything. He must be omniscient. He must be *all knowledge.*

Few of us, on a daily basis, stop to admire God's creation, how wonderful and beautiful it is, and rarely do we stop for a moment to thank God for His creations. After awhile, that thought does not even come into our minds. We are so busy and caught up with our daily lives, with trying to live longer and better, that we don't have time to appreciate the Supreme for this wonderful creation of our complex human body.

If I ask you why a fire burns and what is the motive behind the burning, the answer is because it is the nature of fire to burn, and it is part of the cause and effect chain. It's the same way if we want to say God, or Truth, projects the world, because it is Its nature to do so. It is the nature of the Creator (truth) to project the world as the fulfilled (infinite), and It can have no craving (desire) to create out of incompleteness. That is why logically, we are infinite, we are blissful, we are existence, and we are awareness, and we are being.

If God is both the material and the maker, then you can always ask the question, "Where is God now?" Just as we discussed before with the cloth and the cotton, can you separate the cotton from the cloth? You can't. However, the weaver who is the efficient cause is different from the cloth, but cotton is not different from the cloth. That is why, when we buy textiles (the cloth) we don't bring the weaver along with us. On the other hand, where the effect is, there the material cause must be, which is the cotton. That is why however forgetful you are, it is not possible for you to leave the cotton behind and bring the cloth along, just as you cannot forget the clay when you bring home the pot. Or when you bring an ornament, you are not leaving the gold behind. Where the creation is, the material cause is. That is why the Lord is both the material and the efficient cause.

I gave you previously an example of your dream world that I am going to use now to help explain the creation. If you ask yourself who is creating your dream world, you can always simply say it's your brain and your sense organs, your four stages of sleep, and the REM (rapid eye movement) sleep. In your dream world, if you see mountains and palaces, beautiful trees or lakes, whatever, even if your mind is creating them, *you* are the creator of that dream world, and you are the material of it. Even if you say your own memories are the material cause for the dream creation, the memories came from within you to create that dream. The material cause is you, and the efficient cause is yourself. You are both the efficient, as well as the material, cause for your dream world. In a similar way, the Lord is the efficient and also the material cause of all of creation.

Therefore, the universe (the world) is apparent cause, and it is the material; the Creator and the efficient cause is the Lord. So now you can see that God is not up in "heaven," and He cannot be outside the creation, and He cannot be inside the creation, He is *the* creation. If you say He is inside, how can He be inside the creation and do the creation? If we say he is outside, this does not make sense because the space itself is creation. Therefore, God *is* creation.

God Himself manifests as the world, and He created the world out of Himself, and so God, therefore, permeates the entire creation, and he governs it as well with his laws of nature being changeless. As I said in the beginning, it may take some preparation of your mind to understand this and you may have to read this book more than once.

All human beings have a topic of common interest when it comes to the state of affairs in today's world. When we look at the world, we see the disparity among the people, the rich and the poor, the violence, suffering, injustice, cruelty, natural disasters, and exploitation of innocent people. We wonder why God is showing this kind of disparity when He is supposed to be just, kind, and loving. We wonder how can He watch all of this sorrow in the world and why doesn't He do something about it. Since He created this universe, certainly He could do something about it. Why did God create all these miseries? Why didn't God only create a wonderful, beautiful world, with happiness only? Even geniuses like Einstein had the comment, "I wish to know the mind of God." Marconi, who invented the radio, said to his friend, "I know how it works but I don't know why it works." This disparity is fodder for people who are atheists or nonbelievers in God. They often ask the question, "How can a God who is supposed to be kind and loving of all creatures allow such misery and unhappiness in this world?"

There is so much suffering and misery in the world, and if God created only happiness, we have to conclude or realize that the suffering is our own making, and God did not create suffering. God's creation is vast, beautiful, joyous, giving, and it works according to His laws, which are the laws of nature. *We* create our own little worlds of likes, dislikes, tensions, worries, jealousy, competition, pollution, noise, and wars. We create our own traffic jams and smog-laden concrete jungles. God did not create those. Specifically, He gave us "free choice," which we used to create these problems on our own. We cannot blame the Creator for our choices. This being the case, we should discover our own purpose of life on the earth and try to fulfill it. Once it was said, "Find a purpose, the means will follow." If you have the curiosity to learn about yourself, the understanding will come automatically. And then you'll understand the cause and effect chain where the material cause, which is the creation, and the efficient or intelligent cause, which is the Creator, are both part and parcel of the Creator.

As I mentioned before, matter can neither be created nor destroyed. Nothing is invented. It is already there. In a similar way, knowledge is already here, and we are shedding our ignorance or incognizance little by little. However, even though the Supreme Lord is the original Father and original Teacher of our knowledge, we still must appreciate and salute the great teachers who have tried to understand before us a great deal about the universe and creation, and who devoted and dedicated their lives for the betterment of mankind. With self-knowledge you will realize that the world is a "furnished house" that is meant to be enjoyed by all. Its kitchen serves food to every creature, whether it is a bee or a bird or a human being, and all beings are equipped for survival. Human beings come with nostrils to draw oxygen from the air; a fish has gills to draw its oxygen. Everything is well designed, including the human machine, which is capable of lasting a hundred years. In an objective creation, a thing is available for perception by all observers. It exists. Therefore, you and I and others can see it. However, its author only perceives the subjective creation. For example, when you are dreaming, you see mountains; you see beautiful scenery or other objects in the dream, which nobody else can see. And that mountain you see in your dream is not an objective creation. You are seeing it only in your mind. Therefore, it exists only in your dream. We discussed a pot created by a potter, and the potter knows what a pot is and how to make it, and he knows what to use as a material and how to shape it, and what tools he needs. In other words, a potter is the one who has the knowledge and skill to make the pot. A bird has the knowledge and skill to make a nest. A bee has the knowledge to make a honeycomb. If you look at the whole of creation, it is like a great magic trick, with an unseen magician creating the illusions.

So what is available for public knowledge and handling? That which is present for everybody's perception is the creations of the Lord. We all perceive this world and this universe as objective creation. You can project your private opinions and values and see a different world, which is your private subjective creation. Both what is projected by your mind and what the Lord projects are from awareness alone. Clay does not undergo any change to become a pot. Water does not undergo any change to become waveform. Without undergoing any intrinsic change, things can be born. Clay is real, the pot is apparent. The pot exists when clay exists, but when the pot is gone, the clay still remains. Similarly, awareness is also that in which the creation exists, but which itself is free from the entire creation.

The world we see, even though it appears to be real for us, is like a person who is dreaming, and he is the dreamer in the dream. As we see the world, it is constantly changing; it cannot be real, and if we are experiencing it, it cannot be totally unreal either. Then the dilemma comes, what is it, real or unreal? However, the fact is that it is the nature of the truth, of God, and we have to understand that the world is only relatively real—therefore, it has an appearance. You can never experience your absence, so the "self alone" is absolutely real.

We are part of the world, or the universe, and the universe is part of God, and all that there is in the totality (universe) exists also in the individual.

• *Chapter 13* •
The Triangle of You-Universe-Creator

One day, my twin daughters came to me with a question for their theology project. Their teacher told them to ask five people who they are and who created the world. When they asked this question, I told them, "I am awareness, which is the universe, which is part of the Creator." They looked at me with strange expressions on their faces! I told them that when I finished writing this book, they could read it and then talk to me to see if they have the same impression they have today. The reason I mentioned this to them is that the spiritual quest always goes on, depending on one's level of interest, intelligence, and desire.

As you know, various people have desires for many different things. One likes to eat gourmet food, one likes sports, one likes to watch movies, and another has the desire to read. In a similar way, some people have spiritual quests. If you read about the ancient mystics, they also discovered that they were not separate from God, the Creator and creation, and that all is in one. They discovered that there is no separation, and if you think of yourself as separate from others and the world, then you go from death to death; otherwise, you can end the cycle of death or experience no death, only continued existence. The reason for this is that if you separate everything from yourself, then you are experiencing everything as a different entity and separate from you. Thus, you create a "heaven," which is another transitory illusion, because in the ever-changing world of duality, everything must transform into its opposite.

There is always an opposite to that which exists. For example, if you have pleasure, there is also pain. If there is pain, there is also pleasure. And if there is life, there is death, and if there is death, there is life, so it goes on and on and on. On the other hand, if you look at everything all in one, without separateness, without duality, then you have accomplished liberation. You have to realize that the world of duality changes constantly; the only thing that does not change is the reality, which is the truth itself, (the Hindus call it "Brahman"). The rest is called unreal which is "maya," which means illusion, and is caused by the perception of this great oneness as a myriad of separate things. The belief in the liberation from this illusion is called "nirvana," which basically means "enlightened state of oneness with God." Nirvana is just like a wave in the ocean. If the wave knows, or if the wave has the knowledge of the Lord, it knows that it cannot exclude itself from the ocean. The wave can only say, "I know I am one with the ocean."

In a similar way, with this knowledge, you can say that you are one with the universe, which is part of the creator, the Lord—just as the wave knows that it is the same as the *ocean,* which is also water. Without this knowledge, the wave thinks it is separate from the ocean, and automatically, it is limited. On the other hand, if the wave has the knowledge that it is composed of water, the same as the ocean, and they both are the same, that thinking process and knowledge can bring limitlessness, because the ocean is a limitless entity. Even though physically the wave is different from the ocean, they both have water in common, and water is the whole wave creation, and the ocean is the whole water, and the ocean creates millions of waves.

With proper "vision" that comes from self-knowledge, one is able to experience the presence of God, the Creator, everywhere and is also able to see the connecting link between the human being and the totality that is the Lord. You see, as an individual or "I," we are limiting ourselves with our egos. On the other hand, the Lord, who is free from ego, who is all knowledge, is limitless. You can see why God is limitless because, as human beings, "I, me, mine, myself" possesses the opposite qualities of God who is universal, limitless, pervasive, and omnipotent. However, in gaining self-knowledge and experiencing our self-awareness, we can realize that we are the same as God, limitless, in an *implied way.*

It may not be physically possible, but mentally, you can make the "I" full, contented, and happy, but for that, there must be a means of knowledge. You have to realize the truth behind this apparent world. I gave an example before of the gold and different kinds of chains. You do realize that, underneath all these different forms of chains, the main element is the gold, and if there is no gold, there is no chain. The gold can exist without a chain, but the chain cannot exist without the gold. The chain is the thing that is apparent, and as we gain self-knowledge, the world around us becomes apparent, and we can recognize apparent as apparent, and real as real. *That is the gift of self-knowledge.*

As we discussed before, from the five fundamental elements—space, air, fire, water, and earth—come the five senses. From the five senses, come the physical body, the gross world, and the five elements that account for the whole creation. The truth is that where there is life, there is this gross world, and when it is not there, the body becomes the same as any other inert object. That there is no difference between the different objects of the world and the cosmos is the knowledge and the truth. However, the Creator is behind the whole universe. Everything that is living and nonliving, inert and in motion, that is God. He is everywhere, including in the life of the individual. Thus, we have a relationship between the individual and the Total, that is, the Lord, who is the Creator Almighty. He created life, and man conducts his life as a limited being because of the limitations of the physical body and the sense organs. Living in our limited capacity, we cannot experience the limitlessness and, therefore, man has the individual notion that "I am limited."

With simple thinking and without acquiring self-knowledge, it becomes a very hard question for us as to how to give up the notion of separateness. However, with the means of self-knowledge, if we can identify ourselves with the universe, which is part of the Creator, we can acquire limitlessness and contentment as seekers of knowledge. The easy way to remember this whole concept of self is very simple: *always think of the ocean.* It is an entity, and a wave is an entity also. Waves come from the ocean and the ocean, as well as the waves, is made of nothing but water, so wave is water, ocean is water. As long as you can compare your relationship to God as akin to the relationship between a wave and the ocean, you are acquiring the self-knowledge that is a stepping-stone for the means of happiness, and you are closer to the Lord who has endowed you with infinite knowledge and other noble qualities.

By just acquiring pure awareness and realizing that there is no difference in the nature of awareness, and there is no difference between life, the individual, the Lord, or the level of consciousness, you are acquiring self-knowledge. And you are being liberated from all the daily opposites I already mentioned such as grief, sorrow, sadness, unhappiness, and discontentment. We can overcome all of these negative qualities on a daily basis. Even if we come face to face with them, still we do not have to attach them to ourselves and live in the past. We can acquire self-knowledge by daily practice, by shedding our incognizance just like the snake shedding away its old skin. That is liberation while you are living. What it means is that ignorance or incognizance is dispelled so that one is revealed in the vision of one's own essential nature, which is self-knowledge.

Another simple example is that if I pull a hair from your head and ask you whose hair is this, immediately your answer is "mine," or, by DNA analysis, forensic experts can tell that the hair belongs to you. Theoretically, let us say that if we give life to that single hair and ask that hair who *it* belongs to, the answer from that hair will be that it belongs to you. Just like that, the creator, or God, created this universe, which is only a small particle within Him. Hence, we belong to the universe, and automatically we belong to the Creator, and we are part of Him, just like a hair belongs to your body. When I say that the Creator (God) and you are not separate and that you are part of God, some people might continue to find this illogical and nonsensical.

Of course, there is a difference between the Lord and us in regard to our form. Having only two hands and two legs, we are definitely limited physically, and this question can be raised by someone: "How can you be God, or how can you be limitless?" He or she can conclude that it is all nonsense. But as I have already explained, both the Lord and you have the same existence, awareness, and limitlessness, even though Lord is whole, comprising all forms, in contrast to us. However, your form, created by the Lord, is included in His all-pervasive cosmic form.

In regard to the "self," the Lord and you enjoy a common existence, awareness, and limitlessness. Just like the wave and ocean have their being in the same water, you and God are one, limitless awareness. Just like water can see itself in regard to the ocean as a total, or in regard to the wave as an individual, the same, too, with us. In regard to the wave, it is limited, born a minute before and soon subject to death. However, even if the wave cannot appreciate itself as water, it can at least appreciate the fact that the ocean is that from which it is born, by which it is sustained, and into which it returns. Seeing its form included in the ocean, the wave surrenders itself back to the ocean. Even if you look at water, it always constantly flows, from a stream to a river, from a river to an ocean. Once it mixes in the ocean, it is part of the ocean, and then it is no longer called a river, stream, lake, tributary, or canal.

In the beginning, we look at our cosmic relationship as a triangle: the human being, the universe, and God. As you acquire self-knowledge and truth about yourself, this triangle slowly disappears, and you come to see everything as a single whole. Then you appreciate the knowledge of the self. Then everything comes naturally for you. You recognize the divine qualities we talked about, and your mind becomes simple, fresh, and appreciative of the universe and the Lord.

Self-knowledge throws light on what is as it is, and this knowledge throws light on the basic fact that there is no difference between the individual, the world, and God. Just as your eyes are the means of your vision for seeing a rose or an object, or your ears are the means of hearing sound, the words and sentences in this book are the means of self-knowledge. There is no other way but reading and discovering the truth about your self. The senses we have and which we trust the most can sometimes deceive us, which we know by the example of looking at a rope in the dark and thinking it is a snake.

You cannot hold on to old notions or prejudices and understand this knowledge. You must have both open mindedness and a "fresh" mind. Knowledge and doubt can't coexist within you. Nor can knowledge and vagueness. Where there is knowledge, there is no vagueness or doubt. When you put this knowledge to the test against all questioning and doubts, with systematic arguments raised by others, and if the logic stands, and you are able to answer all the questions, that is the true knowledge.

I will give you another example about the earth and yourself. The earth itself is a "guest house." You come into this world as a guest and enter this planetary guest house. You don't bring a truckload of supplies. You bring only the carry-on baggage, which is your physical body, and you know very well that you will be taken care of. Just for a moment, look up at the sky. What a beautiful ceiling you have for your guest house, with enchanting, ever-changing colors. And the guest house has provided beautiful scenery all around you so that your eyes can enjoy the colors.

Your ears can hear the symphonies and the songs of the birds. You can smell the scents of the jasmine and the rose. And there are things beyond your sense organs, which you can discover and enjoy with your intellect. Everything is provided for your comfort and enjoyment. You need only to make use of it. When your stay in this guest house is over, you leave it as it was when you arrived. You don't possess anything here, and you don't take anything with you when you go. This guest house of the world is meant for your enjoyment as long as you are here, and then you leave it to others. So you should make your stay a pleasant one and leave with pleasant memories. You should not forget the benevolent Host who has provided for your stay here in this beautiful guest house with beautiful flowers, and lakes, and scenery, and so many wonderful things to enjoy throughout your entire stay. If you try, you can see the Creator in every creation He has made, and you should be thankful for all this creation and for all He has made. You should appreciate Him in all your perceptions.

When natural disasters devastate human lives, it is natural to blame the Creator. But the Creator gave us free will to decide our actions and reactions. We, ourselves, make ourselves miserable or happy. Once you act on something, the ultimate results are according to the unwritten laws of nature. Our lives are neither accident nor chance, and God is not responsible for the inequality among us. God does not create negative activities for us. He does not induce people to act, nor does He create the fruits of actions. It is nature's laws that create the results of actions, and God does not assume anyone's sinful or pious actions.

The world is an illusion according to some scriptures and religious believers. It is always changing from what it is into something else without ceasing. This does not mean the world is not important; it means that what you see is not the real world. The true world is beyond description and beyond the concept of time. It does not mean you have to run away from the world. It means you should work in the world in order to reach the true knowledge. We witness duality in the world like right and wrong, good and bad, rich and poor, day and night, to name a few. The illusion (false knowledge) of our nature makes us forget our true nature. When you come across true knowledge, false knowledge disappears just as when you turn the light switch and the darkness disappears.

• Chapter 14 •
Where Did We Come From?
Where Do We Go?

If we ask the question of what happens to us (our spirit) after death, science cannot answer it because science deals with what we can see or measure. Science can only explore the phenomenal or physical world. It cannot explore the human spirit. That is the illogic of science, even though science is logic. So, if we cannot unequivocally explain life after death, then it remains a mystery. That is why many of the great mystical traditions of the world advise us to cultivate an acceptance of the unknown, or the unknowable. This allows openness to a deeper intuitive understanding of life and death, beyond our ideas and concepts.

Remember, matter can neither be created nor destroyed. By the same token, at the end of the day, everything must come to an end, each of us must go to sleep, and when we sleep, we dream and go to different worlds, which is another mystery. No matter how scholarly we are, or how ignorant we are, or what a scientific mind we have, one thing we all have to do is to face the mystery of death for ourselves. Even if we look at the great people in any branch of science or religion, everybody has to perish or die and leave the body. We do not know *for a fact* what happens to our souls. Not even the greatest people of our millennium.

But, if we try to acquire self-knowledge, perhaps this awareness will serve to remind us of the mystery of our present life here on earth. We want to live at least one more day than the day we are supposed to die.

We do so many things to beat the odds and constantly try to achieve a longer life. We are born, we live, and we die according to the laws of nature. These laws are always there. They cannot be changed and new ones cannot be made. However, they can be discovered and used to our advantage. An example of this is going to the moon. For thousands of years, man was unable to go to the moon, but eventually we acquired the scientific knowledge that allowed us to get there. However, this feat was always possible within the existing laws of nature. We did not create anything new. That is, we did not create any new laws of nature. We only became aware and used to our advantage the laws of jet propulsion that already existed. The same principle applies to our self-knowledge and happiness.

Once upon a time, you were so and so, born as so and so; you grew up and lived all your life. That is the analogy: Like the water in a river, the journey is our life, and joining the ocean is joining the Creator. Even then, you are not losing your self because, even though you may not appreciate the universe in one particular form, once you "join" the Creator, whether you will have another form or not, still you are a part of the creation and part of the universe. That is a truth you have to understand as part of self-knowledge. If necessary, review this again and again. When you understand, it becomes automatic, and you don't have to think or make an effort, for the knowledge is *yours.*

Whenever I ask anyone, "What is your ultimate desire—having no pain, no limitations, no sorrow, rather happiness forever?" The answer is always "Yes!" because that is what we are and that is already a part of our one's self. That is why we try to get rid of our sorrow, misery, sadness, frustration, and why we always welcome, invite, and look forward to happiness. That is why we take vacations, seek material gains, try to improve our positions, earn more money, try to invest wisely, or constantly have the desire to make even more money. It's through these material things that we find happiness, which is always a part of us, and we don't want it to be different. On the other hand, sadness, sorrow, and misery are not part of one's self, and that is why we want to get rid of them. It is as simple as that.

Every individual heart is seeking freedom from the limitations we have imposed on ourselves by our misunderstanding of the fact that we are already unlimited. If you understand and acquire self-knowledge, you fill up your heart, and you make yourself see that "I" and the Lord are not two different things, but one.

With self-knowledge you'll understand the real meaning of "ownership." We may claim "this is my body," and claim the ownership of it, but ownership is simply a notion. You do not own your body or anything outside of it either. We owe to hundreds of thousands of factors for any achievement. We simply live and enjoy the things that are provided for us. That is the glory of the Creator.

I can explain very simply why no one can claim to own anything, not even one's own body. First off, your mother can claim responsibility for your body because she brought you into this world. Your father is also partly responsible for your birth. Your spouse can claim you by marriage. Your children claim you as their parent. Your employer claims you as an employee. Your country claims you as a citizen. The vegetables, the wheat, the rice, the beef, the pork, and the chicken you eat have a claim because *they* provide the nourishment that keeps you alive, and the earth has a claim because everything is born of the earth, the five elements we talked about. Fire can register a claim for keeping you from freezing in winter. Water, air, and space have claims to your existence because they are always accommodating you, as are the organisms in your body. But still, we say, "This is *my* body." Do you see? When you look *globally* at the total reality and the truth of your existence, how silly it suddenly looks to claim ownership of anything when we realize that we owe thanks to hundreds and thousands of factors for any achievement or anything, including our bodies, that we claim to "own."

If you know the Lord, you know the whole world, because the Lord is the cause of all creation, and He is the material cause of the whole universe, and He pervades creation. Therefore, in knowing the Lord, everything as well is known. Remember the metaphor for this concept is that each and every wave is water. While a wave has no independent existence and depends entirely on the water, the water can be totally independent of the wave. Therefore, wherever water exists, we cannot say automatically that it is in the form of wave because, even though water is the material cause of the wave and it sustains the wave, it is not the wave. *In the same way, the Lord is not creation, even though the lord pervades the creation,* because of which, the creation comes into "being." That means the creation comes into "life or being," and because of the Lord, the creation is sustained, until such time as the creation will dissolve into the Lord, who is limitless existence, which is awareness. So there is no question of anything being apart from that.

In this life nothing belongs to us. We come into this world empty handed and we leave the planet empty handed. How many times in a day or even in a month or a year do we remember that truth? Most of the time we fight and try to blame other people and point fingers at others for our own greed or desires. Even though we know we come, and we also go some day, still we are caught up in the cycle of life and constantly try to overcome death by whatever means we can. Some people resort to trying special exercises and diets, taking lots of vitamins and antioxidants, investing in plastic surgery, dying their hair, using cosmetic makeup, and experimenting with a multitude of other youth-enhancing techniques and products. We do many of these things because the desire within us never goes away. We want to live forever, and we want to stay young forever—even though we all know the truth that we are born with this fragile physical body, and we leave this body one day because the body is perishable. When we have wrinkles, some of us go to a plastic surgeon to mask them in order to look younger. Even though chronologically we've reached a certain age, it doesn't come naturally to us to tell our exact age. We do not bring oxygen with us when we are born, and we do not bring food to last for sixty to eighty years; these things are all provided by the Creator. Even the oxygen we breathe to stay alive is provided, not by us, but by plants. They take in the carbon dioxide we excrete as a waste product and turn it into breathable oxygen. Of course, this is how we mutually help each other according to nature's design. We have come to this fully furnished guest house, and we cannot claim the authorship of anything found in the creation. We are not the authors of the creation, we cannot be the owner, and we cannot be the creator.

The Lord is the Creator. He is the author, and He is owner of this entire creation. The laws of nature are responsible for the materials with which we build or construct, and they are all drawn from the creation. The brick is not your creation; it is made possible by the Lord, who provided the clay. So, what exactly is your creation? You are just rearranging things around you that are already created. One can say that he owns something, or we boast to ourselves that we created many inventions. Man was able to go to the moon, thanks to the knowledge that came with research and discovery. We have been able to achieve many amazing things with our intellect, which was also provided to us by the Creator. With that intellect we explore, discover and make use of this world. This is true of any achievement of any age, or era, or millennium, whatever. The wind that blows and the sun that shines belong to the Creator. There is no special power that belongs to anyone here. All things belong to the Creator, who is the Supreme.

Let's say that you think you have lost your keys and search everywhere for them, but then you realize that they were in your coat pocket all the time. Now tell me, how difficult is it for you to reach into that pocket? There is practically no effort required to reach into your pocket and grab the keys. Likewise, to recognize yourself as limitless does not require a great effort; it is not a big thing or a big deal. You don't have to discard your social life, or family life, or your profession. You don't have to shave your head and put on orange clothes, or grow a beard, or sit in one corner in a temple or a church, devoid of desires and continually doing meditation to know yourself. The point I am making here is that your *limitlessness*, like the keys you didn't know were already in your pocket, is just waiting for you to discover or acknowledge it.

There was a gentleman I was riding with one day to a meeting. I was telling him about this book, and he got very curious. He asked me a question, "Dr. Pasupuleti, when I die, what happens to my soul, or one's self?" When I explained to him as I have to you about one's self as part of the universe, which is part of the Lord, his eyes seemed to light up as if he had won the lottery. Similarly, with many people I talk to, once I start the discussion and explain to them a little bit, immediately their eyes brighten and they feel as though they are closer to knowing true happiness. Hopefully, once I invoke this thought process in you, then you, too, will have a realization, and you'll understand that there is a truth that cannot be shaken by anybody, nor can it be improved on by anyone. The knowledge always exists, and we are the ones who have to shed our incognizance or ignorance. Once you have done so, you'll understand that God is limitless. And you'll refuse to accept that you are anything less than limitless, because that would be against the experience of life, against logic, and against the law of nature. Once you understand this truth, you will be free from limitation, and you will be content.

Like the examples I gave before, no matter where the water is, when it is flowing, even if you construct a dam, it always tries to rise and go beyond all obstacles until it reaches the ocean. We always see that the rivers are joining the ocean. This is because the water doesn't reconcile that there is a dam and it doesn't have to flow any further. Water keeps on exerting its pressure on the dam, raises its level and does whatever necessary to flow further, continuing the journey to the ocean. That is why we see water flowing all the time, because it has the "vision" of the ocean. That is why the flow does not stop. But once the mighty river, even though it is water, flows into the ocean, automatically it loses its name and becomes part of the ocean. As flowing rivers themselves disappear into the ocean, losing their special names and distinct forms, in a similar way, I answered the gentleman who asked me what happens to his soul after his physical body disappears. This probably explains it the best. Like a river merging with the mighty ocean, once we give up this physical form, we become one with the mighty Lord.

When I am talking about self-knowledge, if you come forward and ask me, "Where is the proof? Show me the proof for the things you are talking about," I will have no problem saying that I cannot prove them. It is up to each individual to arrive at his or her understanding that the soul never dies, that one's self never dies. Neither I, nor *anyone*, can prove that the soul survives after death. We would be attempting to support it with intellectual logic, for there is no physical logic to prove it. The logic we would be attempting would be illogical because all we have to back this postulate up is "awareness," and awareness is either there or it is not. Logically however, it does make a lot of sense when we say that the one thing common for every person is awareness, which is limitless and infinite. When I say that we must have something in order to be conscious, and the "something" that makes us conscious is not just the presence of awareness, it is that "something" which manifests awareness. That "something" is what is called a subtle body. I mentioned this before to you, when I was discussing the self, the soul, the subtle body, and the gross physical body, but everybody has the question, "When the physical body dies, can the soul realize or be aware of the universe?"

This is very complex question, and I will do my best to make it simpler. I will give you an example: Let us say there is a tree that dies. Anything that dies must have the subtle body inside its anatomy, which makes the thing alive. So, this gross body has a subtle body within itself. As long as that subtle body is there, or as long as the physical body is capable of retaining that subtle body within itself, the body is "alive." On the other hand, if for some reason, the subtle body leaves, the gross body cannot remain alive. The "subtle body" plus the consciousness is what is called the soul or the life. And that soul travels, continues to exist, until it discovers the fact that it is identical with awareness, which is the "truth." That is liberation. Therefore, for a person who attains self-knowledge, there is no "hangover soul." The soul does not hang around indefinitely after the death of the gross body. Rather, it blends itself into God as a crested wave blends itself into the ocean.

For different religions there are different concepts and perceptions regarding the soul and what happens after it leaves the gross physical body—whether it moves into another body or not. Nobody knows, nobody has come forward and said "This is absolutely without a doubt what happened to so and so after his physical body died." Of course, for centuries we have heard so many stories about reincarnation, especially in Asian countries like India. Lots of Westerners thoroughly studied those incidents, but the accounts of the persons who claim their previous births were so and so, never turn out to be solidly proven fact, and they never have more than sketchy details to back up their claims. To me, reincarnation always seemed like an enigma, which is an unanswered question. For me, after reading the scriptures and various religious books, my understanding is that after the physical body dies, the self is nothing. It becomes nothing but the symbol of the Lord because anything can become a symbol of the Lord since the Lord is omniscient, pervasive, and everywhere. For me, this makes more sense than the idea of my soul occupying another body after this physical body dies.

In Buddhism, the moment of death is a particularly powerful and spiritual opportunity to become enlightened. Buddhists believe that the soul at that particular, profound state of loss that we call death—at that very moment—the soul is face-to-face with God, and it is "spiritually mature." If that soul is *spiritually mature* and has used its human life to develop wisdom and compassion, it measures with the love light and dissolves into God like a drop of water into a mighty ocean. In the same way, the Hindus and swamis say that for an enlightened being there is no death because in reality, there is no birth, there is no one to die, but only ever was, and is God, the Supreme.

I will try to make sense out of this for you. Think about this for a while, and see if you can grasp the concept that nothing in this world really ends. Matter does not get destroyed, nor does energy. We have known for centuries that matter can neither be created nor destroyed. The only thing that happens is that one form may be converted into another form, but it does not disappear altogether. Remember the basic five elements I discussed. There is no logical basis of thinking that can conclude the conscious being comes to an end. You are the conscious being, you are the one possessing (wielding) this body-mind complex, you only have to realize that the conscious being does not die when the body, which comprises only matter, dies and disintegrates. Death only means that association of the life with a given physical body has come to an end. Knowledge of you as the limitless being is always there. You are just shedding your incognizance and becoming aware of yourself as *awareness*.

When you understand the Lord, the universe and the creation and when you worship the Lord with devotion, with the attitude of oneness and limitlessness, the individual is dissolved into the Lord. Not like a salt crystal in water, but like water into water. There is only one Lord, who expresses both the inside and outside of you. The individual is a notion. All is the pervasive almighty Lord. You dissolve into God as the wave dissolves into the ocean and, what goes is only your notion that you are different. It is dissolved in the ocean of knowledge. If you think that devotion to the Lord is better than devotion to self-knowledge, it is irrelevant. Actually the two are identical because the Lord makes no distinction between devotion to God versus complete self-knowledge.

Life and death are inseparable mirror twins. Life begins with birth and it ends with death. There is no birth that does not bring death along with it. Everything that begins must end. What is born must die. In every human being's life, the time will come when all of our sense organs slowly decline in their functions, like our vision, our hearing, and our muscle power or coordination, perhaps even our mental faculties. Everything is born out of the Creator, sustained by the Creator, and dissolves into the Creator. The oneness between the life and Creator is called knowledge of "awareness." The knowledge is based on understanding. Hence, there is no error, doubt, or vagueness in it, so you are free from confusion because all wrong notions are no more for you.

• Chapter 15 •

How Many Gods and How Many Heavens?

If God's wisdom is infinitely superior to what we are capable of as human beings, and if He created all of us, the whole universe, why would he choose one kind of people over the other such as the way some whites have felt superior to blacks? This does not stand up to logic. Only one percent of the whole body is pigmentation. The rest of the body is essentially the same for any human being. The same is true for any ethnic group that claims to have earned "God's preference." This does not show intelligence. Even the so-called higher authorities in some religions demonstrate the same narrow mindedness, claiming that *their* God is the only God and they are the only chosen or preferred ones. Because of this, they want you to convert to their religion, and they go to different countries, especially to poor people, trying to make them become converts. You have to understand the basic principle that it is not by numbers that one religion is superior. When I was talking to one physician about his religion, he began boasting how many millions of people they have and how their number is growing. Quantity does not make one religion superior to the others.

Who can disagree with the concept that there is some Superior Force maintaining and sustaining the universe? As a child, I always had unanswered questions like, "Why do we put our faith in the so-called Bhagavad-Gita (a well-known Hindu religious book, which is like the Bible to Christians or the Koran to the Muslims)?" and, "Why did certain things happen only in India—why do Hindus have Krishna and Rama happening in India only?" and, "Why does the Arabic world have Islam, and why does the Western world have Christianity?" Also, I wondered, "Why do Christians believe that Jesus is their Savior?" and, "Why do the people of Islamic faith feel that the Prophet Mohammed is their Savior and the Koran is their bible, and they have to visit Mecca during their lifetime?" and, "Why does Judaism worship their god, and Buddhists have the Dalai Llama in Tibet—they also believe in reincarnation, but why do they worship Buddha?"

These questions puzzled me even when I was a child, and I was not exposed to a tremendous amount of knowledge, nor did I have the resources children nowadays have through TV, the Internet, and other technological advances. In America, we can find out about almost anything just by punching the computer keypad. Practically every household has a computer with Internet access. Many libraries also have access, and children of today have more exposure and knowledge about the world than when I was growing up.

Recent statistics show that in the world the primary religious groups are Christianity (about thirty-three percent), Islam (about twenty-six percent), Hinduism (about thirteen percent), and Judaism, Buddhism, Taoism, Confucianism, and others (about eighteen percent), and those claiming they have no religion at all come to about ten percent. I've had a chance to talk to many different religious people who have studied their religion in depth. I've had lunches with them, spent two to three hours talking with them, as well as with some of my religious patients when I am doing procedures. I've found it interesting that almost everyone thinks their religion is the greatest religion, and their God is the only God. I also got this impression while talking to some renowned religious leaders. They too do not consider any other religion or people to be on an equal basis. Instead, they feel that they are somewhat better in the eyes of God. It always makes me wonder why that is their blind belief, and if there is any logic to it. In some cases, when I tried to suggest that, to God, all religions are exactly equal, they would get very upset or angry, almost to the point of quarreling with me. I have a world of tolerance for other religions, and even in my own religion I look into the scriptures logically rather than blindly saying that you just have to have faith.

Let us say that Roman Catholic, Christian, Muslim, and Jew all feel that their God is superior, their God is the only God, and they may even think, "Why do Hindus have thousands of Gods?" In Hinduism, different Gods are given different names and different forms with more than two hands and powerful weapons. On the other hand, if you are open minded and think that God is universal, that God is for everybody, then you do not come to any dilemmas or confusions.

Here is an analogy: Let us say that three people who are about to die each believe with all their heart that God favors their religion over all others. One, an American gentleman who's involved in an auto accident is praying fervently for God to save him. At the same time, in a remote country, another man is hanging from a cliff and calling out vociferously for God's help. Also, in South Africa, an African lady, who is going into premature labor, is begging God for help. For discussion's sake, where should God go to offer help? To the lady in South Africa? The gentleman in America? Or the person in the remote country? After all, each person very strongly believes that God would automatically choose him or her over another person of any other faith.

On the other hand, let's say each person believes there is one God who can exist in many different forms and that it is irrelevant how you worship Him. These people have no problem because they know that God can be present in many ways, forms, or methods. They realize there is absolutely no competition for God's favor. So each form can help each person who is praying at that moment, no matter how many are praying at that moment. Therefore, simultaneously the paramedics can arrive in time at the scene of the accident. A hiker can throw the cliffhanger a rope, and a midwife can show up to deliver the baby.

And one more analogy: Three men of three different religions are riding in the same car when it is broadsided by a semi-trailer. Each is slowly dying, and each begins praying to God. However, each one, upon hearing the other two praying, feels he is more deserving, and each begins praying even harder, asking God to "Ignore the other two and save *me* instead." Which prayer should God answer? Perhaps, you may be thinking, it would serve them right for God to ignore all three. Actually, if God were to answer all three of their prayers, all three would die. Suddenly, however, one man has an epiphany and says, "God, don't worry about me. Please save the other two." And the other two, upon hearing this, also have a change of heart, and they both ask God to save the other two. Now what happens when God answers *each* of their prayers?

See how simple? The reason I related the analogy is to demonstrate that no one religion needs to be considered superior to another—and to hopefully make it clear to everyone that the Supreme is only One and is available to everyone, regardless of belief system. To put this in another way, suppose you set up a thousand mirrors on your lawn. The sun will shine and reflect in all those thousand mirrors, but it is only one sun. However, for the thousand objects that capture the image, it looks like a thousand suns. This is just an example, and you can take any number of mirrors or any number of analogies and apply them to the universe and our human lives. There is only one God and He "reflects" whatever way you look at him through whatever means or object. This applies to all religions, whether it is Islam, Judaism, Hinduism, Buddhism, Shinto, Taoism, Christianity, Confucianism, tribal religions like Animism, Spiritism, and Shamanism, or whatever. *All* are reflections of the same *one* God.

God is in all religions, as He is in all things, and no one religion has a special claim to Him that others do not. A religion or a group having a special claim to God is as illogical as a religion or group having a special claim to the sun, which others do not. The sun is for all, as God is for all.

Please understand. I am not trying to contradict any religion. All I am saying is that it is important to use our thinking faculty and not blindly follow. For everything we cannot explain, we should not simply say, "It is a miracle," either. My goal is to help enlighten the thinking process and help bring "awareness" into people's minds.

I find it interesting that when I talk to various people in different cultures and religions, some have a curiosity about Hindus. They want to know why Hindus pray to so many gods, and why they have so many stone statues, but they don't stop to think that there are many branches of Christianity. Some people I know in my own town who belong to one branch of Christianity don't want to associate with certain other persons who belong to another branch. This always makes me wonder why. If you accept Jesus as the Son of God and believe in His message of "Love thy neighbor," why would you have those disparities, especially with other Christians?

Another example is if you look at beautiful scenery such as in Hawaii, with magnificent trees, flowers, birds, and water. As you sit and watch the sun set, it looks so magnificent and you wonder at the beauty of the experience. But the same sun shines and sets everywhere, even in a slum, but that type of place, to just about everyone, doesn't look as beautiful. It is not the sun's fault; it is your mind's perception that views the beauty, serenity, happiness, or sorrow.

In any religion, the supreme state is that God made everybody equal and did not create sorrow or sadness. It is you who feels that. For example, if you won a lottery and got up in the morning, everything would look beautiful and wondrous to you. On the other hand, if you lost your job or had a calamity, everything would look gloomy and sad—the beautiful surroundings, the people, everything—but it is your mind that perceives this. The external world, or so-called outside objects, always remain the same.

There are famous scholars who say, "It is all in our mind." The mind itself can make a heaven of hell, or a hell of heaven. In the modern era where most of us are materialists, we like to believe what we see, but we know that our senses have limitations. For example, some people cannot see either near or far, which is why they wear glasses. And we use powerful telescopes, which are the only means by which scientists and astrologers can describe the Milky Way and other galaxies. Some materialists believe that a heavenly life after death is just a wish-fulfilling fantasy. Many mystical traditions would agree that paradise is a sort of dream state, which probably prompted the saying, "Rest in peace." There are ancient beliefs that when we go to sleep every night, we die a little and visit different worlds beyond our world. That is why the ancient Greeks have the god of death and also the god of sleep, Hypnos. You can see how beliefs differ among us in reference to heaven.

In one of the Hindu books, one thing that really strikes me as interesting is the saying, "The spirit of man has two dwelling places, both this world and the other world. The borderland between them is the third, the land of dreams." But the bottom line is, if heaven is "all in the mind," is it real? That question always comes up. However, if you look at all these great mystical traditions of the world, and if you read the descriptions of the heavens and even if you go in a deeper sense into Hinduism and Buddhism, they answer that it is real to those who experience it. This world is real to us, and when you go to sleep, you are in a dream world, but the reality is that you have to wake up from it, but some people believe that the existence of ourselves is a dream, and ultimately a dream from which we must be awakened.

One famous theosophist said, "This is part of the model dream of life, dreaming that he lives, a man dreams that he dies." The more you read the mystical traditions, one thing becomes very clear, that all these traditions believe in a Supreme Reality, and some call this God. It is like the light of a film projector on a screen of our own conscious awareness. If you perceive that you are living in a film, you can turn and see the light of the truth that lies beyond both earth and heaven.

When we start asking religious pundits the fundamental question: "What was before this? For example, who was before Christ? Who was before the prophet Mohammed?" They stop you there and say, "This is it. He is the God, or He is the Savior, or he is the Son of God." Nobody can answer logically because you have to have belief. But, an intelligent mind is used to having proof for everything, not that we expect God to be shown to us, but when we ask them about different religions and why is their God the only God, and what about the other people on the planet, they have no solid answers. They say, "You just have to believe. God said this or that and here are the miracles we have written in the scriptures. That's the proof."

An intelligent mind with a quest cannot stop there. That is where the "problem" comes. When there is a problem, you look for a solution. Am I not right in saying that? If anybody abruptly answers with a statement like, "You believe it or not. This is it," in my mind, with whatever intelligence I have, that is not enough. You cannot just say, "Don't question God," or, "Don't question this or that." My immediate reaction is, "Why not? Why can't I question?" Why should you "just believe it" because some so-called authority figure says it is so? For me that's not an acceptable reason. When I ask certain religious leaders or scholars, "What about the other religions?" often their answer is, "Well, it is their belief. Unfortunately they don't believe in our God," as though they are showing pity for them. Even well read, highly educated and sophisticated scholars have shown narrow mindedness when it comes to religion. Whenever you think, "My religion is the greatest. My God is the greatest," it actually shows that your religion is not the greatest, because that is biased belief. If you constantly feel the need to try to rub it in on other people, your religion isn't serving you well. We have six billion plus people on the planet today, so how can you say "My God is it, and everyone else is damned to perdition if they are not worshipping my God"? That is utterly egotistical. That is not going to give you the salvation you seek, that is not going to give us the answer, and that is not going to put an end to the big problem in this world of ongoing religious quarrelling and warring.

On the other hand, if you believe that there is only one God but we all have different faiths, and we all worship Him in different forms and shapes, then there is a chance for an end to the fighting between Palestinians and Israelis. There would have been world peace a long time ago, and Hitler would not have victimized innocent Jewish people, and the New York Twin Towers would not have been destroyed by the religious fanatics like the Al-Quaeda and Taliban terrorist groups. This feeling of religious superiority is all because of somebody's madness or distorted thinking and limited mentality. For that, sometimes the world suffers, not only those people who blindly believe God favors them, but those who commit crimes in the name of their religion.

I am not trying to be a world peace leader; I am just sharing my free-floating thoughts with all my fellow human beings. I also strongly believe that one person can make a difference. We have so many examples like Albert Einstein, Mahatma Gandhi, Martin Luther King, Rosa Parks, and Mother Theresa. They all believed in humanity and human well-being. Some of them also sacrificed their lives for their belief and were assassinated by zealots. With that same belief, I do my best to help advance mankind, even though I am a single person without any strong ties to religion, class, groups, or racial organizations. Still, I express my voice and make my statements and views very clear. I have made a difference in the professional and social lives of other human beings in my community. That is the reason I am showing this much enthusiasm, and why I am sharing this with all of you toward the achievement of self-knowledge and happiness. We all face situations in our lives socially and professionally where there will be one person who rallies people just like Hitler did, or some other leaders did in history. This person has political motivation in mind to climb the ladder at the expense of others. He first starts with one or two good deeds, begins accumulating followers, and gets more and more power hungry. If anyone tries to make him aware and open his eyes, he crushes them using his political power, which I often see professionally (and, granted, on a smaller scale) at my work place.

I do not believe in maintaining separatism because you belong to a group or a race. We all have to stick together. I have been strongly against separatism since I was a child. I had friends who did not belong to my religion, and I invited them to my house and shared food and drink with them, even though our parents and grandparents objected out of their narrow mindedness and prejudice toward other religions, other races, or classes. I never stopped doing this since I was a child. I am doing the same thing here now at my work place, and in my local community, even though I face so many hurdles and much antagonism from people who are afraid that their power might slowly be diluted. They come vindictively, strongly against me, but still I do not lose my confidence, my resolve, and I don't stop doing what I feel is best for all humanity. I mention this to you because sometimes we all face these situations and we get frustrated, depressed, and feel like giving up.

My point here is that you should not give up and you should not make yourself miserable or unhappy because of the negative situations surrounding you. If you realize that you are content and you are like anybody else, you can face these situations more easily with a strong mind, and without falling apart.

I have read many books on Christianity, Judaism, Buddhism, and Islam, and I try to understand the basic messages of those religions. After reading this book, I am sure that many of the religious leaders will claim that what I said was nothing new, and everything is in their book, or their prophet said everything in their holy scriptures. I am not going to try to contradict or deny any religion because that is not the purpose of this book. Whatever examples I give or methodology I have used to bring awareness to everybody's minds, it is all found in a variety of religions, and that is the basic concept that I am emphasizing here. Even if they were to come on TV shows, or in newspapers, or on radio talk shows and claim that I stole their ideas or modified them, I will not disagree with them. As I have said, I've done my best all these years to study many different religions, and I've tried to understand the basic meaning of every religion and to put their concepts into a book in a way that the common man can understand them and make good use of them. A Hindu can say that everything I said here is in the Bhagavad-Gita, or a Muslim can say it was in their Koran, or a Christian can say everything I said was in their Bible. The basic qualities of human beings are the same. The only thing that differs is the way we practice, or the way we think from religion to religion, culture to culture, or country to country.

Whatever religion you observe or follow, you still have to have discriminative and analytical thinking to make yourself aware of what is real, and what is apparent. It's just as if you put a candle in a container in which you have made several holes, when the candle is lit, the light comes through all the holes and spreads across the room at different angles. If you put a big chandelier in the middle of a hall, it also spreads the light. Essentially, there is no difference in light coming from a grand chandelier or from a single candle in a container with holes. Light is light, regardless of the source. And that is how we have to look at knowledge. Knowledge is knowledge, regardless of the source. We can improve our knowledge by keeping our minds open for all the various discussions, comments, and analytical statements. With an open mind you can absorb more and enlighten your self more.

• *Chapter 16* •

Heaven vs. Hell

If you sit down and think of all the various religions and read a little bit about every one and what they preach, like Mohammed, a prophet for Muslims, Jesus for Christians, and many gods, as you know, for the Hindus of India. The religions are all similar, showing that if you behave and if you do good things in life, you will reach heaven. A lot of people have claimed that when they had a near-death experience, they "crossed over." However, if we ask "Did anybody actually see Heaven"? and the answer is no. When we ask, "If you did go to heaven and return, please describe how heaven is, and who is living in heaven, and where does God reside, and what does He look like," they cannot give a definitive answer. Now, if somebody goes to France and comes back and describes that country to you, if you have any doubt, you can visit that place, check it out with your own eyes and see for yourself if what they said was accurate. It's not the same way with heaven or hell. Everybody believes in those places but there is no validation of them except for a few selective stories we hear now and then, here and there, from people with near-death experiences, which are, once again very biased and often based on the beliefs of their particular religion. So we really don't have an answer for that. But in every religion, depending on the intellectualization and imagination of those reporting, we have many descriptions of God and heaven.

If we think logically, putting our religious beliefs, faiths, and superstitions aside, and ask ourselves, "Where would we place heaven in this vast infinite universe?" we get a variety of answers. When I discuss this with my patients, religious people, and even my colleagues, automatically they look up, as though heaven is upward in the sky. When I ask them whether they see the stars, the moon, and the sun, they immediately acknowledge the solar system, the galaxies, and the infinite universe. Then I take their thinking process further and ask them whether they believe in different heavens for different religions, like one heaven for Christians, one for Hindus, one for Muslims, one for Jews, and so forth. Immediately they look at me with a frowning and puzzled face, realizing what I am trying to say.

If you think about it, when you look up, "up" is the direction of the planets, stars, and galaxies, and when you look down, "down" is the center of the earth, which has proved to be super-hot molten liquid and gases. So if heaven is not up, since *up* is occupied by the other planets and galaxies, and *down* is occupied by gases and molten rock, where can heaven and hell be? Consider this: heaven is everywhere and in everything, just as God is everywhere and in everything. Perhaps it exists as another dimension. Thus, to your immediate right or your immediate left is heaven, but you cannot see it or feel it or know it is there because it exists in an alternate, undetectable, immeasurable universe that is here and not here at the same time. Perhaps heaven is in the space between the molecules that make up the things we *can* see and touch. And what about the hell? Perhaps it is merely a concept with no substance whatsoever. The same as existentialism is a concept. Or transcendentalism is a concept. In other words, what if we look at hell as merely a philosophy, or a way of thinking, intent on using fear as a motivational tool for inducing good behavior?

The universe, like God, is infinite, and if we think globally and logically with an open, unbiased mind, it doesn't take a scientist's brain to understand that we can't place heaven or hell at some specific place in the universe. However, using logic can sometimes create doubts and uneasiness within us. A part of us doesn't want to look like a fool for believing and following the myths of our own religion that have been accepted for centuries, and we can't swallow the bitter pill that perhaps our religion is *not* the greatest one on the planet earth. It gives us more comfort and happiness to believe that our religion is the only religion that takes us to heaven. Each week when we go to our church, temple, mosque, or synagogue and listen to the preachers or priests or rabbis praising our God, it reinforces and assures us that ours is the true religion and ours is the real God and true savior. Just as we look in the mirror and admire our face and beauty, we do not want someone telling us we are not who we think we are.

It is difficult for us to admit that the other religions are no different (that is, no better, no worse) than the one we follow. It is hard for us to admit that there is no heaven or hell because we all firmly want to believe in going to heaven after we die. It gives us great pleasure to believe in heaven, and to keep social order and justice; we need to believe there is a hell as the ultimate end result for immoral behavior.

In many religions, we are taught that with our improper conduct and behavior, God will punish us by sending us to hell, whatever that may be. As you know, not everybody has an interest in learning about the creation of the universe, or *who* is God, and *where* is heaven. They simply go to their church, temple, synagogue, or mosque and pray to God for a good life and forgiveness for their sins. They all want to go to heaven after they die. Not everybody probes into the subject matter of where is heaven and what happens after death. But philosophers, thinkers, and curious minded people do probe into these questions, and there are many, many books written on religion, theology, psychology, and philosophy that deal with topics like God, heaven and hell, life after death, reincarnation, meditation, body-mind-soul, how to see God, how to feel God, how to attain God consciousness, and on and on.

We all have questioned at one time or another that if there is a heaven, where is it and how does it look, and will everybody be admitted there, or only a chosen few? Where is this paradise and how do we get there? Will it last for all eternity or is it a stopping off place between successions of human lives? If we believe in the reincarnation theory of Hinduism, this question will come up too. Then, there are the attachments we have to our loved ones. Are we going to see them in heaven when we die? Will they welcome us? What will they look like—the same as when they died, or will they be or younger versions of themselves? And will we recognize them? Everybody has had all these unanswered questions at one time or another. Or, with some people, we can call it a fantasy. If you look at the whole of history, even before Christ, all persons from various cultures have asked these types of questions, be it the scholars, pundits, or the common people. And they've all tried to solve these questions, explaining them to us in different ways, sometimes with myths and superstitions. But because we are in the modern twenty-first century, we should probably try to explore these questions in a logical way. Because with logic we can better hope to obtain the truth, and truth is awareness, which is real.

Once again, remember that I am trying to illustrate these concepts in a simple manner, so that all people, regardless of their level of education, can understand them. That is the goal of this book. That is why I am not giving examples from each and every religion, every culture. A discussion of what each and every religion believes would be a huge book itself, and this would only serve to confuse different readers with different backgrounds. However, wherever there is a reason to quote or mention a religious belief or faith, I will do so to make a point I wish to illustrate or to make something easier to understand.

We are all certain of our birth and death. We all know that we are mortal and will die one day, but we are all uncertain about our ultimate fate. What is going to happen in the next minute, the next day, or how long we are going to live? This is very evident, especially in my practice of neurology when I go to the hospital to see patients.

It has happened that two persons were in a fatal auto accident at the same time, in the same car, with the same head-on impact, but I would have to declare one patient brain dead on arrival and the other one at a much later time. Sometimes there were even days and weeks difference between the two before I'd declare the second victim brain dead. When this happens I always wonder to myself, "Same age, same impact, and same time the accident happened. Why were they were not showing brain death at the same time?" This always reminds me that the timing of death is never certain. Nobody knows exactly when a person will die. All the time in my profession, I hear physicians saying, "You have three months to live," or "six months to live." With all the new studies we have on the different diseases, in my specialty, brain tumors, I always tell my patients that I am not God. I don't have a crystal ball and do not know the future, and I do not know when a person will die, but overall, I explain to them the outlook or what we call the "prognosis." I always make sure they are aware that there are unexplainable factors that defy science and medicine, and that especially with a positive attitude, one can prolong a life way past the prognosis or "predictive norm."

Because of our modern medicine and advanced technology, more and more people are brought back to life after having been pronounced clinically dead, or after a cardiac arrest. Often these people who "died" on the operating table claim they have visited the afterlife while temporarily dead. This is commonly known as a "near-death experience." These people claim that they found themselves outside of their own body and they saw in detail the doctors frantically trying to resuscitate them, and they could hear their relatives and friends off in other parts of the hospital. Then they described themselves moving down a dark tunnel toward a beautiful, loving place, and then they describe a deity, or Jesus, or an angel, depending on their personal expectations. The majority of them describe it like a light at the end of a tunnel. Some people even claim that they met their deceased family members or other loved ones. Some people claim that they came back to this body because it was not time for them to leave the earthly plane, and they had to return to their body to tell their tale to their living ones. However, this near-death experience is really nothing new. It has been described in ancient history.

For the moment, let us talk about heaven. As I mentioned earlier, depending on your culture, your sophistication, or your knowledge, you may envision heaven as a paradise. You may picture it as an idealized place where you have everything, luxury, pleasure, no responsibilities, and freedom from earthly desires.

In these visions of heaven, most of the time it is described or pictured as a fabulous kingdom with palaces and mansions. We fantasize that it is inhabited by the spirits of priests, nobles, and good people who deserved to get into heaven. Probably, if we extend our imaginations, we also visualize that all the valuable stones like diamonds, pearls, and jewels with ivory will be all over, and even the rivers there are probably perfumed, and everything that gives us pleasure is ideally there. In some cultures, depending on the visionary, the people who live in heaven are even given wings, and they don't walk on the floor, but transport themselves by floatation.

If we believe in heaven, there are also the questions of what if we are not good enough to get into heaven, and yet we are not bad enough to go to hell? Where do our souls rest or stay until the decision is made about which way we go?

Different cultures have believed in different places where heaven exists. Even in more modern times, some people describe heaven as being on earth with the entrance at various locations. If there is an approach, it is not approachable by mankind. Usually it is in some ancient and remote area. They believe that the unapproachable area is where there is a great river, which is the source of heaven. For example for Hindus, Mt. Everest is the place of Lord Shiva, and they describe it as Mt. Kailasa in Tibet. Even today, devoted people visit this place and climb over 3,000 feet high in search of heaven's gate.

The Hindus and Buddhists have a belief of reincarnation where, depending on your actions (karma), your future lives play out. Also you go back and forth from animal to human lives, depending on your actions, and ultimately reach heaven, "moksha," which is the eternity and ultimate liberation beyond the death and rebirth. It is also thought to be even beyond heaven.

Who are the inhabitants of heaven? This question then arises: Are they all male gender, female gender, or both genders? Again, this is also divided and different among different cultures or beliefs. For some, there are only males, and for others there are beautiful women in heaven and also the angels, who some believe to be messengers. Some of us believe that the angel messengers come to earth to do good deeds and help people in need, and by doing so they gain extra feathers on their wings, or they might stay for a longer period in heaven. If they did something bad, as a chance to redeem themselves, they come to earth to help people in need, and by doing that, doing a good deed, they can return to heaven for good.

Some religions, like Hinduism, believe that in heaven there are no relationships. Everybody is independent there, and each soul is different. All the bonds and relationships exist only on the earth. That is what they call, in their language, "bhandha" (bondage).

Then the question arises, Who gets there and how do we get into heaven? The majority of religions do believe that being noble, being pure, living a clean life (e.g., in Christianity, living a "Christian life"), without adultery, lying, stealing, cheating, and other vices, gets you a free pass into heaven. In some religions, it is even believed that if a warrior dies in battle, he goes straight to heaven. And it goes on and on, with many beliefs and many variations within each belief.

The Hindus see heaven only as a transit area for a long spiritual journey through many lives, the temporary resting place where a soul reaps the rewards of its good deeds. In their descriptions, the Hindu heaven has no conflict and all desires are easily fulfilled, but there is no opportunity for spiritual growth. That happens on earth. In their descriptions, they have many kinds of heavens, or as they call them, "lokas" (worlds). Heaven is one among them, and it is ruled by a king. They also describe a heaven of jeweled palaces, bright country with a lot of music, pots of gold, and here the dead enjoy untold pleasures, and they are served by beautiful maidens. The crystal water of the Ganges falls from the higher heavens, and they have pools containing blue, red, and white lotuses. Fragrances of those lotuses extend for thousands of miles.

Buddhists, like Hindus, also have many heavens, all of which are temporary resting places between earthly incarnations. Their description of heaven and their beliefs are similar to those of the Hindus because Hindus believe that Buddhism is a part of Hinduism, and that Buddha, born as a Hindu king, then with spiritual enlightenment, started teaching Buddhism and traveled toward Tibet. Hence, Tibetans believe in Buddhism and pray to Buddha as their God. In Buddha's teachings, enlightenment "is not heaven, but is the supreme spiritual goal." He also teaches that paradise is only a more pleasant form of "present," a transitory illusion that cannot last and leads only to another human rebirth.

The question then comes: Who created each of these heavens? If God created these heavens, then who created God? Depending on the imagination, we give God different shapes, forms, and decorations. Some of us even believe that the angels are not only seen as the spiritual powers of paradise, but that they surround us invisibly on earth to guide us toward our heavenly home.

Some patients of mine, if they almost died on the operating table, claim that their souls were watching the entire operation, seeing the medical staff talking and frantically trying to save their lives. I've always had a simple question in my mind since I was a child: "If there's a heaven, and if a husband and wife die at different times, and one or the other remarries, do they reunite there? Or their children, when they die, which pair of parents are they reunited with?" Christianity answers this dilemma by saying that in heaven there is no marriage. In a lot of traditions and religions, there is only love in heaven, so there is no place for jealousy or animosity, regardless of what happened on earth. Furthermore, the angels and all other inhabitants are asexual.

Once again, in most religions, to answer the question of who gets into heaven, it is almost always a reward for a good life, or a good deed, or living clean with great purity of mind. Of course, there is always some sort of judgment, which is often imagined, created, and fantasized, as well as expanded on, according to the sophistication and knowledge of the prophet, scholar, or writer, but it all boils down to pure thoughts, pure words, and pure deeds get you through the gates.

Some religions even have ancient books to teach the believers or followers a methodology on how to get to heaven step by step. We are all familiar with the so-called saints, monks, and the like, sacrificing their lives without any material enjoyments, or giving up their lives in search of purity and in search of God. Some of them pray to God every minute and live a very simple life, and in some religions strictly stay unmarried all their lives. In some cases, they eat very little and go to extremes where they even control their automatic senses, believing that by doing these tough disciplines, which almost seem humanly impossible, they will go to heaven by pleasing God with their abstinence.

Some even believe that when they die, they become stars in the Milky Way, and that the Milky Way will be the road to heaven and ultimately the soul will reach heaven through the path of the Milky Way after becoming a star.

There's a description of the Christian heaven attributed to Jesus saying, "in the land of Promise, magnificent things which may not be told or uttered, and the heaven includes a river of milk and honey, and colossal palm trees with clusters of dates and fruits in each cluster." St. John the Divine was permitted to see the door to heaven, and he describes God and His throne and six spirits, with each one having six wings, and many eyes, and hosts of angels. There was no sun, no day or night, and no need for candles. Instead, the light of God illuminated the heaven.

Muslims often portray the Islamic heaven as the Garden of Eden, a valley entered through an emerald gate. Their heaven glitters with many precious stones, and Allah reveals Himself in all His glory. The blessed are also invited to feast with Allah. They are surrounded by splashing streams and fountains that are never too hot or too cold. They drink from silver vessels and are attended by graceful boys and beautiful girls as lovely as coral and rubies.

For my mind, as a child, there was always the question, "Even if we go to heaven, how long are we going to stay there? What are our rewards and punishments if we do not behave while we're there? Or, if our time is up, will we be sent back to earth as humans or some other form of life?" These questions wandered in my mind constantly.

Some in the past and present, including well-known scholars, well-respected people in society, claim that they "mentally" can go to heaven. They claim to talk with the angels on a daily basis, and some people claim they can communicate with the dead through their psychic powers.

Some people describe heaven as fulfillment of material life where souls rely on their senses and God is love, and each soul has a different occupation to suit that soul. There are no idle people in that heaven, and there is always soothing music. As for how the soul is liberated, every religion has a different explanation.

In some old beliefs, in the ancient heavens, the descriptions were of places where there is no judgment, no fighting, only lovemaking, music, songs, games, sport races, and beautiful birds singing lullabies to the drowsy. Whatever a soul wished for, it would receive, yet magically the desires of the inhabitants never conflicted.

For people who believe in reincarnation, as in the Buddhist tradition, heaven is only a resting place on a longer journey of spiritual attainment, the goal of which is eternity and liberation without rebirth. They believe that those who have achieved spiritual perfection need not reincarnate again, unless they wish to return to help others.

The imagination of what heaven is like goes on and on. There is no need of work, and life is easy there, with no storms, no snow, and the winds blow very gently all day. The inhabitants lie in beds of flowers while nightingales rain flower petals on them, scent falls from the sky like dew, and the trees magically supply glasses of wine to supply a perpetual party.

Even for the American Indians, the famous quotation from Chief Seattle is, "There is no death, only a change of worlds." For Hindus, there are more than seven heavens, and also for some primal people, there are different heavens for different people like bachelors, married men, married women, spinsters, and so on. People go to different heavens depending on their roles in society. For example, a king dies and goes to a different kind of heaven than a common man.

In the modern heavens, the notions are a little bit different from the ancient ones. For example, the notions of the afterlife in the Bible are very vague and in the Jewish tradition. Some societies suggest that on death, souls are gathered in a "treasury beneath the throne of glory, awaiting physical resurrection." Some sects of Judaism, just like Hindus, have also developed the idea of an immortal soul that can exist without a body.

One thing for sure with any culture, most people wish to be with God in heaven after death. The famous composer Beethoven, who was deaf, wished that when he died, "I shall hear in heaven." Vaughn Williams, another composer said, "In the next world, I shall not be doing music with all the striving and disappointments, but I shall be *in* music." In other words, Beethoven expected to hear the music and Vaughn Williams hoped to "be" the music, just as many people wish to be with God in heaven after death. For some great saints, the ultimate spiritual goal is to "be God," or Godlike.

Having said these things about heaven, then what about hell? I will also come to that the same way with different cultures, and mystical beliefs. Actually, mythology is just another word for religion. We apply it mainly to ancient religions, although we can sometimes apply it to a few more modern ones also. Just as they have done for heaven, works of literature and different cultures have developed different ideas of hell, and for various reasons. Just as they have described heaven as a reward of good behavior and living a good life, they have also developed different ideas of hell to explain what happens to sinners after death. Also, the concept of hell has been used to motivate people to live a good life and to control people, usually politically, by frightening them with a threat of eternal damnation and torture, and sometimes the possibility of hell helps some people incorporate a sense of justice. If you read about hell in different cultures, it often boils down to one thing. Basically, in society, the concept of hell is an attempt to control different people with different powers so as to maintain some type of order. Just as we consider any pleasant thing that happens to us a reward for being good, in a similar way, we also try to apply chaos or natural disasters as warnings, creating a fear in human beings that we are being bad, and that God is trying to teach us something.

If you look at the ancient cultures from which the creation of myths evolved, and if you look at the way they lived, you learn that basically hunting was the main means of getting food. They created their deities usually in the form of animals that the tribe hunted, and they often depicted them as magical animals with horns. These horned animals played no part in the afterlife, but were there merely to provide a source of predictable food. Thus, these tribes created local deities and worshiped them for protection, placation, and to ensure a good supply of food. Unlike animals that are hunted, these animal deities could not be killed off in case they contained a power, so they had to be demoted. They were relegated to be the custodians of a dark other world.

If you look at prehistoric caves, you see these animal paintings on the walls during the Stone Age. Starting approximately 5000 BC, human beings gradually went from hunting to developing farming and finally to an agricultural civilization. In olden times, for cultivation you needed sun and water. Floods and hurricanes were a threat to farming and cultivation, so the people created "natural" gods in the form of Sun, Moon, and Water, and started worshiping them to guarantee abundance.

In the newer order, heaven was the life-giving sky, with the sun, moon, and stars, so it made sense that the opposite must be below the ground, and the old, horned gods of the stone-age people became the caretakers of the nether world of hell. In reading the traditions of the ancients, it is only logical that the location of the place of the dead was below ground in the "underworld" because that was where the dead were buried. You could say it made for a shorter trip. Also, if the soul was immortal, and lighter than air, it also made sense to believe that it rose upward to the sky and beyond the sun. Again, we realize that the more sophisticated and civilized the culture is, the more this concept of hell reflected that culture. The beliefs are also dependent mainly on the culture itself. For example, Native American people believed only in the concept of heaven and that all people, when they die, go to a better place where they will always have plenty of food and a comfortable living. On the other hand, China has different complex orders of eighteen levels of hell, reflecting the class system of China itself, and in the Roman/Greek era, the more complex the culture became, the more openings they had for sin and immorality.

Just as there are different views about gaining entry into heaven, there are going to be different concepts of consignment to hell, but one thing is clear for a person with a little bit of spiritual understanding: If you want your spirit to be enlightened, naturally every culture and tradition prescribes that good deeds or a good life leads to heaven, and depending on the definition, one who is guilty of the sins of bribery, stealing, lying, adultery, murder, and the like most likely will go to hell. Again, this probably is an attempt by society to create some sense of order, so just as they created a benevolent God for heaven, they created a vengeful Devil for hell. Different cultures have beautified God with different forms and decorations and ornaments. In a similar way, most cultures have also given different forms to the devil, more or less animal-looking with horns, and beastly-looking forms with ornaments such as bones of the dead. Heaven is given to beautiful, bright cities with beautiful stones, palaces, rivers, music, and beautiful angels, but for everything with duality, there is an opposite, so they created a hell with mean and vengeful devils, a place where everything causes displeasure, with boiling blood, fire and brimstone, displays of enmity, beatings, tearing one another to pieces, and various forms of eternal brutality. Exactly the opposite of the way the deserving souls enjoy the pleasures in heaven, the undeserving souls that go to hell are routinely tortured with all means of vile imagination a human being can muster.

Starting from the ancient ages, just as they have described

seven heavens, they also describe nine hells, with different levels of punishment and torture. Of course, each culture has its own set of laws or rules for people to live by, and breaking those rules or failing to live up to those certain standards of morality would be sufficient to cause someone to be sent to hell. The punishment there would be determined and allocated according to the severity of one's sins.

While the description of hell will vary slightly between religions that believe in such a place, the theory is pretty much the same. If you paint a gruesome enough picture, it is hoped that this will generate enough fear to convince the *majority* of the people to behave.

In conclusion, most descriptions of heaven make it seem like a nice and beautiful place to go. Yet even Jesus, whom Christians envision as the Son of God, is quoted as saying, "The Kingdom of Heaven is within you." What this means is that Jesus Himself was not convinced there is a special place "up there," but envisioned heaven as being "within you," that we create our heaven within ourselves. Famous poets in Arabic literature also wrote about heaven and hell, stating, "I myself am heaven and hell, paradise is where I am."

• Chapter 17 •

What Is Prayer?

Why do we worship the Lord? Is it for self-realization that God is everywhere? In fact, God is everything, but when you think of yourself as different from the Lord, your ego is kept under check. The reason you pray to the Lord is because worship brings purity to the mind, which is needed to understand that God is everywhere. "I am everything" is a self-realization. "Lord is everywhere" and "I am everything"—both of these concepts are one and the same. Self-knowledge is to know the fact that you are the self, who is everything, and that God is everything, and God is you.

That is the knowledge for which you require a pure mind, and for those who seek the Lord's grace through worship, prayer is an act of devotion. God is everything, and when you realize that, you will understand all the opposites as well. You love life's pleasures, but you should be willing to accept life's pains. When you understand the laws of nature, there is no wild elation for gain, and there is no deep depression for loss. It reflects in your life in the form of equanimity.

Daily worship of God is a means of good, to live a life of self-discipline and self-growth. Worship is important as long as it does not turn into fanaticism. Having a step-motherly attitude toward other religions is also unhealthy. Some people pray to the Lord and pray that they are able to surrender unto Him. *You cannot surrender unto Him unless you discover that God alone is everything, otherwise it is only "lip service."* The reason we pray to the Lord and surrender unto Him is that the act of praying has a power, and it makes us feel humble in the presence of the Lord.

What about prayer? Prayer itself is an action, and there is always a result. When you are praying you are submitting yourself to the Lord and asking Him for help. When you submit yourself totally to God through a prayer, naturally there will be a result to that action. It may not be immediate, but at some point in time you will see the result.

There can be different forms of prayers; Christians pray to Jesus differently than Muslims pray to Allah. However, whatever the form of prayer, prayer is still an action, and that action is always open to a choice. In other words, you can pray whatever way you want to. There's no right or wrong way to pray.

Even without a language, if you pray to God using visualization, He is able to understand. When I touch your little finger, even though it is a small part of the huge human body, I am still drawing your attention. In a similar way, if God is all pervasive, omniscient, in any form or any shape, with any name, or even without any language, still you can invoke Him with whatever methodology or means you choose. Likewise, if you close your eyes, and I touch the tip of your toe with a soft cotton probe, you know that I have touched you. The Lord is prevailing in the whole universe, and you can invoke Him any way you want to and get His attention.

We all worship God in different forms. We hear gospels, people chanting names for the Lord, and Muslims kneeling on the floor toward the direction of Mecca to pray to Allah. Whatever form you worship God, it becomes relevant if you understand the worship and its meaning. If you do not have the understanding, you may laugh or criticize, or you may be sarcastic toward a fellow religious person about the way he does his prayer to God. You can invoke the Lord in any methodology or form of worship you choose, and it does not matter to the Supreme. Those who make peculiar faces or sarcastic remarks about another culture or religion do so totally out of ignorance.

Language distinguishes human culture from all forms of lower animal culture. There are 3.000 languages spoken in the world today, not including dialects. You can sing the Lord's glory in any language; it is not the language that matters. What matters is your understanding of the Lord and your attitude toward the Lord.

Whether you are a Christian worshipping Jesus as the Son of God or the Savior, or if you are a Muslim and you are praying to Allah, or if you are Hindu and you are praying to Rama, it does not matter. All prayers go to only one God, that is the Supreme, the Creator, and in His vision and in His knowledge, you are not different from me, and I am not different from another person in Africa or Australia. Who you are does not matter. Anything in the creation is only a name, or a form, or a shape. When we go to a temple or a church or a mosque, we see tall buildings with tall steeples. Did you ever wonder why they are that tall? They are constantly in your sight as constant reminders that the Lord is present in all our thoughts and actions.

You see people on TV on the various worship channels. They shout their prayers and sing their songs very emphatically as they praise the glories of the Lord. Sometimes, if we don't have the knowledge, we assume that the screaming, singing very loud, or becoming emotional is an over-reaction. The fact is, when the mind is fully occupied by the Lord and His glories, you are becoming your "self," submissive to God, and your ego becomes smaller and smaller. As I said earlier, the whole creation is the Lord, and all glories belong to Him. Therefore, the more you praise the Lord, the more humble you become.

The agitations we show, the hurts, guilt, greed, jealousies are all a part of our egos. By submitting yourself to the Lord and praying, your ego comes under check, and it becomes smaller and smaller.

When people think their God is the only God and don't have the knowledge or understanding of other cultures that sing, pray, meditate, or chant, they have no tolerance for the other religions and automatically resort to criticizing that religion or the method of worshipping, or make fun of it. When we all understand and realize that God is one and He is everywhere, and that one can invoke Him in any form or by any method, then we understand that whatever that religious person is using to invoke God is acceptable. Without this knowledge and understanding, it is easy to become critical of other religions or other rituals.

I have seen many documentaries on TV with Western pundits going to remote places like Africa and commenting on the local beliefs or the people's way of praying to God. At the end of the commentary, the reporters often imply that these people are "backward" and don't realize that theirs is not really the proper way to worship God. To me, this attitude shows a lack of knowledge and a bias against other religions. You can invoke and acknowledge God in any form you want to. God is omniscient, omnipotent, as well as all creation. We can show our appreciation of the Lord by praying, chanting, meditating, singing loudly, or by just uttering. When I say that God is omniscient and omnipotent, that means that His knowledge and power have no limit. God's knowledge is beyond our concept. Therefore, any amount of praise is going to fall short of really describing the Lord. No one can ever flatter the Lord, nor can the Lord feel flattered, because one can feel flattered only when one is insecure or doubtful about oneself.

There is another thing I have observed back home in India that many people do not understand: There are some who take a vow of silence and stop talking forever. Others in their lifetimes may give up things also. Some may give up eating meat; some people give up smoking, alcohol, gambling, or other bad habits. But think about it—some monks actually give up talking! We may think it is some kind of gimmick, but in reality, it is one of the toughest things to do. We cannot stop talking. If somebody insults us or makes a comment or provokes us, immediately we get angry and we shoot our mouths off. Many of us talk a lot. When I compiled this book with taped dictation, I must have used eighteen to twenty tapes because I love to talk. When I give lectures, I always go beyond one hour, and I have to look at the clock before I realize it's time to stop. One of the reasons everybody says "talk is cheap" is because it is a luxury any human being can afford who can talk, because it does not cost anything. Plus, talking is a diversion. Any other type of hobby or diversion you have usually costs money. Some people have the hobby of collecting stamps or buying antiques. Even though it is a hobby, it is actually a diversion. Going out to eat is a diversion, and watching a movie is another diversion, but they all cost money.

However, talking is easy, and it does not require any money. All you require is someone else to listen to you. And it is also an escape. As I said earlier, much of the time we like to escape from ourselves. For example, if nobody is around for you to talk to, you may start singing. Perhaps you sing when you are taking a bath or shower. Even though you may not have the professional voice to be a singer, it is still a diversion and an escape, and you are trying to be happy. Whenever a thought comes that makes you sad, you may begin to hum or whistle just to shake off that thought, as a means of escape. In a similar way, talking can be an escape, and not always an enjoyment for us.

If you are wondering what I am getting at, it's that when you say something, you should mean it. When you offer thanks, you should mean it. When you wish someone, "good luck," you should mean it. Don't be mechanical. You should exercise restraint from uttering meaningless words. Twenty-four years ago, when I came to the United States, I noticed that the phrase "thank you" is very mechanical and automatic. Other mechanical phrases I have observed are "that's nice," and "I am happy for you," but when I would look into the speaker's face, his expression didn't really match his words. They were usually just randomly uttered words. I do have a problem that most of the time I try to speak the blunt truth. I do realize that sometimes speaking the truth can hurt the other person. I know it should be pleasant, but sometimes it comes out too fast, and too late, a moment later, I realize that I need to exercise delivering the truth in a nonhurtful way.

For example, if you saw someone who was disfigured, and everybody knows the person's condition, you don't need to tell that person he is disfigured. Even though it is the truth, you would be hurting that person, and you have no right to do that. Instead, when we try to say the truth, if we do it in a pleasant way, it makes it easy for you and also for the person who is hearing it. Most of the time, people who speak the whole truth are generally very hard. I am conscious about my speaking the truth all the time, and sometimes people see it as abrupt, rude, and abrasive. I have learned that in my practice. When I tell a patient and family members what I see on the MRI (brain scan), even though it is the truth that the patient has a tumor, I don't come right out and say, "You have a tumor, and you are going to die." That kind of news is a very bitter pill to swallow for the patient and the family. They would feel you are callous or rude, even though from your angle you think you are just giving them the facts. Over a period of years practicing, I realized that and I taught myself not to deliver bad news, albeit the truth, in an abrupt way. Now it is almost automatic for me to discuss those critical issues in a more sympathetic, gentler way, at the same time giving them the hard truth.

The reason I gave you this example is that I am not just writing this book to make suggestions to other fellows about how to behave, how to think, or how to be happy. By giving examples from my own experiences, I hope to provoke thought processes in your mind, to help you understand my reason and logic as you are digesting this book. For example, I also have observed that just being pleasant in and of itself is a beautiful thing because it is not always easy to find a pleasant person these days. It is a kind service to others that has its own reward in the kindness that is paid back to you.

Many people are selfish, and they have the attitude that they are always right and the other person is always wrong. That is why we have so many lawsuits. It is like a virus, not only in the Western world, but spreading to the other parts of the world as well. Instead of learning to do good deeds, everybody learns these hurtful kinds of things. It's like when people are trying to learn a new language, it seems just about everybody comes to learn the curse words first—that is just human nature. In a similar way, even if you are speaking the truth, you should make it pleasing and beneficial; try to have some honey in your words, even though it is a hard thing to do. I also realize that many of our problems arise because much of the time we are being very mechanical and are giving "lip service." I mentioned before that expressed feelings should always be from the bottom of our hearts when we say "thank you," "please," and "that's nice." That gets rid of confusion and it makes you free from conflict, which is nothing but simplicity. We should be humble and simple as much as we can, and we should keep our minds open. Being complex causes conflict; being simple frees us from conflict. When you are a complex person, as I said earlier, you have to remember everything you said before. When you are being manipulative, or are scheming, then you become a very complex person and it becomes difficult to deal with the situations of daily life—and difficult for others to feel they can believe you or trust you.

Devotion and knowledge are interlinked. Without devotion, knowledge is useless, and without knowledge, devotion is merely empty, idle worship. If you want to be the top basketball or baseball player, or the top singer, top actor, or top physician, you have to have devotion in that field, plus dedication and practice. Even if you desire to win a multimillion-dollar lottery, you don't just play one time and think you are going to win. You probably have to play thousands of times, and you may win only a few times and only small amounts. Even then, there is no guarantee that you are going to win millions of dollars. I have known people who have played the lottery all their lives, and spent hundreds of dollars per month for the lottery tickets, hoping that one day they will win that multimillion-dollar jackpot. Even though they don't realize it, there is devotion and dedication involved in playing the lottery.

The knowledge of the One to whom you pray should be free from any limitations. Even a prayer directed to a deity named in reference to a given phenomenon like the Sun or Water or Fire goes to God. A prayer to nature is a prayer to God.

As I've said, you play different roles in life. You are a father to your son, boss to an employer. You are a friend, relative, spouse, teacher, or pupil. However, your relationship with the Creator is different from these other relationships. When you are praying, *you are a devotee,* and that relationship remains same at all times with the Creator. It is an abiding relationship. It is a fundamental relationship born out of recognition. Prayer is not a technique; it is an action, and it results in "Grace." You can invoke the Lord with your prayer in any given name or form. You can express your devotion to the Lord in various forms. If everything in our lives is in order, prayer becomes redundant, and you need not pray. Rather, the way you live your life is like one ongoing, never-ending prayer. Your kind and caring actions are worship and the praise as they reflect the goodness of God.

In one type of prayer you are submitting yourself to the Almighty without any ego. By doing prayer, there is an acknowledgment of the Almighty. In submission there is acknowledgment, and this recognition itself reveals a degree of maturity. This prayer is the acknowledgment of one's helplessness. With prayer you discover hope and solution. The Creator is All Knowledge and All Power, so you look up to Him for help during a helpless state. You establish a contact with God through prayer. Prayer does something to your mind, because there is submission. In submission it is the Will that is submitted, and the Will is submitted willingly. In submission itself, there is Acceptance, that is, acceptance of the past. You go to the Source where help is available, invoking the Lord with your prayer.

We are constantly victims and hostages of fears, anger, self-criticism, intolerance, hatred, unhappiness, and depression. Our sorrows, agitation, and anger all lead to depression, and they all stem from not accepting or understanding our past. Hence, we blame a number of factors like people, political and economic systems, poverty, health, institutions, schools, colleges, society, relationships, the stars, or whatever. When you pray, you realize that no one is to blame, nor do you blame yourself. When you are the victim of your own past, you are apprehensive about your future. You become worried, cautious, and frightened. You see yourself as a victim of your past because you don't accept it. You cannot do anything to alter a fact once it is established as a part of your past. Therefore, resentment of the past is a huge waste of time and energy.

As a baby you had almost no will of your own. You were in the hands of your parents, and later your elders, teachers, and society. Your knowledge as a child was limited. You made conclusions about yourself and the world. Those conclusions formed the basis for your interpretations of the events to come. As an adult you cannot remove the conclusions you made as a child, and therefore you become a victim of your own past. Then you make valid reasons to blame others for your past, including society, which consists of many people, situations, and events—all these are to blame. In blaming there is resentment of a fact, there is rejection of a fact. But a fact is a fact. Your rejection doesn't alter fact. It only adds to your confusion. Whatever has happened is a fact. With prayer, you accept the past gracefully and blame no one.

With prayer, you free yourself from blaming yourself and blaming others. Instead, you acknowledge their contributions to your life. You cannot forget the past, but you can gracefully accept it, and prayer provides the will and strength to do so.

You do not change the self-criticizing mind. You accept that mind with the power of prayer. You accept the mind as it is. You are not afraid of this self-judging mind, this self-condemning mind, self-criticizing mind, and self-pitying mind. Prayer helps you to accept the mind as it is.

Acceptance of the past implies accepting the outcomes in the present and future. What type of acceptance? A simple one? Or one with reluctance and resistance? Your wish list has no end. You wish you were rich or handsome. You wish you had a home where there was better communication and more understanding. This wishing mind is one that resists acceptance. When somebody offers you a flower, you accept it with joy, with thankfulness and cheerfulness. This frame of mind is necessary for total acceptance. This type of mind resolves your likes and dislikes; you are totally objective, and you don't place blame on anyone. You accept what is. You accept the fire as it is—hot! You accept mountains, trees, sky, clouds, birds, and animals as they are. In the same way you accept your past and the people in your past with the same frame of mind that accepts things as they are when you look at the sky. "I accept it!" Is this just a sentence? A mere sentence doesn't imply acceptance. Acceptance implies a certain attitude on your part. The mere word "acceptance," without understanding the meaning and its implications doesn't help. You let the things be as they are. You accept the tree as it is and the sun, moon, sky, mountains, birds, a chemical, sugar—even poison—as it is. Acceptance doesn't imply that you have to use it. You don't blame the sky because it is or it is not cloudy on a particular day.

The reason we tend to hold on to our beliefs, even if they no longer serve us, is that we have invested our time and our hearts in nursing them. But you can change your attitude and work for the necessary understanding. Thus, you can bring better order to your personal life. With prayer you have that "will and effort." You cannot change the past, for it has already happened. But you can change your attitude and your understanding toward yourself and toward the world. Prayer grants you the wisdom to know the difference between what you can and cannot do, and between what you can and cannot change.

Obviously, prayer is one form of devotion, and so is meditation. Many of us are sincerely devoted to the practice of our religions. Some people have a passionate devotion to their careers. Others have a deep devotion to their hobbies. I can't help but imagine how incredible it would be if we were all as devoted to the pursuit of self-knowledge as we are to these other elements in or lives.

• Chapter 18 •
Why Do We Hang on to Religion?

I want to make it very clear to the reader that I am not trying to criticize any religion, any person, any ethnicity or culture. I simply want the reader to understand the basic concepts of the thinking process and how we can make ourselves happy with our own efforts. We do not have to rely on another person, our religion, or our culture to provide our happiness. There is nothing wrong with following a religion, and doing so can often give us comfort. Our ethnicity and culture help us to understand our heritage and what has contributed to make us the way we are. Religion can also bring families and communities together for common causes.

But for some people, numerous questions arise such as: Which religion is the true religion? Which religion should I believe? Which religion has the highest authority? Which religion stands on logic and offers clear explanations based on rational thinking when the ultimate tough questions arise? Which religion looks into discrepancies and does not just blindly say, "Don't ask and don't dare to know further—you just have to believe—this is as it was told in the scriptures and so this is it." That kind of response does not lead to advancement, and it does not challenge the mind to use analytical thinking to get answers. I cannot boast that I studied *every* religion extensively, but by studying many different religions to comprehend what they are trying to say, I did grasp one thing that stuck in my mind. Most religions have set rules, and you cannot ask any further. You are expected to just follow the dogma and believe that this is what God said. For me, this is hard to accept because of the fact that God Himself gave us a thinking faculty with discrimination, logic, and curiosity. The way I see it, the Supreme Authority gave it to us for the purpose of questioning authority.

In studying all of these religions and attempting to understand what they are trying to say, I came to realize one thing: If a religion is telling you to follow their rules without question, that is not progress, and that is not open mindedness; it is closing the door to progress. I am not saying that you should not follow your religion, but that if your bottom line is happiness, we can pursue that in many different ways, including by attempting to understand the self itself.

In other words, don't allow yourself to be "painted into a corner" by a religion, where you end up with no way to go. Don't let religious leaders box you in so you feel you have no other choice except *their* choice. For happiness, it's important to feel that the option of many choices is always available to you. You should never be confined to the belief, "No matter how painful, this is the only way!" Self-knowledge reveals to you that you are always "at cause" in your life. You are the cause of what happens to you—not the effect of set rules that govern how you must think, feel, or believe.

The bottom line is that universally, everybody knows what is right, what is wrong, what is good, and what is bad. Sometimes, depending on your interests, it may be difficult for you to follow a rigid rule, so you bend and twist it a little bit so it will serve your pursuit of happiness.

Self-knowledge is not like that because here there is no external gain. You are basically reaching an understanding about your self, the meaning of the self and the limitless nature of the self so that you can face daily situations in life in a better way. The knowledge does not amount to fanaticism. When I say that the eyes alone see colors, these are not the words of a fanatic. There is fanaticism only if I were to propagate a belief, which is subject to negation as the only truth, or hold onto one means as truth, even while there are many equally valid options available. So the point I am emphasizing is that you can follow any religion, you can have any belief or faith in any God you want to, as long as it is comforting to you and gives you security, happiness, or whatever you are looking for. On the other hand, if you argue with other religious people and tell them that your God is the greatest, He is the only God, and you are one of His only chosen people, it does not stand logic, and it is subject to negation, conflict, and argument. Or, if you try to convert other people to your faith, thinking that your faith is the only faith through which one can reach God, that is also fanaticism.

I remember one time when I was making rounds in the hospital and I used the word "fanaticism" while explaining something to describe a fellow doctor's attitude toward his religion. Even though he was a close friend of mine, he got so upset he would not talk to me for three or four months. Later on, he came to me and apologized. He realized I had only made a statement, which itself was subject to comments, criticism, and negation. If there is room for conversation or discussion, and if I am a wise person with self-knowledge, and if I have the understanding that everybody can see God in any form they want to, because He has no definitive form, because the entire universe is within Him and part of Him, I should not get upset or angry or become fanatic about it. Instead, I should be able to discuss people's opinions with them and test their logic.

This is an important thing we must all understand. When praying to, or when worshiping a form of God, keep in mind that the form is a just concept to give the mind something to focus on, since it is impossible to focus on *everything* in creation, which is what God, the Creator, truly is.

This is like situations that occur when I teach neurology during rounds, or when I'm giving a lecture. If a resident, medical student, intern, or attendant gets up and asks me a question that challenges what I have been telling them during the lecture, I do not get angry, upset, or mad. Instead I try to explain logically why the statement I made makes sense. If I am able to do that, then I am making progress, making the other person aware of the truth.

What I am trying to say is that because the Creator gave us the thinking faculty and reasoning capacity, we should look into everything with logic, common sense, and see what seems right, what seems wrong, or how it can be better. We should always keep our minds open to everything and every discussion, instead of resorting to narrow thinking like the example of the frog in a well. Open mindedness gives us a simple mind, a mind that does not lean to rigid opinions. Any subject matter or opinion has a grain of truth, but from a number of various aspects, it may not be entirely true, so we also have to be able to see other angles and other points of view. If you gain the capacity for your mind to be open and analytical, or to be broadminded, you will have more avenues to learning, instead of closing the door to all but one. Once you shut the doors of the mind, nothing new can enter, and you become limited like a frog in a well.

Most of us believe in God, but blind belief and faith in God does not resolve conflicts and fights between one nation and another, or one religious group and another. Every day, all over the world, we see some kind of war in the name of religion. You have one concept of God, and I have another concept of God, which may be entirely different. But this does not justify a fight between us. We do not require agreement about religion to stop fighting or to solve the problems of the modern world such as moral and ethical decay, but we are required to use our common sense. Religion does not solve modern problems; however, it can solve the human problem, but for that, you have to understand the religion properly.

We have to understand very clearly the relationship between the cause and the world, the cause and the person, and that should be the basis of religion. When you believe in religion with an open mind, it becomes a thing you follow happily. Otherwise, without an open mind, religion becomes an avenue for escape from the world and reality. There are many similarities among religions, and up to a point all religions are similar. All religions are more or less common in their ethics, or values, and they all emphasize prayer. Whether you pray to Jesus, Allah, or Krishna, it is all the same. It is not going to make any difference. Whatever the language you use to sing to or to praise God, whether in Latin, Hebrew, Italian, or Arabic, in effect it does not make any difference to the Lord.

A similar idea is love. Love does not require a particular language. Love is love for all humans, as well as for the lower animal species. The only problem I have observed with some religions is that they sometimes get caught up in their own concepts. Then they start talking about one's liberation and salvation through that belief only. That is the only thing that makes me somewhat skeptical, because if you really have the true knowledge about God, you do not develop egotistic ideas and try to force your concept on other people in the name of your religion. There is nothing wrong practicing your religion in your own way; nobody questions that.

Knowledge does not belong to any one religion. It belongs to all, the whole universe. If some say that the whole of knowledge is coming from only one source, they are not correct because knowledge does not belong to anybody. Knowledge is knowledge, and it is available for everybody. It is there, it has been there, and it has no beginning. But for a religion to claim that by sheer number, by being in a majority, that knowledge belongs to them and that they are thus in the right, is to show ignorance. And just like knowledge, ignorance is also universal. There is no such thing as American ignorance, German ignorance, or Italian ignorance. Ignorance is ignorance.

A true religion tolerates all forms of thoughts. God is an entity without wry feelings or class consciousness. God is formless, timeless, imperishable, an unborn and indescribable entity. At times of violence, feud, social and moral decay, and when immorality is prevalent, prophets appear throughout the world. They not only teach rules of conduct and morals, but also restore peace and order in the society. No prophet's teachings are all that different in any religion, and if you compare them, they all teach same message of kindness, forgiveness, and love toward fellow human beings. These eternal truths are universal to everyone and open to everyone who seeks them. Truths exist forever, and each prophet has just found them independently and given them to the world in his own language.

A final note is that religion is like man's best friend, and we all embrace our best friend in time of need.

• Chapter 19 •

Passing Blame vs. Taking Responsibility

My sharing of self-knowledge with you is to make you aware of yourself and what makes you happy. That is the quest in which we are always engaged. For example, if a short person is not happy with his height, he will look at a tall person thinking that a tall person is happier than he is. We are always comparing ourselves to other people, thinking that the other person has more than what we have, so the others must be happier. This is what actually is the root of most of our grief and sorrow, besides our losses of personal relationships and deaths.

In essence, all human beings feel inadequate. With that feeling of inadequacy, we sometimes cannot face a particular situation because of our lack of understanding of the facts. You may wonder why God has not given everybody the same wealth or happiness. If you look at it logically with self-knowledge, He actually did; He created everybody *equal*. He did not create sadness or unhappiness. As human beings, we create problems for ourselves because of greed for more luxuries, material satisfactions, and other desires.

What "created equal" means is that regardless of our circumstances in life, we all have the same opportunity to be happy. Happiness is not a privilege of the wealthy. If it were, the rate of depression and suicide among the wealthy would not be higher than those of people with average incomes, which it is. It is important to come to terms with the fact that true happiness has nothing to do with your possessions or your net worth. You can be a millionaire or you can be making minimum wage, and with self-knowledge, you can be just as happy in either situation. This is how we are all created equal. We all have an equal opportunity to be happy once we recognize true and lasting happiness comes not from anything outside of ourselves, but only from within.

For example, let's take a look at the sun. Without the sun we cannot live. It gives us light, and life prospers, continues with sunshine. If we don't have sunshine for months, we get gloomy and depressed, which was proved by Japanese studies in the 1980s. Thus, sunlight has an effect on our moods, but just because of that, you cannot blame the sunlight. The sun does not choose whether or not to shine. The sun just is. Another example is the sun's ultraviolet rays. If you are a fair-skinned person, you cannot sit in the sun a long time to get a suntan. Eventually you'll develop skin cancer, which is a known fact now. But because of that, you cannot blame the sun and say, "The sun is bad, and it is not fair." Again, the sun just does what it does, which is shine. The sun does not decide who is harmed and who is spared. *We* make those decisions either consciously or unconsciously when we either heed or ignore the warnings—or the truth.

The more I practice medicine, the more I read medical journals, and with the thousands of patients I see, the more I learn about diseases. In the field of neurology, I've come to realize that I always need to know more. Endless research goes on and on, and that is why we call it *re*-search—we are searching for what is already there. That is why intellectually we are limited, and if you have to wait for the moment of fullness for all these limitations to be overcome, can you imagine how long it will take? Not in your lifetime will you ever get that fullness. However, this fullness is not denied to anybody. We feel unfilled because of our lifestyles or the tragic things that happen to us. If you realize that everyone discovers a moment of joy now and then in their lifetime, and in those times, at least momentarily, they are full. But how can you pick up this fullness in your life by yourself? How do you discover that fullness and limitlessness forever? Obviously you cannot get it from outside of yourself because no object in the world can be called happiness, and material happiness varies from person to person. Even though the sun, the food, the air, the water are all essential for our sustenance and daily living, they do not bring fullness and happiness. There is no place that you can go to get or buy a bit of happiness. There is no object that you can consider as a source of happiness because that same object could be a source of unhappiness for somebody else. This is like the examples I gave of garage sales or houses for sale. Not only that, one time an object is the source of happiness for us and another time, it may become a source of unhappiness. That is the reason why our divorce rate is so high, at more than sixty percent in certain states in America. When a couple gets married, they are not getting married to get divorced later, but that initial happiness usually doesn't last forever for that couple. Hence the same source of happiness, either husband or wife, can actually become a source of unhappiness. We even see on TV many times, the husband who tried to kill the wife, or the wife hiring somebody to have the husband or boyfriend killed.

If you look at the objects I've mentioned many times before, the cars, the houses, the antiques, the vacation places, and other luxuries, you would think they should give you happiness at all times, but that is not the case. We do sell our houses, we do sell and buy cars, we do sell and buy antiques, we do return from vacations because after a while our minds decide we need something else for happiness. Therefore, happiness does not come from an object outside in the world. Happiness is not found at a particular place, either, and if it is there, it is temporary, and it is not present at all times or to the same degree. That is why we cannot say that any given thing or place is a source of happiness. You can go to Hawaii a few times, and maybe you can enjoy it for ten visits, but after a while you do not find that Hawaii makes you as happy as it did the first time or second time you went there. If you ask people who live there, you will find that in the beginning they were very excited to live or work there, but after a while it became routine and monotonous for them, and they themselves go for vacations somewhere else like Disneyland, California, or Paris, France to find happiness and pleasure. This shows that there is no place that is the entire source for happiness. Otherwise, if there were one place where happiness is, all of us would want go to that one place and live there.

You might feel that a particular time is a source of happiness. But we can't truly say that either, because you don't feel happiness only at a certain time of the day, and after that time has passed, you automatically feel different—perhaps even sadness and sorrow. A particular time, place, or person can also be a source of sorrow too. Now we realize that neither a time nor a place nor an object nor a person is the source of happiness, and yet the whole external world consists of time, places, persons, and objects. Then, the question comes, "Where do we pick up this happiness?" Logically, if not from outside, it must come from within you. Then the next question is, "What do you mean by *within?* Within your body, mind, or body organs? Which is the source of happiness?" Actually, if you think for a moment here, you'll realize that most of our body organs contribute to our unhappiness. For example, as a physician I see a lot of patients with headaches, backaches, neck pain, hands or legs falling asleep, tingling and numbness, dizziness, and other maladies. In reality our body itself is often a major source of pain and unhappiness.

Now you can see, with this thinking process, not one particular thing can be our source of happiness at all times. Some say it comes from the heart. But the heart is subject to heart attack; lungs are subjected to pneumonia, emphysema, congestion; and the brain is subjected to strokes, headaches, seizures, and tumors.

When somebody says happiness comes "from within," it is obviously not from our body, organs, or structures. Then they say, "No, don't take it literally. What I mean is in the mind." If somebody answers that way, that the mind is the source of happiness, then what is the source of sorrow? Then you have to say that it is the mind also. Then how can the mind be both sorrow as well as happiness? In that case, do we have to logically conclude that when there is sadness it is the mind, when there is jealousy it is the mind, when there is hatred it is the mind, when there is frustration it is the mind, when there is restlessness or agitation it is the mind? When there is joy, of course, it is the mind. If that is the case, where do you pick up this joy in "your mind?" Does this mean a particular frame of mind? Your mind perceives what you see objectively. For example, if you have a garland in your hand, when I ask you what it is, you will say, "This is a garland," but you don't say, "I am the garland."

On the other hand, let us say you are happy and I ask you where happiness is, you might say it is in your mind. When I ask you where the start of happiness in the mind is, you don't point to a particular part of your brain that's responsible for happiness. You just say, "I am happy." This is an entirely different thing because you don't say, "This is happiness," as if it's an object. You perceive that as the subject, so it means that happiness cannot be an object and it cannot be away from you. That is why your perception is "I am happy" and you are the subject, so happiness is your true nature.

What happiness means exactly is fullness, and this fullness is manifested in the mind when there is no conflict in the mind and the mind is resolved. This fullness is just like the example I gave before of why the sun can make us happy when our minds are nonprojecting, and we accept the sun as it is. The mind can be nonprojecting only when it is simple, when it is not willing, not assuming, or not desiring for a change of the setup outside for anything inside. Thus, a simple, abiding mind can pick up joy very easily. Basically that's what happens to us when we experience something desirable. At that time the mind resumes that simple state, and we pick up happiness because it is our nature, which is fullness. You can always argue about this and say, "I don't want to accept this, because when I am unhappy also, I say 'I am unhappy.'" The mind is unhappy, so I am unhappy. Then what is the truth? Is "I am happy" the truth, or is "I am unhappy" the truth?

That is a very logical question and a question many are likely to arrive at when reading this book. You might also get that in your mind and say, "It doesn't make sense. How can it be that I am always full and happy?" We can settle that very easily. Let's say you go to an ophthalmologist (eye doctor), and complain to him that you are having trouble seeing clearly. His immediate questions will be, "Do you see double? Do you have trouble seeing color? Do you have blurred vision, floaters, or trouble seeing near or far?" However, if you go to an eye doctor with the "complaint" that you can see *perfectly fine*, he will look at you with a puzzled expression and probably say, "You don't need an ophthalmologist, but on the next block there is a psychiatrist you should see," thinking that you are out of your mind. The reason I give you this example is that when you are happy, you want to be happy for as long as you can. On the other hand, if you are unhappy, you want to get rid of it as soon as you can. You are quickly tired of being sorrowful or sad, and then you get frustrated and depressed. But you don't want to get rid of your happiness. Therefore, "I am happy" is the *full* truth of who you are, and "I am unhappy" is only a half truth.

A very simple observation is that you don't congratulate a person who is sad or unhappy. By the same token, you don't console or sympathize with a person who is happy. That would look ridiculous. You don't welcome sorrow, and you are not tired of being happy. Common sense and experience tell you that you do not complain of being too happy; however, you do complain of "being sad." Therefore, happiness is your nature, that's why you don't complain, you don't want happiness to go away from you, and you don't try to get rid of your happiness. You realize that "being sad is not your nature," you don't welcome it, and you don't want to feel sad. You don't want to suffer frustration. That is why you look for the means to get rid of it and to find a way to be happy. That is why we take vacations and we buy luxury cars, even they if is beyond our means. People buy stuff with their credit cards beyond their capacity to pay, and then they get depressed. According to surveys, the majority of the disagreements between married couples are due to money issues. With their mounting debts, they get into arguments and end up with divorce and unhappiness, even though in the first place they wanted to be happy, which is why they bought material objects beyond what they could afford.

God has given us an ozone layer to protect us from ultraviolet rays, but with our environmental neglect causing acid rain, we are gradually destroying the ozone layer. Even though it started many years ago with nuclear testing, and continues today with excessive exposure to radiation, we can get mutations in our genes that do not go away. As a result, our future children may have birth defects. If you look at your surroundings, God is always kind in what He provides us, but it is the human beings who abuse God's kindness. Perhaps the best example is environmental pollution. God gave us water, which is pure and has no contamination, but we constantly contaminate our water supplies ourselves through negligence, ignoring the beauty of nature and the environment God has provided us. Then we blame God for all the calamities with statements like, "He should have taken care of us!" We like to blame somebody else all the time, instead of looking to ourselves to see what went wrong.

That is what so many lawsuits are all about these days, trying to blame somebody else instead of being more careful in the first place. You expect everybody else to be more careful than you, and when somebody gets hurt, the attorney will find a loophole to bring a lawsuit. It is not humanly possible to be perfect every minute in every aspect of life. The legal system often takes advantage of this and tries to profit from it. I am sure the same attorney instigating a so-called "negligence lawsuit" cannot come forward and say he is perfect and he never did anything wrong. But the message they give the public is "that person or company did something negligent, and now they must pay for it." Even though sometimes the situation or the circumstances may not dictate so, they do their best to find fault. This is not to say that *all* lawsuits are frivolous, but that too many of them are based on greed and the opportunity to go after "deep pockets," rather than being motivated by a *true* and passionate concern for public safety.

Taking this argument further, who created the energy from the sun? The Creator of the universe, but you cannot blame Him for the ultraviolet radiation in the sun, which causes skin cancer, because we are the ones abusing the ozone layer. Instead of appreciating the creation around us, we constantly blame nature for the calamities that occur.

I've been asked this question about a hundred times. India is a land known for its positive philosophy, so why are people begging in the streets and some starving to death? The answer for this is that it is not God's disparity. It is primarily the result of greed in a caste system where the privileged few, including politicians, are constantly trying to make themselves richer at the expense of millions of other people.

I will give you another example, a very simple daily experience I go through. I work in three hospitals in my community, and the parking lot entrance gates in two of the three hospitals are never broken. But at one hospital, instead of using the computerized entrance card, people keep knocking the gate with their cars and breaking it. The hospital replaces the gate at least once or twice a week. Why is it different with this hospital? They have security systems, they have all kinds of monitoring systems, but why does it still happen? Again, it is our own behavior. Some people in certain areas choose to be reckless and inconsiderate to other people and do not follow the rules. I apologize if this sounds like a broken record, but I am just giving the examples I observe every day at work or in the community of how differences in human behavior make a difference for the people around them.

We always question God, and if we see a blind person, we wonder why God did this to him or her, or what did the person do to deserve this fate? Some people try to explain it on a genetic basis, and then the question comes to why one family inherited all of these recessive genes. We do not realize the fact that we are suffering the consequences now of radiation or some other man-made disaster in the past, possibly centuries ago, that has passed from one generation to another. Nobody looks at it that way, rather than blaming God. If the original gene is bad, the original material is bad, or defective, obviously the product at some point is going to be bad.

With self-awareness you realize that by nature you *are* happiness and you can be happy all the time. Sorrow, sadness, and unhappiness are not your true nature. If you have those, you want to get rid of them as fast as you can, in any way you can, by any means you can, and you will find a way to get rid of them. On the other hand, there is no place for sorrow or sadness when you invite happiness, and you always want to be happy because your true nature is to be happy. That is why you don't complain to an ophthalmologist, "Doc, I see pretty well!" and you don't make a doctor's appointment to complain that you "feel great!" On the other hand, if your stomach hurts, your back hurts, or when there is any pain, which is a part of sorrow and unhappiness, you want to get rid of it, and you do see a physician for that.

If you look at the self, you do not require any means of knowledge to determine whether it exists or not, because it is limitless. The limitless self transcends time. Time comes and goes, and the concept of time keeps on changing. For example, if you are very busy, time flies, and if you have nothing to do and you look at the clock, it looks like time is passing very slowly. However, it is your mind and your perception that perceive the relative nature of time. The mind gets into different time scales, and it has its own subjective time. When you are talking to somebody you like or your loved ones, the time flies. On the other hand, when you are waiting alone for a bus, you feel that the bus never seems to come on time. That is why nothing is separate from the limitless self, and awareness is not bound by time: it is not mortal. It has neither a beginning nor an end. Here we are talking about the ultimate reality of awareness, which is not subject to time, not subject to a beginning or an end. In other words, it is beginningless and endless.

Basically, the means of self-knowledge we are trying to understand and learn in this book is unfolding the nature of you, the world, and the Lord. When we say our ultimate characteristic is happiness, and this ultimate reality is the truth, then somebody can question, "How can we define truth, because it is all just words? How can we reveal the truth? Any definition represents only one point of view and it is always subject to negation." For example, if you take a cloth, you can define it as a cloth, as a scarf, as threads, as cotton fibers, so you can reduce it to more fundamental substances. You can keep on going, reducing a thing to another thing, to a more and more basic thing, and then the definition keeps changing. Thus, when we say we can define the truth, we know that the definition represents only a point of view, hence the only way you can define the truth is "that which is not subject to negation."

What we are finally coming to understand is that the ultimate characteristic, the ultimate reality, is the truth, which is not subject to negation in any of the three periods of time: the past, the present, and the future. There is nothing complex about it; it simply means that it is awareness, it is being, and it does not change with relative time, and that is the ultimate truth. You can negate time, you can negate space, but you cannot negate yourself, and that is the truth. Even though this statement may look very complex and may not make sense right now, you have to follow the train of thought through the whole book to come to the understanding that you cannot negate yourself.

How can this be? Because you are the subject "I," and a subject is not subjected to negation because who is going to negate the subject? The subject cannot negate her- or himself, so the subject is something that is not bound by time, that is not bound by space. However, the subject itself is in the space in which time is also present. As a matter of fact, the whole creation is in the space/time framework. The whole creation is the "I" that is called the TRUTH. The existence of anything, like the sky, a cloud, time, space, or what have you, can be established only when you are aware of it. That awareness and that existence constitute the common plane in which the whole creation is.

Awareness and existence are limitless, formless, and therefore are fullness itself. That is the reason that whenever you are happy, you are with your true self, and whenever you are with your true self, you are happy. In spite of the limitations of the body and the mind, you are meant to be happy. When you are happy, you are full; when you have the experience of being full, you are happy. If that happiness depends on the negation of all limitations, or if it depends on the filling up of all limitations (for example the physical, bodily limitations, intellectual limitations, perceptual limitations, by the sense organs), you can never become full, because how can you fill up your physical limitations? If you are here, you are not there, and you can expand only a little bit more, but you cannot cover the entire space. You can show a little bit more strength than another person, but you cannot lift a mountain. Your intellectual knowledge is also limited: the more you know, the more you come to discover how much you don't know. The one who knows a lot is the one who knows there's a lot he does not know, and the person who does not know anything usually *thinks* he knows a lot.

I am not asking you to blindly believe what I am writing here, but I suggest you do a little homework: think about it, analyze it, and see if you can make logical sense of this explanation. Also, please don't ever let go of the capacity to think discriminatively. You don't have to agree or follow blindly what I say because of faith. Having faith is okay for comfort and peace of mind, but faith does not give you the ultimate knowledge. You should analyze yourself on your own, and discover whether what I say has validity for you. If my logic makes sense and is appropriate for you, finally you may realize for yourself that *you are happiness*, and you don't have to take my word for it.

Please understand that in absolutely no way am I putting you down or trying to make you feel inadequate. All I am saying is that if you choose, you can realize your own "self" and bring yourself to acquire the knowledge or "awareness" or "being," the blissfulness and happiness of knowing one's true self. That is all I am saying. I'm just asking you to think about this and make the effort to understand and know your limitlessness. I am not saying something that is unknown, and I am not saying that I saw God or I envisioned the Lord or I have mystic powers. All I am trying to explain to you is that you are not limited because we are all part and parcel of the universe and the Creator.

This is the key solution for the problem of unhappiness we experience as human beings. It is you who has to decide what is good for you, and what path will give you the ultimate peace and happiness.

• Chapter 20 •
Preparing for Self-Knowledge

My job in this book is to illustrate the means of self-knowledge through an understanding of what we are, who we are, what happiness is, and what it boils down to—or at least how to be content most of our lives. I am not claiming to be a saint, and I am not asking you to give up your lifestyle or anything in your life. I am just trying to help people learn to be content with what they have instead of running after mirages. If you use your thinking faculty to understand the cause of discontent and try to rectify that, you *can* be content.

God created everybody with the same human qualities and faculties of mind. He gave you the choice, and it is up to you to nurture those qualities or faculties. He gave you the seeds, but if you don't *plant* them, and *nourish* them, as with water and nutrients, you can't expect the *tree* to grow and give you fruit. In a similar way, the basic human qualities are like seeds in our minds, and it is up to us to grow them and enjoy the fruits. I'm speaking of qualities such as to be kind, to be good, to be considerate, and to be compassionate. If we cultivate these qualities, automatically we become peaceful, and we don't have to go for psychotherapy or take expensive vacations to have peace of mind, joy, or happiness. These virtues are important for our attainment of self-knowledge.

I will give you another example, for people question the unfairness of God or wonder why some people are poor or have diseases. Let us say there is a person in your class who is very smart, very good looking, and appears to have everything. If I tell you to be kind to that person, your immediate reaction might be, "What does this person need from me? He (or she) has everything!" You may feel that there is no necessity for you to show kindness to that person. You feel that this person does not need your kindness or charity. On the other hand, let us say this person broke his or her leg, and it is in a cast. Immediately you show sympathy, you sign the cast, and give him or her a get-well card, flowers, or candy. You tell other friends, and you try your best to help that person as much as you can. You do simple little things you would normally do to please a close friend. Your whole attitude and thinking process toward that person changes right away. To receive your kindness, often the other person has to show something deficient or damaged to make you feel that you need to do something, even if he or she is not your best friend. When everybody is happy and perfect, you feel nobody needs your kindness or charity, and you don't realize the value of the virtues of being kind, good, and compassionate toward everyone without a specific reason to do so.

When you are growing up, you are not only in debt to your family members, but to your teachers, society, people around you, and people who are providing you with the daily necessities. Even though you are paying for it, somebody else is growing food for you, making refrigerators, microwaves, air conditioners, cars, and other conveniences we often take for granted. If you think of that in a global aspect, automatically you feel respect for your fellow human beings because of their contribution to your life and sustenance. They don't have to do you a big favor to make you feel gratitude. Just think about it every day, from morning until you go to bed. You have so many people surrounding you who are responsible for the day to go by more easily for you. You grow in positive values when you show your appreciation to other people surrounding you.

For God, all of these virtues are the same. He is the Creator and Giver, and He provided you with all these virtues. With self-knowledge, for the most part, problems like anger, depression, sadness, self-criticism, and self-dissatisfaction can be minimized or even eradicated in our daily life. When we recognize the source of all power and all awareness, we gain self-knowledge. Even if we make mistakes, or if we made mistakes in the past, they become meaningful if they have made us wiser and we become more cautious in not repeating them. With self-knowledge, we are not frightened of our future. We do not become apprehensive. For our mistakes and for our past, we try not to blame others or even ourselves, and gradually we eliminate all forms of blaming. In our daily life we are victims of our own depression, fear, anger, self-criticism, intolerance, hatred, and unhappiness. These are the source of everything negative, including a failing relationship with a spouse, mother, father, sibling, friend, or boss. They're also the source of everything negative in our feelings about death, poverty, society, political or economic systems, health, institutions, schools, media, music, and more. If we lessen or eliminate the tendency to cast blame, which is the resentment of a fact or rejection of fact, that recognition itself reveals to us a degree of maturity.

When I say the truth is the Lord, I hope you understand that the Lord is the creation. The physical creation is the Lord, your thoughts are the Lord, and your consciousness behind the thoughts is the Lord, which is nothing but the truth, which is also the truth of the Lord. I told you before that when I started writing this book, I was telling everybody about it, my family, my patients and their families, my friends, my colleagues, and even my children's classmates and their friends. Whenever I have a chance to talk to them, I ask them probing questions. Interestingly, they do come up with interesting thoughts, but if I keep on probing to invoke their intellectual thoughts, they usually get stuck somewhere during the course of the conversation. Then I tell them I am writing this book to share my thoughts and views on different religions, and I discuss my ideas with them in those terms. Automatically their eyes get bigger, and they say, "I never thought about it this way," and then they let out a big sigh. Self-knowledge is all about "nobody is a failure." That self-judgment is solely because of a lack of recognition of the fact that life is a variety of experiences. We all learn from them, and nobody fails. That is the truth, that is the reality, and that is the knowledge you have to understand for self-knowledge.

Even though there are limitations in terms of knowledge and resources, what is important is that we realize the fact that no one is to blame, and neither do we blame ourselves. Rather, we make whatever effort is necessary to gain self-knowledge and seek the truth of awareness, existence, and happiness. With our ignorance and innocence, we subject ourselves to hurt and guilt, which result in pain. But we can change our attitudes toward ourselves, and the world, with the knowledge we gain, which will be supported by adequate effort by realizing the awareness of your presence. This is the fundamental relationship born of recognition and realization that you have no reason to be sad, depressed, or angry. You seek the strength of will and the ability to make proper, adequate efforts to change and gain the wisdom and power of knowledge of self. When you read this book over and over and you practice the life lessons, eventually you'll feel that there is a difference in "the meaning of happiness." You will lose your desire for the transient nature of material happiness and the pleasures of your past. Your attitude toward the real meaning of happiness and toward your fellow human beings, your colleagues, and even your relationships with your own family members will change. I can assure you that enlightenment through self-knowledge will make that difference.

We tend to get caught up with our day-to-day life in society and in the world, which is "apparent" and does not have independent reality. The problem comes when this apparent world becomes real for us. We must remember that the body, the sense organs, the mind, and the world outside, all are the creations of the Lord and the grace of the Supreme. We have to understand that even though the universe and the creation are apparent, reality exists only in the usefulness of the creation, as a pot is a useful creation, chains and ornaments from gold are useful creations, a table from wood is a useful creation, and cloth from cotton is a useful creation. So all the creation is useful, but it is only "apparently real" because when you carefully analyze it, it resolves into something else. That is the difference between what we project, or our imaginings, and what the Lord projects, the useful apparent reality.

A person can be made uncomfortable by many small things, such as his or her own gray hair. In looking at our gray hair, we feel that we are getting old and we may dye our hair to a different color, but that coloring lasts for only a short time and we have to redo it to keep the hair looking dark, brown, blonde, or whatever the color may be. On the other hand, if we willingly accept the fact that getting gray hair is natural, we don't feel depressed or disappointed, and we don't fear that we may be disliked because of our appearance. A simple understanding and change of our attitude turns around the results 180 degrees.

When you understand your self, you develop a special attitude, and you appreciate that the result of every action comes through the laws of nature and that nature's laws are instruments of the Lord who gives you the result of actions. It is one's attitude toward an object that makes all the difference. When you take communion or when you receive an object like wine, wafers, or a flower in a temple or in church you view the object as coming from the Lord, so you accept it differently than if you had acquired the same object some other way, like buying a flower or wine in a grocery store. If a flower comes from a garden, you may smell and enjoy the fragrance. On the other hand, if a priest in a church offers it to you, you place a different value on it and have a different attitude toward the flower. What prompts this change of attitude? What prompts the attitudes you feel toward any other object you receive in a temple or a church like ash, water, sugar crystal, or a piece of bread? At that time, you are not concerned with who gives you the object or how much you have received, you just consider it a blessing from the Lord, and that is enough for you. What is making the difference in your mind or perception? The same thing goes for success and failure, but they are only relative terms. They are only attitudes you develop.

Once again, please remember, I did not create anything you are reading here. I am just trying to give you logical explanations to draw your attention and your concentration so that eventually you will understand this and become self-aware. AWARENESS is the key for all our knowledge and the source of happiness. All you have to do is get rid of your incognizance and enlighten your knowledge, which is already there. Just as the snake sheds its old skin and gets a new skin, you can shed your incognizance. With a little preparation of your mind, a little enthusiasm and effort, you can achieve this, and you can be happy as long as you live. This does not mean you won't face troubles or problems at home, at work, with society, money, materials, and relationships, but you can still pull through very happily, with understanding, and with the self-knowledge you have acquired. You can make the painful situations less painful; you can soothe your painful thoughts very easily and with minimal emotional attachment.

You can overcome daily hurdles and day-by-day living problems. You can handle life with a little bit more understanding and compassion than you do now and live more wisely. That is all I am trying to accomplish with this book.

We all have cognition of our existence, and that is our waking state of experience. When we go to sleep, with our mind, memory, and projections, we go into a dream state and that is another experience. We also go into a third state, deep sleep, where there are no dreams. There is no qualified experience when you are in that deep sleep. When you get up in the morning, you feel that you had a good night's sleep and you are well rested. In reality, the third state where you are not experiencing anything in particular is itself an experience even though there are no objects or projections or awareness of you being a dreamer. Deep sleep is a completely tranquil state in the third state of awareness. In that state there is absence of objects of any kind. That awareness is one without subject and without object discrimination. The basic misunderstanding we have is that we falsely identify ourselves with our own body, senses, and mind.

However, we do not realize the true nature of the self, which is the timeless, limitless AWARENESS. That awareness is without subject-object discrimination, and it is not the waking state, it is not the dream state, it is not the deep sleep state; it *is* the one's self. I will give you another example. Let us say there is a famous actor, and he portrays three different roles in a stage play or in a movie. Let us say in one role he is a king, in another role he is a beggar, and in a third role he is a saint. You enjoy all three roles portrayed by that actor and you want to know who that actor really is. For that actor, those three roles are three states of experience for him, but his "real" self is the fourth state of experience. In fact, the actor playing those three roles is only one. The one is real, and the three roles he played are apparent. If you realize that shift from many roles to one, the many being apparent and the one being the real, that shift itself points out the nature of the self, free from all changes, free from limitedness, inadequacy, insecurity, self-judgment, and self-criticism. That is what you have to realize and understand through day-by-day practice until it becomes automatic to you, just like learning to ride a bicycle and swimming.

In every situation you face on a daily basis, you must realize what is apparent and what is real, and that will limit your sorrow, sadness, and frustrations and give you a different outlook in every situation, without going to extremes. That means that your self-knowledge will make you liberated from bondage. When an actor plays a beggar role, he becomes so immersed in that role he thinks he is hungry, sorrowful, and impoverished. In reality, he is a well-fed and well-paid actor. This simple analogy is meant to demonstrate what is real and what is apparent as part of acquiring self-knowledge. If you use your rational mind and thinking faculty, you will not be shaken by any illogical reasoning or thinking. Just as the dream experience you have every night when you go to sleep does not shake your conclusion that you are the physical body, the "I," so wrong thinking can be shaken off by right thinking, which only comes from knowing, from seeing, and learning. It does not come from experiencing.

Then you may wonder what about all the techniques they use to make your mind useful, ready to learn, ready to see. I have no problem with those techniques or practices. They may be helpful but, like physical exercises, or certain diets, only if you understand their purpose. In my opinion, they all prepare your mind to acquire self-knowledge. I think it is the same in any branch of knowledge. I always emphasize that you must have proper preparation for learning, just as you have to learn how to read before you start studying advanced literature.

In a similar way, to understand self-knowledge, you also have to prepare your mind, whatever methodology, practice, physical exercise or diet you use, or whatever healing places you choose. When I am giving lectures to my interns and colleagues, if they just sit there and listen to my lecture without paying attention, they will not get a whole lot out of the lecture. On the other hand, if they pay a little attention and try to understand what I am trying to tell them, they probably take home some message and are able to utilize that in a proper way when a situation arises. For example, let's say I give a lecture on headaches, seizures, and strokes. In that one-hour lecture, a young doctor understands by paying attention, preparing his or her mind to listen and learn the different types of strokes and what types of medication we use. When this doctor sees a stroke patient, even if I am not there, he or she can treat the patient properly with the knowledge acquired during the lecture. This is probably the most basic example I can give you, taking my profession into consideration, to make my point about preparing your mind.

Self-knowledge basically teaches you what you are, and with it you are using logic for the removal of doubts, to give clarity to your vision, your thinking process, and your mind. With certain reasoning, you are removing the blocks of incognizance that are impairing your vision—and once they are removed, your vision becomes very clear. The blocks we have as incognizance are always irrational, but you can easily remove them with reason. Some people might have trouble with what I say about experience *not* being your best teacher, but you can also use your experiences; you can accumulate your experience in terms of knowledge. However, you should not forget that you don't require a new experience in order to see your self because, your self is not an experience; it is a fact. There is no other source of happiness or blissfulness, and the vision of that which we call fullness and happiness is nothing but you. When I gave you the examples moments of happiness you experience when going on a vacation to Hawaii, having a gourmet meal, buying an expensive car or house, basically you are experiencing your essential self itself. Liberation is not something like going to heaven after you die. Liberation is about knowing your self. Your self liberates you and you are ever free once you have self-knowledge. All human beings universally feel that everyone is confronted with limitations like pain, sorrow, and death. The ignorance is nothing but incognizance about the real nature of the self. However, the self is limitless, indestructible, and unborn. This is knowledge. *Until one discovers one's self to be a completely adequate self, life continues to be a series of problems.*

You also have to understand that when we say you are learning about the self, or learning the truth of one's self, or your true nature, it is not an intellectual conclusion, and it is not something to be reached by experience. You don't have to go to a particular place to reach that conclusion, and you don't have to have a bodily experience for your self to understand that as the truth. There is nothing to become, and there is nothing to transform. You simply have to understand that you *are* the truth that you are seeking—and that self-knowledge is a means of knowledge, like an instrument that shows you what you are. What you are is not an intellectual conclusion from certain data you gather or that is available from a logical conclusion where you say, "I reached this conclusion and inference." Self-knowledge does not work that way. Self-knowledge is basically an understanding about your self, what you are, what your true nature is. One thing that you should not forget is that your existence itself does not require any kind of conclusion or inference. The point I am trying to emphasize is that we fail to know about ourselves due to incognizance, not due to lack of availability of our self. The knowledge is always there. The only thing is, we are removing the incognizance and acquiring the knowledge. When you enter a dark room, what is there is there even though you cannot see anything. Just because you cannot see what is in the room does not mean it is not there. On the other hand, if you have a candle or flashlight in your hand, the room is illuminated. Then you can see the whole room and what is there. This is how self-knowledge works. You see what was *always* there, and you see it very clearly.

In this book, the whole explanation is about human life being complete, being adequate. And the sense of inadequacy arises only from misunderstanding the real nature of the self. Sometimes one can help solve another person's problems by simply listening patiently. A person who commits himself to the pursuit of knowledge is generally supported by a society that values the knowledge. In modern society, scientists are provided with grants and resources for research. They may or may not discover anything, or their hypotheses may be proved wrong, and it doesn't matter; they continue to do research. Society will not disown a person who pursues knowledge. Good is a relative word and what is good today may not be good tomorrow. For example there is no such thing as good medicine. The very same aspirin tablet that can prevent a heart attack in one person can also cause serious side effects in another person who is allergic to it.

We all want to achieve freedom from the limitations of sorrow, mortality, and ignorance because we do not know this freedom is already achieved, just as removal of the imagined snake (that was really a piece of rope) is already achieved. In reality, you did not do anything to remove the snake because it was never there. It is just the incognizance that made us frightened and fearful. A wise person does not depend on anything for happiness, and so he lives in the world without fear or attachment, moving about as freely as the air. Such a person can enter or leave any situation without a problem. He can be involved in all events but not get caught up in them, just as an ocean will not flood when rivers come and join with more water. In a similar way, the wise person who gains the knowledge remains unchanged once he gains peace, unlike the one who desires objects. *Like the ocean, a wise man's heart is ever full, and that fullness does not depend on the arrival or departure of anything.*

In contrast, a person who depends on material objects in order to be happy will be elated by getting what he or she wants, and depressed by not getting it. We can compare these people with a pond that dries up if the rains do not come or overflows when it is filled to the brim by one shower. The preceding ocean analogy sums up very simply the nature of understanding one's self, the meaning of limitlessness, the fullness, the awareness, the being, and the oneness. You have to understand that this knowledge of limitlessness is not a state of experience. It is the vision of the mind brought about by the knowledge that one is free from all limitations. In awareness there is no distinction. Through knowledge you realize that happiness is not something to be gained. It is already contained in one's self, and understanding one's self to be happiness is all self-knowledge is. Happiness does not depend on the presence or absence of things.

When you appreciate the laws of nature, you understand that they are nothing but instruments of the Lord. You then appreciate the fact that results come from the Lord, your attitude changes, and you accept the results with an open mind and without apprehension. You don't have an overwhelming reaction, whether or not the results are according to your expectations. You may not have any expectation in the first place, just an open acceptance that *whatever* outcome transpires, whether you see it immediately or not, it is *always* for your greater good.

Instead of depending on *things* for your happiness, you know that in reality you are a full, complete being, in which all things exist. The world exists in you too, and if the world does not, yet you do exist. Therefore, that which has no independent existence is called apparent. The self is real, and the world is apparent. You must appreciate the simple truth about yourself that *you* are real and the *world* is apparent. This is the greatest magic. The magician is the Lord, and that Lord is in you. *Without undergoing any change, you and the Lord both have produced the whole creation, and it will dissolve into the Lord again.* This is the king of all knowledge, and of all the disciplines of knowledge we have. This is the king of all secrets, the most exalted thing of things that purify, that which can be known directly. The results of this knowledge cannot be destroyed. This is the most sacred among all the secrets, and it is easy to learn for one who has a prepared mind, but it becomes very difficult for the person who is not ready for this knowledge. Therefore, you have to prepare yourself for a life of study about yourself, the secrets about your self.

If you did not understand this concept and the truth about yourself, that means your mind is filled with likes and dislikes, and you have to prepare your mind more. It's just like taking an exam. If you fail the exam, you know that your preparation was not enough, so you prepare again. The second time you study much harder, and you pay more attention to the subject matter to understand it well so you can answer the questions better. Even though life is not an exam, in this case, because we are here, we have a curiosity about ourselves, the creation, the universe, and God. And we want to know the true meaning of life and to be happy at all times. There is no third source of sorrow in this life. Either we want something or we don't want to lose what we already have.

You have to recognize that all your results come according to the laws of nature, which were created by God. Thus, those laws of nature are proper. If you develop that attitude, by attaining self-knowledge, your likes and dislikes can be neutralized and your mind becomes much clearer, free from reactions, and you will discover yourself as someone on whom the whole creation depends. There is no transformation involved here, no becoming somebody or changing into somebody else. It is just purely giving up your incognizance and learning the secret of life, the secret concealed by yourself and within yourself, which you reveal to yourself by getting rid of your incognizance and acquiring self-knowledge.

A person who has knowledge of limitless self does not experience ups and downs with the comings and goings of things in one's life, and this wisdom brings poise and tranquility. At some time poise and tranquility are necessary in order to gain the knowledge, and knowledge is necessary to gain the poise. This is not necessarily a vicious cycle. One cannot discover peace through a life of agitation. When the mind is peaceful, it is open to teaching and understanding the knowledge. A peaceful mind will automatically remove the likes and dislikes that occur within the mind. All of us have those likes and dislikes in plenty. Nature does not program us to act in a prescribed way like animals do. Using our thinking faculty, the faculty of choice, and using our free will we choose, picking up likes and dislikes in the process. Starting from childhood, we grow up with likes and dislikes. The more sensitive one is, the more vulnerable one becomes to the power of likes and dislikes.

I will give you another example of how, with knowledge, our attitudes change. Let's say a man loves a woman and decides to marry her. Then he learns that as a baby, his bride-to-be was abducted at a big carnival, and foster parents who did not know this paid to adopt her and brought her up. At the same time, the man remembers that his own baby sister was abducted at a festival when he was a little child, and with further investigation, he comes to know that his bride-to-be is actually his own sister. Immediately his attitude toward her changes, and now he regards her as his sister, not as his future wife. Thus, a change in attitude was brought about by knowledge and awareness.

With self-knowledge and the right attitude comes understanding and acceptance of results of actions gladly, automatically, and naturally. Learning to ride a bike, if you fall, you get up and try to ride again. You don't quit riding the bicycle. For example, if you see your presence in society not as an unfortunate accident, but as a logical incident, you will consider yourself important and approach life with a purpose. On the other hand, if you focus only on a segment of your life, you may find reasons to condemn yourself and complain about others. If your vision is clear and wide, you'll have an understanding of the whole totality, and there will be no complaint or condemnation. Your vision should not only be wide, it should be cosmic. If you look at human anatomy, each cell has a function. So, too, in the cosmic pattern, each individual contributes. If you understand this, you just perform your duties no matter how insignificant you may appear to be in the grand scheme of things, and you keep the Lord in view all the time so you will acquire self-knowledge and understand the truth of the totality. Then you still continue to do your work, achieving what you want, and you don't get hung up on likes and dislikes or desires all the time.

Simply put, if you understand yourself and if you look at everything in totality in the cosmic vision, you cannot hurt another person because it is impossible for one to have animosity toward any part of the totality that includes yourself. If your teeth accidentally bite into your tongue, you don't knock out your teeth in anger because they bit your tongue. If you remember this, and with this understanding, feelings of restlessness and sorrow will subside, and the cheerful mind will see the truth unfolded by knowledge. This is just like the wave discovering "I am water" and becoming one with the ocean without undergoing any change.

This knowledge will give you the right attitude toward the action and the result. So here the question really should not be, "What is better?" It should be, "What do you really require?" That is a mind free from likes and dislikes and that naturally enjoys everything that takes place, without positive or negative feelings or over-emphasis on the results. You must also recognize that your demand for praise from society is due to your incognizance. You must appreciate that everything is given to you, and you should not claim authorship of anything, because you create nothing. Rather, God is the author of everything—you only "uncover" because everything is already there, so you cultivate a peaceful mind to discover the peace that is one's nature.

A person with self-knowledge, who has no likes or dislikes, and who isn't hung up on the positives and negatives of life, has no fear of the world. That person enjoys happiness at all times. And the source of his happiness is himself. It comes very natural to him, just like a person who has learned how to ride a bike or swim in a pool. It comes automatically to him, and he does not have to practice every day. You do not grieve over things that deserve no grief.

I hope this will help you understand the true nature of yourself and your association with God, the Creator. I hope this will help make your confusion go away about what is right and what is wrong. I hope this will give you a vision of yourself, and you will know that you are full. You are happiness, free from all bondages and belongings, cravings, likes, dislikes, and the desire to be different. With this knowledge, your incognizance will be gone.

The fundamental source of dissatisfaction comes from one's pursuit of happiness through material possessions ranging from the basic necessities like food to the luxuries of cars, computers, resort homes, diamonds, TV, and the like. If we rely on them for ultimate happiness, they will disappoint us because they are not permanent.

Lasting peace and happiness do not come from external material sources but from the understanding of one's self through self-knowledge and the way one perceives the world with a positive, undemanding attitude.

* * * * *

As for myself, I did work hard, and as everybody says, America is the land of opportunity, which is true in the sense that I came here with nothing and today I am, at least in the eyes of my peers, colleagues, friends, relatives, and other people who know me, a successful professional. I am thankful for that. However, my zest and my striving for new goals never was buried or stopped. Even after becoming successful, my zeal for teaching others or explaining to others my experiences, or sharing my knowledge to help them understand complex subjects by using simple language has never stopped.

If we have a desire, usually we work at it, and once accomplished, immediately we desire for another form of happiness. We don't say to ourselves, "I have exactly enough." Also, we often have this unsatisfied feeling when we compare what we have with what others seem to have. Some may call it jealousy or envy. Whatever you want to call it, and whatever sophisticated form you use, this is our basic human nature, regardless of what culture you belong to. I will give you an example, a small story here.

Let's say there is a place called heaven. A minister or another religious leader with a very kind nature is constantly praying to God, and whenever possible, doing good deeds. Upon his death he goes to heaven. Now let's imagine that this heaven has beautiful buildings, crystal-clear lakes, flowered landscapes, beautiful music, and beautiful angels—a place full of serenity. The minister is given a lovely little cottage there and he is very content, but then he notices that there is another person with a big mansion a little way down his street. He recognizes the man as a reckless alcoholic taxi driver he knew of on earth. Because of his drunkenness and careless driving, whenever passengers got into his cab, they were scared practically to death. He had had so many near accidents, it was a wonder he was able to keep his license.

The minister went to the angel who had assigned him the small cottage. The angel was surprised to see the look of consternation on the minister's face and wanted to know what the problem was. "Why do you look so sad and unhappy?" the Angel asked. "After all, you are in Heaven and everything here is designed to be completely enjoyable and stress free."

"Well, not that I'm jealous or anything," the minister replied, "but there is one thing which is bothering me. On earth I was always a believer, and I happen to know that my new neighbor, the taxi driver, never went to church a day in his life. So why does he have a bigger house in heaven?"

"Yes, you are right, the taxi driver had little faith," the angel replied, "but whenever anyone took a ride in his cab, even if they were atheists, they started praying like mad to God."

The moral of the story is, no matter what we have, we'll almost always be jealous, envious, or upset if someone we think is less deserving has more.

Even if you have everything, or more than enough in other people's view, you may still be unhappy or unsatisfied and try to seek more. You can have a happy family life, wonderful children, a great job, a nice income, and a comfortable life, but still you may compare yourself to somebody else. For example, if another person has inherited his millions, and just goofs off all day long, often, especially if you are a hard worker, this will bother you even though you are well off. We all know that no matter how much money we have, after certain basic needs, everything else is icing on the cake. We may know this intellectually, but still we continually seek to acquire more than what we have.

Animals accept what they are because they have no choice. For example, there is no carnivore that tries to kill more than it can eat. They search for food and when their stomach is full, they are satisfied. A pride of lions does not try to kill a whole herd of wildebeests or zebras so they can boast about having more than a neighboring pride, but look at human beings and how dissatisfied they are with so many things. They are not happy with their bodies, so they have plastic surgery. They are unhappy sometimes with their given names and go to court to change their names. They change their friends, change their jobs, and they even change their food. (For example, even if you start out as a meat eater, you can become a vegetarian if you decide you want to. This is a conscious decision you can make, whereas a cow eats only grass, and a lion eats only meat.) Unfortunately for humans, our unique traits of greed and jealousy are often the root causes of our unhappiness.

I do realize we sometimes experience frustration, anger, and a state of helplessness because things don't go the way we want them to, or because we expect different results from those we got from our actions. However, the type of results you get, positive or negative, depends on your action and cannot always be controlled by you. A lot of people, when you are talking about happiness, immediately try to show off their superiority and cleverness. They start asking you difficult questions. For example, they might ask, "Why is there so much poverty in third-world countries?" and, "Why are people so disease ridden?" They talk as though living with material comforts is the only proof that they are better off than others. As I said before, even if you have a billion dollars, you cannot buy happiness, and whatever you buy to achieve happiness will be temporary because it is external. It does not come from within yourself and you have to struggle constantly to keep your internal happiness going by attaining one material item after another, because everything tangible is short lived and always temporary. On the other hand, if you develop inner happiness by acquiring self-knowledge, it is forever.

In the case of poverty in third-world counties, there is an effect that is not visible to you. For all situations, positive or negative, there is always a cause and reason behind them. It may be a people's lack of self-effort and their lack of improving their virtues, which were given to them by the Supreme. Perhaps over a period of time, they forgot or resigned, and they no longer make the effort to improve. Naturally if this is the case they will suffer. This is just like having money in a bank account. Even if you have a million dollars, you have to use it or invest it wisely. If you think that you have so much money you don't have to make an effort to spend it wisely, in no time you can lose it. There have been numerous examples of celebrities, such as movie stars and sports figures, who made millions of dollars, but at the time of their deaths, friends and relatives had to raise money for their funeral services.

To be complete and to be happy, to be knowledgeable, is a natural urge for all human beings. Often on many news magazine shows like "60 Minutes" and "20/20," you see murderers who are being interviewed. They usually express a desire for their children to be happy, and they want them to be educated and knowledgeable. They don't want their children to make the same mistakes they did. Freedom from limitation is a most desirable pursuit of life. Everybody wants freedom from sorrow now and forever, but to achieve it, we have to realize that self-knowledge is the solution to the problem of sorrow. Thus, self-awareness naturally becomes the most desirable end for human beings.

There may be thousands of books on topics such as religion, heaven or hell, God, or life after death. There are many others on secular subjects from fashions to makeup, to movies, or anything and everything else in the world—all promising some kind of a payoff. But what is the basic, fundamental thing that human beings are looking for? It is happiness. It could be in different forms for different people, but how can we gather all the information in all the varieties of topics and put it all into the basic concept of self-knowledge? When I teach about seizures or strokes or headaches with the knowledge I've acquired over the years to doctors, interns, residents, and attendants, it is with the experience and know-how I've gained by shedding my ignorance about a particular topic. I make the lessons simple and use a methodology based on repetition, so that even those who are not neurologists can understand the complex subject matter and realize how they can utilize it in their daily practice. In no time, they can make a quick diagnosis of what type of headache a patient has, how to intervene, and how to treat it. That is the goal I always have when I teach neurology in community hospitals.

In a similar way, I am trying here to use a methodology of repetition of simple examples and metaphors so that a common person will be interested in knowing about the truth about life, learning more about one's self, and attaining self-knowledge. You may come across the same concepts in different books stated in different ways, or in different discussions from different sources. As I said earlier, and just as I emphasize in my practice, nothing in this book is newly discovered. I did not make up anything new. I just compiled various sources of knowledge into one book so that it will be a reference for your source of happiness whenever you are down, emotionally shot, upset, discouraged, disappointed, or frustrated. You can read the book again and understand the reality and the true nature of one's self to give you immediate comfort. Some people go to psychotherapists and psychologists for stress or emotional and relationship problems and engage in half-hour or one-hour sessions with the therapist over a long period of time. Sometimes it works, and sometimes it doesn't, which I have seen in my experience with my patients. Sometimes they resort to tons of medications to keep themselves calm. Here in this book, I am not attempting to replace those treatments or methodologies. I am not contradicting them, and I am not saying that they are not useful. Simply, I am saying that using self-knowledge and the realization about one's nature of self could help immensely in dealing with your daily problems and situations. You can think about and look at the situations differently after acquiring self-knowledge. Let us say you know a married couple at your church, and when you see them, they look like the happiest couple on the earth and have the most well behaved children. But before you can turn around, that couple is divorced or their children are in trouble in school or with the law. Why is this?

Almost everybody wants to show that they are happy with their possessions or accomplishments. Unfortunately, many people measure their happiness by their material acquisitions in life, believing that the more they own, the happier they must be. Many people make the mistake of considering success and happiness to be the same thing. The problem is, success demands more success, and you can never rest.

On the other hand, happiness is all inclusive. When you are happy and content (regardless of what you own), then you don't need more of anything. Thus, seeking material happiness is like chasing after a mirage.

We should not exalt somebody just because they go to church or temple frequently, and often talk with groups of people about life or philosophy. I had my own experience with this, including certain doctors who go to temple or church to pray, discuss values or humanity, and contemplate God, but once they leave the doors, their behavior and attitude are entirely different. They have no problem undermining a fellow human being's efforts to fulfill a desire for advancement. I am not saying all the church- or temple-goers are pretentious, but there certainly are some who have a false belief that going to a place of worship will instantly make them good, or that God is automatically going to bless them. It is not an exaggeration if I say that they go to church for the social gathering, or for political interest, or to remind themselves once a week that they have to make a show of good nature.

Some people take up golf. It is one of the most popular sports in the Western world where some people go merely to make acquaintances with important people. I have often seen this with my medical peers. Even people who are not Westerners, when they come to America, they'll pick up golf just for the socializing and political gain, even though they had no idea before what golf was. At the same time, some of my patients enjoy golfing, and I often recommend it for the relaxation or exercise it provides. Whatever you do, if you do it with full enjoyment, that's fine. On the other hand, if there is a self-driven motive behind it, then it is not your real nature.

I am giving all of these examples simply for your awareness. I am not out to criticize somebody or make fun of somebody or insult somebody, rather to help you understand the meaning of self-knowledge, which leads to true happiness.

True happiness originates *not* from outside stimuli, but from within. It comes from implicitly knowing that you already have all that you need to be happy. God created you happy, so you don't have to go somewhere else, do something else, have something else, or be something else other than what you are right now. But this is not to say you shouldn't try to better yourself in life—just that you shouldn't *feel* that you *have* to better yourself as the only way to be happy. *You are created by God to be happy in whatever state or place in life you are in, and happiness comes when you fully recognize this.* In this instance, trying to better yourself becomes more of an entertaining experience or a game, with serious effort to succeed, but no serious attachment to the outcome. This is because you realize you've already won. You are a winner even before you start.

If I have explained this to people in a way that it is easily understood, my goal is accomplished. Somebody can always have a question like, "What is the source of this knowledge?" If I say that I have acquired this knowledge with a quest, from various sources including the modern teachings of the scholars, then the question still remains unanswered, because my key point is that the knowledge has always existed and has no beginning and no end.

There is no difference in the sadness of all people. Sadness feels the same to us all, even though the means of removing it is different. For example, a beggar who has lost his begging bowl will be happy if he gets another begging bowl. But a king who lost his kingdom is not going to be happy or cheered up by getting a begging bowl. My point is that sorrow or sadness is a result of a mental projection, and you are grieving for a reason that deserves no grief.

Many people have a lot of information, but they do not have a lot of wisdom about life. They do not have the knowledge that converts a sorrowful life into a happy one. There is no legitimate cause for our sorrow. We contrive sorrow; it does not just happen naturally. For proof of this, look at the animals in nature. Have you ever seen a bird that looked depressed and unhappy? Have you ever seen a squirrel that appeared to be deeply saddened? Animals have moments of fear, especially if they are a food source for other animals of prey, but once the threat is gone, they are back to their happy, contented selves.

An animal in nature will not spend a day in a deep state of depression. This is because the natural state of all animals is contentment, but human beings, with their advanced brains, have actually figured out a way to be depressed or sad for long periods of time. But as a part of the animal kingdom, this is actually *unnatural* for us. Despite our higher intelligence, we are still within the animal realm, and thus our true overall nature is to be content. However, we have *unlearned* this truth and have come to believe that being depressed or sad is *normal* for us. In fact, it is *abnormal* to be discontented with our lives.

Often, our discontent is derived from unreasonable standards we have set for ourselves that we cannot reach. As I said earlier, we often compare ourselves to other people and use them as yardsticks to measure our own happiness. We also set up a false equation for ourselves that the more we have means the happier we will be. Thus, if we see someone who has more than we do, we equate that to mean we must not be as happy as they are. And if we lose something we own, we equate that to mean we are now less than we were before. Our reasoning may run along the lines of, "I just lost something that makes me happy, so I can't be as happy as I was before." But when you understand that happiness is your birthright, your basic God-given nature, the flow of material objects into or out of your life has no effect on your happiness.

Let's say a squirrel is saving up acorns and storing them in the bough of a tree that stands on the bank of a river. One day, lightning strikes the tree and it falls into the river and is carried away, acorns and all. When the squirrel discovers its stash of acorns is gone, does it go into a deep depression, give up all hope, and wish it were dead? Does it consider jumping in the river to literally drown its sorrows? No. As if the loss never happened, the squirrel simply starts gathering up more acorns and storing them in a new place. It does not become paralyzed by loss and sorrow.

In humans, sorrow develops slowly, and it is built up even though happiness is natural to us and sorrow is not. If sorrow were natural, we would be happily sorrowful, but we want to get rid of the sadness. You can get rid of it because it does not belong to you. It looks like happiness comes and goes, but it actually does not. It is only that your confused mind and unfocused thoughts sometimes keep you away from enjoying the happiness that you naturally have. Some people may think that this world makes you sorrowful and that giving up worldly pleasures and pursuits is the answer, but you cannot give up worldly pleasures and pursuits totally as long as you are alive. No one can remain without activity even for a moment. It is possible for a human being to give up some particular actions, but not all actions, as long as one is alive. You perform actions using your choice, intelligence, and thinking faculty and take the results as they come.

Once you embark on the path of self-awareness, during that process your likes and dislikes will be neutralized and in time your mind will become pure and prepared for self-knowledge. You will come to understand the true meaning of freedom of choice, which was given to all human beings, and which is not present in the lower animal or plant kingdoms. This knowledge about yourself, about your true nature, is the most secret of secrets, even though it has been revealed in scriptures for a long time. Unfortunately, without self-knowledge, we are not pursuing it, and we will not come to understand that secret.

In the next chapter, I will give you the *Five Golden Rules for Happiness*. With repetition and practice, you will be able to unravel the secret that has eluded so many for so long.

• Chapter 21 •
The Five Golden Rules for Happiness

I have already covered each and every golden principle in this book with many examples from my life—personal, social, and professional experiences—or from various religious sources and teachings of scholars, philosophers, and prophets. But now I am going to capsulate these *Pancha* (Five) *Sutras* and put the concepts into *Five Golden Rules* so you can more easily put them to good use. I will follow them with appropriate examples, even though there is some crossover between some of the rules. The bottom line is that there is a simple secret that eludes us all until we can fully grasp its monumental significance. The secret is, *the inner peace you are seeking is already within yourself, and it has nothing to do with what is happening around you.*

For a particular time or era, one country may be considered the top one in the whole world. If you look at history, Rome had its days, Great Britain had its day, and India had its time when people sold diamonds on the streets. Now it's America that is the number one country power-wise and economy-wise—and many foreigners want to immigrate to America more than any to other country. When I was a child I heard that in America people never used to lock their houses. Even if you lost your wallet or purse on the street, if there is identification, people would bring it or send it back to you. Now you see that almost everybody has high-tech security systems and possesses guns for their safety. Things change and everybody has their ups and downs, but that should not make us lose our thinking process, or our basic fundamental qualities.

As a physician, with all my accomplishments and the relentless service I provide to all my patients, I still notice a lot of red tape and experience discrimination and political manipulation on the basis of my race, religion, or certain people's perception of my power. However, this does not stop me from going to work each day and taking care of my patients. As I've said, the truth is like a fire, and many physicians continue to refer their patients to me for neurological consultation, believing that I provide good service and that I don't have any political, religious, or monetary entanglements or deals. When they want to have good service for their patients, they refer them to me, despite the prejudice they witness in some of their peers. Some people might have the perception about me that I have trouble with social adjustment, am not easy to talk to, or have a very sharp tongue. This is probably because I do not hesitate to state or stand for my principles, even if I have to oppose the views of a politically prominent person with a lot of followers who are politically in debt to that person and who try to oblige their leader by antagonizing me. This does not make me afraid because I do believe that truth is powerful, and no matter what, the good end result is always yours if you are honest and straightforward.

As long as I consciously do things for the betterment of mankind and for my patients, I am not afraid of the hurdles this effort creates. I am giving my personal examples here to illustrate a point that whatever position or the job you have, whatever social circle you have, you can't avoid problems with other fellow workers, superiors, and colleagues, no matter what race, religion, or culture you belong to. If we understand the basic concept of self-knowledge and awareness (see the italicized sentence at the end of the first paragraph of this chapter), it makes things easier. It makes us live happily until we die, and then the rest of it is up to the Supreme. If there is a heaven or hell, let Him be the determinant. I understand that it is very hard for us sometimes not to be greedy and not to be upset when we don't get what we want. Still, by acquiring self-knowledge, we don't have to feel miserable even if we don't accomplish or gain something, and we can wait patiently for time to decide when it is right.

In life, you may have a lot of adversity or opposition, and some people may even try to ruin you if they can, because you are an obstacle to their desires and greediness. As long as the truth is with you, it acts like a weapon, like fire, and fire can engulf anything.

I felt I had to give examples here and there about my own life, how I face negative situations on a daily basis, so that you can understand that I haven't always had it easy, even though for some people it may look like I am a very fortunate professional and an over-achiever. I believe I've had to struggle harder than most in my profession to get where I am today, and I will never stop standing against any kind of political groups at my workplace if I feel they are going to hurt my patients and their care. Even if I am one against hundreds of my colleagues, it does not make me weak and I do not get scared. Temporarily, I may not be invited to everybody's house for dinners, or they may try to make me an outcast. Despite my entire professional and educational background, and the good name I have among patients and peers, certain people don't stop doing things to oppose me. If I give up and join them, play by their rules and standards, then the purpose is lost. Then I am also like people who have no interest in attaining self-knowledge.

I am giving my own example for the benefit of the readers who may think, "Oh! It's easy for him because he made it. He has a medical degree." But that has not always made my life easy—and in some ways has complicated it. I tell everyone that I came from a middle-class family in India, and after coming to America, I have never boasted that I came from a princely family, and that we have thousands of acres of land and many servants back home, thinking that nobody would check up on me. If you keep on fabricating yourself with untruths, you have to have a perfect memory to remember all of your lies because this is a small world, and there will be somebody who knows you from back home and may reveal your background. When the time comes, somebody will appear who knows exactly what your true nature is. Then, whatever house of cards you have built will collapse one day when the truth is revealed about you.

On the other hand, if I am truthful and tell everybody what I am, without inflating or boasting or hiding my true basic identity, I do not have to remember what I said before because it will always be the truth when it is double-checked by somebody else who knew me from back home. The qualities you have, the actions you do, the life you lead, is what makes you great.

At social gatherings, the first thing people want to know of me is what part of India I'm from, what my caste system was, and how rich my parents were. When I tell them as it is, often the other person looks stunned and shocked. But even for a simple person with a simple life anything can be accomplished, as long as you have that basic knowledge, or self-awareness.

I talk to my patients at their bedside when I am doing the testing to distract their minds from the procedure. Whatever direction the conversation takes, religion, politics, medicine, philosophy, I talk to them according to their interests and backgrounds. For the past three years I have been telling my patients that I am writing this book, and I try to explain to them about self-knowledge to make them aware. When patients come to see me with pain (headache, backache), if I impart some self-knowledge to them when they leave my office they usually feel quite happy and are motivated to learn more.

When I make my daily rounds in the hospital, many physicians, working personnel, patients, and their families, make me feel like a celebrity, and this has been going on for more than twenty years. Every day I learn more and have more enthusiasm to become a better person than I was yesterday. This is simply because of my daily actions and not just my thoughts. Yes, I do sometimes show anger, but not irrationally. I won't say that I smile all the time or that I am like Mahatma Gandhi, or that if you slap my cheek I'll show the other cheek. I don't do that either.

Since my childhood, I always have had the eagerness to bring awareness and do what is right. I have always fought for truth and justice, not just for myself, but for everybody. I don't hesitate to show my opposed views, even if the other person is politically prominent, or if people tell me that this person is going to crush me, make my life miserable, see that I don't have a practice, or my fellow people will boycott me socially. I have never been afraid of that. I tell my wife and my children that "if you don't like yourself and if you are not happy by yourself when you're alone or with your own family, and if you are always looking for places to go, or spending time with other people, inviting them to your house or going to theirs, going to bars, spending hours and hours on the telephone, that means you are trying to avoid being yourself." You are afraid to be yourself. You are unhappy by yourself. This is not the case with me. Even if I am by myself, I can enjoy my own thoughts, or read a book or a medical journal, which helps me take care of my patients better than yesterday.

I don't mind spending a lot of time with my family members. Sometimes, I think my children are bored with me because I am always with them when I am not at the hospitals. I don't take vacations without them, except for the medical conferences I go to. I spend hours and hours with them. Even when I had a small office with only two rooms and my twins were four years old, my wife worked in my office. She started working from day one when I started my own practice. Some people have problems when they are a husband and wife working together, getting on each other's nerves. I don't say every minute was pleasant, but even if we had an argument or disagreement, we vented it out, discussed it, and came back to normal. Because we cared for each other, we didn't have to be pretentious.

My children used to sleep in my office, come in with us, and go home with us. Even my youngest daughter, when she was born, from her third day onwards, grew up in my office. All my patients knew her, and I made it a family thing, even though it was in my office. My patients were all comfortable with the family atmosphere of my office. At least, no one ever complained, and I think it made many of them more comfortable with the physician/patient relationship. To them it felt like we were not that different—that we were one and the same, working toward the common goal of good health for everyone.

Today, I am a consultant in neurology, and I may see patients only one time to give my opinion, at the request of their family physicians. Even if they didn't know me before, after half an hour with me, they feel like they have known me for a long time. This has to be natural. You don't have to put on a show, you just have to be yourself and not be afraid to speak the truth. People may say this is not good for politics, and you have to always have tactfulness and diplomacy. That is not true. If it were, I wouldn't have so many patients, their families, and other physicians who have a great admiration for my work.

Even if there are some people who perceive you as a threat to them and try to portray a negative image of you, you should not be afraid of them or let it get you down or become depressed. Never lose your self-image or strength of character, and never surrender to the people making those comments. That is what I want to emphasize to you, using my own life and profession as an example.

I donate money to temples and organizations and show my generosity because I came to America with nothing except a medical degree. By the Supreme Grace I am doing fine and I am very content with what I have. I try to show my willingness to help other fellow human beings when I donate money or my personal time. At the same time, if I need some work done at my office, at my house, or somewhere else, I get a few estimates, and I observe the workers I hire. If I feel that they are trying to take advantage of me, immediately I make them aware of that, and I express my unwillingness to pay whatever the amount they are asking for. Why is this important? Because, you want to be kind and nice to fellow human beings, and at the same time, you don't want to be taken advantage of by others. Becoming soft or a pushover is not the lesson I am giving in this book.

I will give an example to help you understand. Whenever I give a lecture for my colleagues, interns, residents, or the general public, I always use lots of examples in the form of stories because I think that is the best way to teach or make a point to others. So, there was a king cobra crawling around in the bushes, hissing and biting everybody who came across his path. Soon everybody in the village was scared of that king cobra. One day, a saint was passing by on the path where the cobra lived, and the cobra tried to bite him also. This saint had the ability to communicate with animals, and he said to the cobra, "Why are you behaving like this? Just because you have poisonous venom you cannot just go around biting and killing everybody for no reason." He added, "You are committing a lot of sins, and you will have a terrible afterlife. The cobra repented, realizing the mistakes it had made all its life. He slithered onto the saint's feet and cried. The saint said, "I just brought awareness to you, so at least from now on you can live a decent life and not be harming innocent people."

The cobra went back to its hole and stopped hissing and biting people. Soon, kids in the village who came to know over a period of time that the cobra no longer hissed or bit began throwing stones at it and beating it with sticks. The cobra took all the beatings and bodily injuries but still never bit another living creature. It came to the point where the snake got weaker and weaker and was almost in a deathly situation. One day, the same saint passed by and saw the cobra in a miserable physical condition. He asked the cobra what happened. The cobra told the saint that it was following his advice faithfully by not hissing or biting. Then the saint told the cobra, "I gave you self-knowledge, awareness, and enlightenment. I told you to be nice and good to other living creatures. But I didn't tell you not to defend yourself. You did not understand that your nature is to scare people and make them afraid to confront you. When people approach you, just hiss at them, but don't bite and kill them. With just that fear of you, they will run away from you, so that your life won't be in jeopardy. And you don't have to get hurt physically or die, to be good to others."

This story explains my attitude toward people whom I feel are acting unjustly or are hurting their fellow human beings just to serve their own greed for money, material gains, power, or whatever. I don't just bow my head and say, "Okay, Master," and fall in line just because that person has hundreds of people behind him playing "follow the leader." I do not care that those followers would embrace me, give me a fancy social life, and invite me to all of their dinner parties. If that happened, I may enjoy superficially the attention given to me, but in my inner soul, I would not be happy because I would be projecting what I am not. On the other hand, if I stand for my views and my beliefs, with my determination and ambition, I will be helpful to fellow human beings and make sure justice is served. If I see something immoral, unethical, unprofessional, I do not hesitate to tell that person or the administration, or to bring the awareness to the patients or their family members. If it turns out that a certain group of physicians may end up not liking me, so what! As long as I serve my community well, I will always have a practice. Many patients always will demand that their physicians refer them to me. I don't have to be afraid that someone is going to control my practice, either the hospital or any group of physicians.

Another example is that for the last fifteen years I have been taking care of all kinds of patients at the hospital, and I've increased my workload, but I have not asked the administration to give me a raise. No other physician on the hospital payroll has done this, and the administration is quite aware of that. One time, when the hospital was financially at risk, they asked all the staff physicians to take a cut in their salaries. When they came to my office and asked me, I agreed without hesitation. Later, I found out that only one other physician out of all the rest, agreed to the pay cut. I am not telling you this to boast about how great I am, but to make a point to you that even though we all want money, depending on the circumstances, taking less money is okay as long as it is not going to make you starve or put you on the street, as long as you have food on the table. It is a sense of contentment that makes you feel that you do not have to claw and fight for every extra dollar you can get.

For the good of all concerned, sometimes you have to stand up against some bullies, and you get the strength to do so with self-knowledge. This is because you come to know that you do not need everyone's approval to be happy. You just need to uphold your values.

For Christians, the belief is that Jesus is the Son of God, and that He was born as a human being to show mankind that "even as a human being you can have supreme qualities or divine qualities, equal to God." Throughout the Bible, we are told to be good and to be contented. People who work with me, if they read this book, might ask, why then am I not content as the Director of Neurology, if I were to decide to run for a higher position, like Chief of Staff. To answer them, it is not greed or lack of contentment, but sometimes you have to do what is right, what is good for the institution, the workplace, or for the welfare of other people. If an institution is being controlled by a certain group of people for their selfish ends, ignoring the needs of other people, or trying to suppress others, depending on your capacity, stamina, and the truth behind you, it is your duty to oppose them and their views.

God created all of us equal; *we all have the same innate inner qualities and inner power*. Nobody should feel that they are less powerful than others. You may look at other people and think of them as more powerful because thousands look up to them for their position or wealth, but you have to understand that those people cannot give you anything of real value. Nor can they give you anything you don't already have inside you. Even if I have the political pull, if I am not a good physician, I cannot serve my patients well with proper diagnoses and management, and nobody else can keep my license in good standing, and nobody else can keep my practice busy forever. On the other hand, if I have the human quality, professionalism, a good bedside manner, and timely service I provide to critically ill patients, and if I don't lose those qualities, wherever I may be, even if I am in a small boat in a mighty ocean surrounded by many sharks, I will pull through. This is the type of thinking I have always had, I always will, and this is what keeps me going. Nobody, and nothing can pull me down.

I hope you understand this point because my whole book is about self-happiness, awareness, and how to be content, and these are my personal experiences in my life that I have hurdled across since childhood, not being the rich kid, not belonging to the uppermost class in the society. Despite this, I still breezed through my early education and medical school. Since coming to America twenty-four years ago, I have never been afraid to speak the truth and stand up for my beliefs. I hope this gives you some insight into self-awareness, self-knowledge, and how to be content and happy. When I go to work, I enjoy talking to patients, their families, physicians, nursing staff, and paramedical professionals. Anybody, whoever is there, I don't mind talking to, and I enjoy that moment of time. I don't feel it's necessary to have a party or take a vacation in order to enjoy myself and to have a good time. This is because I am *always* having a good time, no matter what I am doing. People who don't understand this, think that if sometimes I work seven days a week, seemingly killing myself, it's because I'm greedy and want to make much more money. They think that the only way to make oneself feel good is to throw parties or take vacations, but after a while they discover they're not enjoying themselves, and once again they have to give bigger parties or go to more distant places in order to be happy.

If you have happiness within yourself and surrounding you at all times, why do you have to go places? Of course, it doesn't mean that I never take vacations or that I don't visit places. I thoroughly enjoy taking vacations and visiting tourist attractions with my family. As I said, I am with them as much as possible. Even though I teach them my philosophy of finding happiness from within, I still don't want my family to be deprived of valuable life experiences, so I provide these things to my family members as much as I can. However, I make sure they realize that true happiness comes from within and that the exterior pleasures can only be temporary, which I am sure they are picking up here and there from my "boring lectures" to them almost every day. They are young and capricious now, but I take heart in knowing that they'll mature and come to appreciate all I've tried to teach them about self-knowledge one day. I've already seen this in my older children when they didn't demand to have "open house" parties for their graduation just because "most of the *other* kids are having them!"

You may say, "Well, it may be true for you, but maybe it is not true for everybody. Besides, in the scheme of things, I am only one humble person." For that, I always say one humble person can make a lot of difference socially, scientifically, or any way you like. Examples include Mahatma Gandhi, Albert Einstein, Martin Luther King, Jr., Mother Theresa, and Rosa Parks, to name a few. There have been so many "humble" individuals who made a difference for centuries, millenniums, like Jesus Christ, the prophet Mohammed, and Buddha. Each of these was "one humble person" who made a huge difference, but millions of their followers think of them as God-like, because they also have that special quality of standing for what they believe more than most common men and women are able to do. That is why they were recognized in the whole world as somebody different and unique. Because they showed the basic human qualities we all have, which they understood, and which led them to live their lives as an example of those qualities. That is what made them special and eligible to be honored or worshipped.

We all have problems that come up at work, and none of us can truly say, "I have the absolute greatest job in the world." Even if you ask the richest person on the planet, I doubt that person will say he is extremely happy simply because he has an abundance of money, which you and I don't have. I am unequivocally sure that he will have his own problems and headaches too, either professionally or personally. The point here is that there is only one way to be content and happy, and that is by being content and happy with yourself exactly the way you are. I am not saying that you don't have to have goals or that you shouldn't try to achieve or to better your position in life. Nor am I saying that it's okay to live like a lazy person, and just sit around and watch TV. Whatever you do, give your best effort, and that is all you can do. Always be thankful and content with what you have—and not envious of what you don't have.

Again, I can give you many personal examples. I have been teaching at this one hospital for more than fifteen years. As of today, some medical residents who don't belong to my religion and don't share my circle of friends don't like me personally because of entanglements our differences cause them within their own groups. However, they still value the opportunity to spend time with me in neurology for a month or so to learn whatever they can from me. Because of political, religious, or social differences, I have never received the "Best Teacher Award" from these medical residents or the "Pinnacle Award" from this particular hospital, but I have received the highest praises from medical students after their elective rotations—and many of them were born and raised in America.

I realize that the final decision on the awards is politically based, religiously influenced, and depends on who has ties with whom and who dictates who should get them. Despite this pettiness, I don't get upset, and I don't stop teaching there. Whether a person is African-American, Muslim, Jewish, or Christian, it does not matter to me as a teacher. I always give my best. When the medical interns take an elective in neurology, I try to spend three or four hours a day teaching them, which is more than what's required. I not only teach them neurology, but how to be a good physician, how to have a good bedside manner, and how to treat patients without bias and irrespective of their race, religion, socioeconomic status, philosophy, morals, or ethics. All these things, I combine in my teaching. When these medical residents go out as practitioners, they may refer their patients to their own group or set of physicians based on their social, religious, or economic ties, but it does not bother me. I always do my job the best way I can, whether or not I ever receive an award or accolades for my efforts.

Sometimes a resident will go to the program director, twist the facts, and try to portray me as "too tough a teacher," but when the administrators sit with me and come to know the facts, they then come to see the truth as it is. I have explained before that truth is like fire. Even if a medical resident tries to manipulate the situation, because I have the truth with me, I don't have to fabricate or manipulate in return. I tell it as it is and in the last fifteen years, I have not been proved to be wrong in my teaching methods, my professional attitude, or my unbiased relationships with residents, interns, or fellow physicians. Yes, indeed, I do bring certain facts to the administration, such as my awareness about some physician or resident who I feel is jeopardizing patient care. It doesn't make me feel afraid that they may do something to try and get even with me in the future. No matter what the ups and downs are in my professional life, with self-knowledge I am easily able to cope.

Soon to come are the *Five Golden Rules for Happiness*. However, when you reach the last page, you cannot just say, "I read the book, I memorized the *Five Golden Rules*, so where is my "ongoing happiness?" Happiness is an exercise you have to practice, which in the beginning operates at the conscious level and later on becomes automatic for you. To make it automatic behavior, you have to show a little effort and work at it on a daily basis. Just like the examples I gave before: to become a physician, or an artist, or to play an instrument, you have to practice and exercise. In other words, you have to take a personal responsibility. This is not a cookbook where you read the directions, mix the ingredients, and suddenly there's a casserole or a pie. You cannot just say, "I read it. Why am I not happy?" This whole thing is to show you, to make you aware, and to guide you to your own means of self-knowledge.

When I speak of the *Five Golden Rules for Happiness*, they represent all the knowledge you can acquire by means of self-inquiry. But first you have to prepare your mind. You have to have a curious mind and an interest other than in seeking material happiness. In other words, you should have an interest in appreciating the reality, and the truth, and to know and understand the knowledge. The more content I feel, the more I feel the zeal, the urge, and the quest to share that contentment with my fellow human beings. That's what is driving me to write this book, not that the 6.5 billion people on our planet will acknowledge, admire, or agree with my ideas or thinking process. This never happens. There is always an opposite view and contradictory statements, criticism from other types of believers—with which I also agree. I don't mind sitting with them, discussing with them logically and helping them understand why these *Five Golden Rules* make sense. I am not promoting any kind of quick cash-in or quick-fix type of scheme here. This book is just to enlighten you, to make you think, and help you to become aware of your own self in a simple manner with examples from life.

I thank you for your patience and your willingness to take the journey that is encompassed within this book. And now, at long last, I give you the condensed version of the *Five Golden Rules for Happiness*. As you come to understand workings of life and come to have the basic knowledge of one's self, the *Five Golden Rules* to incorporate are as follows.

1) God created only *happiness*, not sorrow, sadness, hatred, or misery. Hence, my true nature is happiness, and I must always *think globally* (benevolence toward others) in terms of expressing this happiness.

2) *I am happiness*, which is freedom from an attachment to my possessions, freedom from prejudicial likes or dislikes, and freedom from the desire or need to be different from the way I am. Hence, I'm contented, complete, and limitless.

3) The Creator (God), the world (universe), and I are not three different and separate entities, but the truth is that all are one reality, sameness, or *oneness*.

4) *Incognizance or ignorance* of the truth about one's self creates the source of grief, sorrow, hatred, and unhappiness. My removal or shedding of this incognizance results in *self-knowledge*, which leads to happiness.

5) Self-knowledge is *existence* (being), *awareness* (knowledge), and *fullness* (contentment).

These are the *Five Golden Rules for Happiness* I have come to understand. As I have explained in a previous chapter, it does not matter that we have different Gods, different religions, different prophets, different beliefs, or different faiths. What I am emphasizing is *let us all be happy here on the earth* while we are living, instead of having to wait to experience "heavenly happiness." Whether or not there is a heaven or a hell, we can still live a golden life here on the planet earth by understanding these *Five Golden Rules*.

To make it easier for you to remember the *Five Golden Rules for Happiness*, I have written a shorter version of each in ALL CAPS, followed by an explanation (*in italics*).

Golden Rule #1
I AM ALWAYS HAPPY
(Because God created only happiness, and I express this happiness through my kind and loving actions toward others)

You constantly try to get rid of your sorrow or sadness because happiness is your true nature. As I have repeatedly said, the Creator, God, the Supreme, has created only happiness. Due to the lack of this knowledge, and due to our own incognizance or ignorance of this fact, we keep on looking for happiness with the same attitude: "I want, I need, I must have…" and we change our desires constantly. But with self-knowledge, what we seek is our self, so (and this is a very essential point) *you are that which you are searching for*. In other words, our self-knowledge, our awareness, keeps telling us, "Hey, you are that!" So we each have to realize finally, "I am that truth, I am that awareness, I am that fullness, and I am that happiness."

Just for a minute, consider that you are the subject and everything else is an object of your knowledge. The sun is an object of your knowledge. In the same way, the moon is an object of your knowledge, and the stars, the earth, the trees, plants, flowers, men, women, and children. All are objects of your knowledge because if you reduce the whole creation, then you end up with only two factors. One is the subject, that is the "I," and the rest of the world is the object, which is the "YOU." The things you don't know, when you learn about them, or when you realize them, become the objects of your knowledge and the face of your experiences. Thus, you create ongoing happiness when you *fully* learn and appreciate that *happiness alone* is your true God-given nature.

When you think globally, you realize that you are not different from your fellow men, and you start to treat everyone the same way you would like to be treated by showing love and compassion for others.

We have to understand that even though we are all mixed, yet we are all the same. The whole human race progresses through the contributions of *all* of the various races and religions. Through a multitude of means, everyone on the whole planet is supporting each other. Since the beginning of time, no one race has ever completely dominated the others, and no one race is ever going to completely disappear from the planet. Thus, it is vital that we find unity in our diversity.

Global thinking encompasses the realization that there is only one universal truth, and mankind arrives at it in many different ways depending on the culture in which each of us was raised. Exercising tolerance through global thinking, that is, global acceptance of other races and their diversity, raises your consciousness and quickens your path to self-knowledge. You then realize and accept that no other race, no other religion, no other people on this planet is ever a threat to you. This type of global thinking leads to the self-knowledge that no one on this planet can take away your contentment, your fullness, or your awareness. *Your happiness comes from within, thus it cannot be touched; it is always with you, and it is always yours.*

Golden Rule #2
I AM CONTENT, COMPLETE, AND LIMITLESS
(Because I am free from needing belongings, free from prejudicial likes or dislikes, free from needing to be different from the way I am)

By not being attached to our possessions, our likes or dislikes, or a *need* to be different, we are free from the uncomfortable sensations these things would normally cause us to feel. We may still be aware of them, but their ability to make us feel uncomfortable or unhappy is greatly diminished, and our reaction or response to so-called *displeasures* becomes more of a "take it or leave it" attitude. Thus, we just go about our business as if the discordance doesn't exist or is irrelevant one way or the other to our happiness.

As I mentioned before about material happiness—which is derived from things like going on a vacation or buying a new car, a new house, or a new *anything*—after enjoying it for a while, the second problem for human beings arises, which is "Now what?" because that experience is over.

Many of our beliefs about ourselves and what will truly make us happy are the result of false perceptions. To demonstrate this, let us say that you are standing next to a wall that stretches in both directions, farther than the eye can see. From your perspective, you are "inside" a compound. However, you know that there are people on the other side of the wall. From your point of view, those people are "outside" of the compound, but if someone were to look at the situation from an overhead or aerial perspective, that person would see that everyone is "inside" a wall or "outside" a wall, or that neither of you is truly outside—you are both inside a wall. So the feeling of being either inside or outside is just an illusion and not a reality. It's the same way with awareness. There is only one limitless awareness. There is no second limitless awareness. We are all within that one awareness, but we all perceive things differently with our physical bodies and minds.

Once you perceive that there is no difference, no separation between objects, you, and God, you can attain a lasting happiness that is free from a need to covet possessions, free from likes and dislikes, free from needing to be different from the way you are. You will have the knowledge that you are content, complete, and limitless just as you are right now. You can still have possessions and appreciate them, but you will not *need* possessions in order to be happy. You can still have opinions, but not get caught up in their importance. You can still strive to better yourself, but without basing it on a feeling of inadequacy.

Without self-knowledge, most of us have the belief that it may not be possible to be secure here on earth but that going to a place like heaven will *finally* make one secure. The fact is, if freedom is what you want, that freedom happens to be available in the form of self-knowledge. Therefore, if you want true security or freedom, you should gain an understanding of your self. You should understand that the ego, the "I," is the one that's insecure, is inadequate, and has hundreds of opinions about yourself. Your ego is the one that buys into a lot of opinions of others about yourself. All of your bondages are due to incognizance of the fact that you are already complete, and you need nothing material to make you whole or to make you happy.

If you realize the truth of the above paragraph, you are getting closer to understanding the meaning of self-knowledge. Then you acquire the freedom from the feeling of having limitations without choices, which is our basic human problem. The seeking of meaning in life through your acquisitions comes from incognizance. On the other hand, if you know that you cannot seek things that you already have, then you are beginning to understand self-awareness. Nobody would ask the Lord to give him a head over his shoulders because he already has one. This is like looking for something elsewhere when it is always there with you all the time. If you know the fact that you are limitless, you know that even the Lord cannot give you what you already have. It becomes clear that getting things that you already have doesn't make sense, and there is no necessity for it. That is what self-knowledge gives you.

I will give you an example. Once a man was reading, using his reading glasses. Somebody came to see him, and the man lifted his glasses to the top of his head and started talking to the visitor. After the visitor left, he wanted to continue reading, but due to the distraction, he forgot where his glasses were, and he began searching all over. They were not on the table or on the floor, and he could not find them. He started looking all over the house, shouting and screaming, "Where are my glasses?" His children and his wife stood there watching the fun because from the beginning they realized that the glasses were on his forehead. Finally, the youngest child pointed at the glasses on the father's forehead. The man realized that the glasses were with him all the time and he had been searching foolishly all the while. This is what I have been saying about self-knowledge, that the limitlessness, the awareness, the existence, the blissfulness, and the joy are all within you all the time. It is pointless to search for or try to gain something you already have.

I will give you another example. When you have moments of happiness, during that time you see yourself as a free person in spite of your being "small" in the scheme of all things. That means there is another version of yourself, which is diametrically opposite to what you think you are. That version is desirable because "I am a wanting person" is one version of yourself, and "I am not a wanting person because I am unhappy when I'm wanting, and my true nature is happiness" is another version of yourself. So the second version can be the basis for trusting what we are trying to understand about the truth. When someone talks about the truth of yourself, you would not have the same trust in his words as you have when you operate with your own eyes or ears. For example, when someone says, "Look here," you immediately open your eyes because you trust that by opening the eyes you will see. In a similar way, by trusting your awareness of your true self, you acquire self-knowledge.

Golden Rule # 3
I AM ONE AND THE SAME WITH GOD AND THE UNIVERSE
(Because I perceive all three working in unity and harmony with each other)

I have often said that the human being, the universe, and the Supreme are all one and the same because the universe is part of the Supreme, and we are part of the universe (as the molecules of water are part of the wave, which is part of the ocean). You are not alone in the world. When you look at all of this as one, you feel more joy and more wonderful feeling than when you see it as different entities. If you are different from the universe, then God is different from you. When you look at it as separate, instead of as one, there are always sorrow, misery, and problems. I will give you an example. If there is a disagreement, it takes two people to fight. For a conflict there has to be two. It takes two for a crime (the perpetrator and the victim). It takes two for violence, it takes two for jealousy, and it takes two for hatred (the hater and the person or thing hated). Even if there is only one other person, one other creation in the universe, if you look at it as divided, there are always unhappiness and problems. Look at the wars the world has gone through between two countries, two religions, two places, two families, and even two siblings in the same family. There is almost always a fight when there is divided mentality and the feeling of being different, but if you look at yourself as part of the universe and the universe is a creation of the Supreme, the Lord, and all three are one and the same, then there is only happiness and joy.

Let us say there is a person talking loudly, and if you don't want to listen, immediately you feel that he is just making noise and he is disturbing you. On the other hand, let's say you went to a concert and paid a lot of money for the ticket and a performer sings with a loud voice, reaching his or her highest octave. Do you complain about that as a loud noise? Not at all, as a matter of fact, you admire it and say, "Oh my God, look at how that singer is reaching the top note!" You don't feel that he or she is making noise because you want to listen to the music or the singing. However, it is also a loud sound, and as you can see, the difference is in the perception. What it all boils down to is what you want and what you don't want. When you look at everything as different from you or inharmonious with you, then you always want to get rid of something or want to gain something or acquire something, and in this strife there is no harmony.

If you take a symphony orchestra in which each player is playing her or his instrument according to the musical score of the symphony, it sounds beautiful and is pleasing to our ears. On the other hand, if a couple of musicians are playing their instruments out of tune, and it becomes predominant, then they create disharmony. It's similar with a family. If we have several members in a family, even if they have different opinions, notions, or tastes, if they are all able to accommodate each other, you'll find there is harmony in that house, love in that house. Otherwise, there will always be fighting, and the couple is likely to turn to the court for a divorce. Thinking of everything as one and the same brings more love and joy than thinking of everything as different, like you are different from me and I am different from you—different from my color, my height, my culture, or my socioeconomic status. If you constantly think that you are different from everybody else, then you *are* different from this world, and you are different from God. There will always be conflict, uneasiness, agitation in your mind, and there will be no tranquility. Some people think that they can buy tranquility by going on a vacation, enrolling in a membership in a health or healing place, or picking up a hobby like golf, but the tranquility these bring is transient and temporary.

Sure, the game of golf may bring you some peace and tranquility, but you cannot play golf 24 hours a day, 365 days a year. What's more, you cannot avoid your daily problems, either. But if you make a little effort to understand one's self, the meaning of self-knowledge, you will see the facts of one's self and the truth. The meaning of one's self is that there's something that is common between you and the world, between you and the Creator of the world. If this is something that you do not perceive, you can acquire this special knowledge through the continued practice of the *Five Golden Rules for Happiness.*

It does not take a scientist or physicist to know that silver is silver, copper is copper, gold is gold, and iron is iron. What you require is good eyes and your own experience to notice that the colors are different, the properties and value of each metal is different, and each metal is used for a different purpose. We can easily see that each one is different from the other, and we don't need to know a whole lot about physics to realize this. On the other hand, it definitely takes knowledge and physics to know that be it gold, copper, silver, or whatever the type of substance, they are all only one thing, and that is matter, which is convertible to energy, and that energy can become matter. That is the equation $E=MC^2$ defined by the Nobel Prize winner, Albert Einstein. In other words, there is only energy, which itself alone appears in different forms.

With self-knowledge you realize that God is no different from you, that God has no particular form and no special shape and that He is omnipotent, He is everywhere, He is all pervasive, and He is in every object. It is a common error to visualize God as different and to looking upward to Him as a separate object or a human-like form. The moment you see God this way, the trouble starts. Most of the time we visualize God as a person (usually elderly, wise, long white hair and beard, and wearing a white robe), so then we have to invoke God through that particular form. My point is that you can invoke God in any form, living or nonliving, even as a stone, because He is everywhere. He is ubiquitous. You see, it depends on how we look at a symbol. You may not want to accept that stone as God unless you have the understanding and the knowledge that God is everywhere else at the same time—as well as in the stone. In the beginning of this book, I mentioned that a lot of people wonder why Hindus pray to many different Gods and in different ways. They pray to stones, to animals like snakes, cows, and elephant heads, but for them, it is not the object they are praying to or invoking; they are simply invoking God *through* that form.

It may help you to think of God in relation to water. Water has no particular shape. It is not round, square, or triangular. Rather, it takes on the form of whatever vessel is holding it. Likewise, God is the shape of everything you see—the shape of plants, animals, humans, houses, cars, mountains, clouds, planets, and stars because God is in *all* of these.

With self-knowledge, there is no separation. You constantly perceive that you, the world (the universe), and the Lord are one and the same, that the Creator has no particular form, and that He is everywhere. The universe is within Him, and we are within the universe, so we are within the Lord, and automatically we are part of the Creator. If we fully realize this concept and permanently have this knowledge, then we understand and experience the limitlessness of one's "self." Then we do not look for God in one place or another because He is not located anywhere. He is everywhere.

In the beginning this may sound confusing or illogical. Even if it is not making sense to you that *you are the universe, the Creator is the universe, and you are part of the Creator*, you can come to understand this by reading it several times. If you keep repeating it over and over in your mind, eventually it will become a part of your being.

Golden Rule # 4
I AM FREE OF ANGER, SORROW, HATRED, AND OTHER NEGATIVE EMOTIONS
(Because I've removed my incognizance and realize negativity does not belong to me)

By understanding and implementing these *Five Golden Rules*, you can achieve true happiness. It could happen very quickly, or it may take a few months for you, reading them over and over again, so that you can grasp the essence of this whole book, but with practice and repetition, you can enlighten yourself with that self-knowledge or self-awareness. The day-to-day life most of us live offers very little self-knowledge, and it frequently presents obstacles or challenges that test us and remind us of our weaknesses, our faults, our vulnerabilities, and our "humanness." Because of this, when you tell a person that as a reflection of God, he or she is "omniscient, omnipotent, and almighty," immediately that incognizant person questions, "How can I be almighty?" Similarly, when you say to someone, "You are limitless," you are imparting information that is quite opposite to what we generally think about ourselves.

For some, it may seem that negative forces must be conspiring to subvert our attempts to maintain a constantly positive attitude. For some people, hardly a day goes by that some type of problem does not arise that appears to stand in the way of ongoing happiness, but anger, sorrow, hatred, and other negative attitudes do not belong to you. Through incognizance, ignorance, or lack of self-knowledge, you have *decided* that they are a part of you, even though God did not create them for you to hold onto. Anger, sorrow, and hatred exist only so we can know and appreciate their opposites. How could you know and experience deep love without the knowledge of hatred? How could you know joy and ecstasy without the knowledge of sorrow? And how could you know forgiveness and acceptance without anger? Negative feelings, emotions, or attitudes serve only to remind you of what you are NOT, so there is no need for you to cultivate or nurture them. You need only to acknowledge them and then dismiss them so you can embrace love, compassion, and happiness instead.

Golden Rule #5
I AM EXISTENCE, AWARENESS, AND FULLNESS
(*Because I'm always complete and require nothing outside of myself for my happiness*)

It is common knowledge that you are alive, that you are an individual, and that physically, psychologically, and intellectually you are bound by your own body, mind, and intellect. You are spatially limited, and your powers and abilities are limited. To realize this, you don't need to study any scriptures, and you don't need a scholarly brain to figure it out. You do not require any schooling or any kind of special education to make this observation. However, to realize that one's *self* is limitless and has blissfulness and awareness—for that you need special knowledge, which is attained by the means of self-knowledge. Because we lack that special knowledge, we are always looking for something to make us happy. Because we have a sense of smallness and limitedness, we are constantly *seeking* happiness until we understand the universal truth about sameness and the meaning of one's self.

The experience of joy and the experience of sleep both have sameness. In other words, whether you are poor or rich, white or black or brown, we all experience sleep. The feeling of joy is the same in everybody regardless of what the cause may be for that joy. As sleep and joy are both experienced the same, so too is one's self the same for all human beings.

If you do not understand this explanation, please read it again, because the whole concept of happiness exists in this. The whole concept of awareness, the principles of one's self-knowledge like awareness, existence (the being), and blissfulness (the joyful nature) exist in this. This is one of the most important concepts in this book—how to be happy without perceiving differences and limitations. When we look at the all pervasiveness and awareness of our self, naturally we realize that we are limitless awareness.

Think of anything, and it is awareness. I do realize that for our physical bodies certain things do look like they are outside of our awareness, but if we look at it globally, we find that they are not outside of our awareness; they are only outside of our minds. Certain objects are outside the reach of your mind and out of your thoughts. Actually this is good. If it were not so, the whole of creation would consume your mind.

Awareness is common for all of us, and in that awareness is the sense of time and the sense of space, and in that space is the object. However, that object is outside of your mind. That is why it looks like everything is outside of you, but remember that it is not outside of your awareness.

Let us take a simple analogy: You have a black jar with five holes, and the jar is in a room that is dark. You put a bright lamp inside the jar, and you now have five beams of light that come out of those five holes. Each beam of light illuminates a different object in that dark room, whichever objects lie in the path of each beam of light. If you look inside the jar, there is only one light, but the light beams coming out of the five holes are illuminating five objects in the dark room. This is the same way we can look at our whole human physical body with the five sense organs. The sense organs light up their respective objects: the eyes light up the form of colors, ears light up the sounds, nose the smells, tongue the tastes, and the sense of touch the various forms and textures of objects. Each of them, like the five holes in the jar, can be linked to a beam of light as it lights up the object. But behind the sense organs there is one light, which we call the mind, and all these five sense organs "shine" from that mind. The mind, with its moving pattern of thoughts, itself lights up the sense organs, which in turn illuminate the respective objects.

That is why you are limitless: You are awareness, and you are being. That awareness itself is limitless, so you cannot become bigger than what you are because you are already limitless. The physical body we refer to all the time as "I" actually is also an object of your own awareness because you are aware of your physical body. The mind, which is an object of your awareness, cannot be the one who is aware of it because your memories, your knowledge, and your incognizance all are objects of your awareness. This awareness itself does not have a form, and yet all forms are objects of this awareness. The entity or person who perceives the awareness is the one who is the self we are talking about.

If you acquire self-knowledge, you will discover yourself to be in the state of being full in the present moment (EXISTENCE), the state of knowing you are not separate from God (AWARENESS), and the state of having freedom from wanting (FULLNESS).

* * * * *

I have explained to the best of my knowledge, the *Five Golden Rules*, or *Pancha Sutras* in the preceding chapters and have given you shorter versions in this chapter. I hope you have increased your understanding of what is self and what is self-knowledge. As I have been telling you throughout this book, as a human being *you have the ability to choose, and with the freedom of choice,* once you act, the end result is according to the laws of nature, created by the Creator.

You can choose to be happy by understanding ones self, with the help of self-knowledge through the *Five Golden Rules.*

In closing, I wish you well on your journey of self-knowledge. That is, incorporating the *Five Golden Rules* into your daily lifestyle—and coming to the understanding that everything you need to be happy is already inside of you. This journey will take some effort, but it will be one of excitement, adventure, and fun, and it will ultimately lead you to ongoing happiness each and every day. This is my grandest, most loving wish…HAPPINESS FOR EVERYONE!

• *Note to Readers* •

Both the condensed version and the short version of *The Five Golden Rules for Happiness* are reprinted on the following pages for the purpose of making copies. I suggest that you tape one or both in an area of your home (e.g., refrigerator, closet door, near your computer desk) where you will see them and be reminded each day. This will assist you greatly with incorporating them into your daily life.

The Five Golden Rules for Happiness
(Condensed Version)

As you come to understand workings of life and come to have the basic knowledge of one's self, the *Five Golden Rules* to incorporate are the following:

1) God created only *happiness*, not sorrow, sadness, hatred, or misery. Hence, my true nature is happiness, and I must always *think globally* (benevolence toward others) in terms of expressing this happiness.
2) *I am happiness*, which is freedom from an attachment to my possessions, freedom from prejudicial likes or dislikes, and freedom from the desire or need to be different from the way I am. Hence I'm contented, complete, and limitless.
3) The Creator (God), the world (universe), and I are not three different and separate entities, but the truth is that all are one reality, sameness, or *oneness*.
4) *Incognizance or ignorance* of the truth about one's self creates the source of grief, sorrow, hatred, and unhappiness. My removal or shedding of this incognizance results in *self-knowledge*, which leads to happiness.
5) Self-knowledge is *existence* (being) *awareness* (knowledge), and *fullness* (contentment).

The Five Golden Rules for Happiness
(Short Version)

Golden Rule #1
I AM ALWAYS HAPPY
(Because God created only happiness, and I express this happiness through my kind and loving actions toward others)

Golden Rule #2
I AM CONTENT, COMPLETE, AND LIMITLESS
(Because I am free from needing belongings, free from prejudicial likes or dislikes, free from needing to be different from the way I am)

Golden Rule #3
I AM ONE AND THE SAME WITH GOD AND THE UNIVERSE
(Because I perceive all three working in unity and harmony with each other)

Golden Rule # 4
I AM FREE OF ANGER, SORROW, HATRED, AND OTHER NEGATIVE EMOTIONS
(Because I've removed my incognizance and realize negativity does not belong to me)

Golden Rule #5
I AM EXISTENCE, AWARENESS, AND FULLNESS
(Because I'm always complete and require nothing outside of myself for my happiness)

• *References* •

Adams, Robert and Maurice Victor, eds. *Principles of Neurology.*
McGraw Hill, 2002.
Cragg, Kenneth. *The House of Islam.*
Houston: Wadsworth, 1988.
Craze, Richard. *Hell.*
Berkeley: Conari Press, 1996.
Freke, Timothy. *Heaven.*
Berkeley: Conari Press, 1996.
Hinnells, John R., ed. *Living Religions,* 2nd ed.
New York: Penguin Books, 1997.
The Holy Bible, Revised Standard version.
New York: William Collins, 1971.
Kurtz, Paul. *Science and Religion: Are They Compatable?*
Amherst: Prometheus Books, 2003.
Mankind's search for GOD.
New York: Watch Tower Bible and Tract Society of Pennsylvania,
1990.
Schumacher, Stephen and Gert Woerner. *The Encyclopedia of Eastern
Philosophy and Religion.*
Boston: Shambala, 1994.
Smith, Houston. *The World's Religions.*
New York: Harper Collins, 1991.
Swami, Dayananda, *The teaching of the Bhagavad Gita.*
New Delhi: Vision Books, 1997.
Viswanathan, Ed, *Am I a Hindu?*
San Francisco: Halo Books, 1992.